Schools Council
Research Studies

The Moral
Situation
of Children

This is the final report from the Schools Council
Moral Education 8–13 Project (1972–1976),
directed by Peter McPhail at the University of
Cambridge Department of Education.
John Sutcliffe was statistical adviser.

Schools Council
Research Studies

The Moral
Situation
of Children

J. R. Ungoed-Thomas

Macmillan Education

First published 1978

ISBN 0 333 22755 7

Published by
MACMILLAN EDUCATION LTD
Houndmills Basingstoke Hampshire RG21 2XS
and London
Associated companies in Delhi Dublin
Hong Kong Johannesburg Lagos Melbourne
New York Singapore and Tokyo

Text set in 10/12 pt IBM Press Roman, printed by
photolithography, and bound in Great Britain at
The Pitman Press, Bath

British Library Cataloguing in Publication Data

Schools Council Moral Education 8–13 Project
    The moral situation of children. – (Schools
    Council. Research studies).
    1. Moral education (Elementary) – Great Britain
    I. Title II. Ungoed-Thomas, Jasper Rhodri
    III. Series
    370.11'4   LC314.G7

    ISBN 0-333-22755-7

Foreword

This report by Jasper Ungoed-Thomas describes in detail the survey work and findings of the project's research, which he administered and organized with the help of the other project team members and serving teachers. It contains a wealth of detail, including verbatim accounts of the childrens' responses, and gives a unique insight into the moral world of the child.

I believe the report will be influential and continue for many years to be of great interest and practical value to all those who care about the wellbeing of children.

The project has used the report findings in two ways, both described in the central book of our publication programme. We have evolved from it our understanding of the moral learning process of the 8–13 year olds. In addition we have applied what has been learned about that process, especially about their positive motivation for considerate treatment of others, to the production of moral education techniques and materials and suggestions for research and curriculum work in the schools.

The identification of childrens' needs from their descriptions of their condition is basic to all our work.

Peter McPhail
Project Director
1972–1976

Contents

Tables

Introduction

The various parts of this report are interdependent, and it is hoped that its readers may discover both the time and the inclination to sit down and read it from cover to cover. However, the pressure of life being regrettably what it is, it may be helpful to indicate which parts may be of the greatest interest to those who have some, but not much, time to spare.

In Part I, Chapters 1 and 2 are brief and essential to an understanding of the purpose of the study. Chapter 3 deals in detail with the methods of the inquiry, and perhaps will be of most interest to those who are themselves concerned to initiate research using a similar methodology, and to those who wish to investigate how the outcomes described were achieved. Chapter 4 considers, primarily in terms of moral philosophy, the justification for the questions asked in the research.

Parts II–V, and particularly all chapters except the first in Parts III–V, deal essentially with what the children wrote, and possibly will be of greatest initial interest to those whose major concern is with children. Teachers and parents may find it most rewarding to turn first to these chapters, which form in any case the main substance of the report.

Part VI investigates, through analyses of interrelationships of variables, a series of hypotheses related to the main aims of the study.

ACKNOWLEDGEMENTS

The author would like to acknowledge the invaluable contribution to this research made by John Sutcliffe as statistical adviser, and by David Ingram, David Middleton and Caroline Rennie in carrying out field work and data analysis. He would also like to thank the project consultative committee and the staff of the Schools Council for their help.

Part I
Aims and design

1 Background

The present research was carried out as part of the work of the Schools Council Moral Education 8–13 Project. Consequently, it is concerned with children attending schools designed to provide for the middle school age range. It is a characteristic of the education system in England and Wales that a wide variety of types of school caters for these pupils.

The Schools Council Moral Education 8–13 Project was established to continue the work of the Moral Education 13–16 Project, under the same director, Peter McPhail. It operated therefore according to a general rationale and within a network of organizational relationships with schools and local education authorities which had already been successfully established. Further, the work of the 13–16 project was widely known through the publication of its *Lifeline* programme (McPhail et al, 1972) which took place immediately following the establishment of the 8–13 Project. *Lifeline* both spread awareness of the existence of curriculum research in moral education, and aroused expectations concerning the nature of further work under the same direction in the field. So the present research was, for all practical purposes, part of an ongoing exercise, and did not start with a *tabula rasa.*

The 8–13 programme of curriculum research was designed in two phases. In the first phase, a National Survey was carried out to obtain reports from children about the moral situation, or culture, in which they found themselves. The team considered that, without an insight into the moral world of children, it would be difficult, if not impossible, to design educational materials which would be motivating, relevant and appropriate. In the second phase of the curriculum research, programme materials, derived from interpretations of the National Survey data, were designed and tested in schools.

This report, therefore, is presented both as research which it is hoped will be considered of intrinsic interest, and as an integral component of a complete curriculum research programme. It is the considered opinion of the team that research and curriculum development are not separate entities, but interdependent concerns (Ungoed-Thomas, 1973). Research in moral education should be designed to provide outcomes which can be employed to provide practical assistance in schools, and curriculum materials should be based on relevant research findings, whenever possible.

For those interested in the full programme of the project (rather than particularly in the research which forms only a part of the whole), the team has published a teachers' guide. This gives an introductory résumé of the research findings, discusses the process of moral learning (with particular reference both to the middle years as an age of dependence and to children's needs to learn morally through observation, experiment, and play within a context of reliable and loving relationships), explains the nature and use of materials, and suggests techniques by which teachers may develop their own curriculum materials and approaches. The project's *Startline* materials are firmly based on situations discovered from the research to be of significance (and therefore motivating) to children; they are flexible and designed so that they may be adapted in a variety of ways to the needs of children, and they are − at the same time − sufficiently clearly structured to offer children the security and confidence which they require for satisfactory development. More specifically, the classroom approaches proposed include the use of a variety of types of illustrated and ordinary work cards, photographs and posters, tape-slide sequences, and educational games. Details of the teachers' guide and materials produced by the project are given in full in Appendix F.

2 Aims

The problem of how to provide moral education for children is one which has aroused perennial concern. The recent resurgence of interest in moral education has seen the initiation of research in several major areas. Such research in psychology is reported by Wright (1971) and Kay (1968), in sociology by Sugarman (1973) and Kay (1975). By general consent the most influential research into the moral reasoning of children has been carried out by Kohlberg (1969). The philosophical aspects of the problem have been considered by Wilson (1967), Hirst (1974) and Peters (1966) among others.

However, one area which has not been directly investigated is the moral culture of children. Mead (1952) and other anthropologists have established that the ethical practice of individuals is influenced by the behaviour codes of the societies in which they live.

The Opies (1959, 1969) in their account of the lore, language and play of children, have gone a considerable way to substantiating their assertion that 'however much children may need looking after, they are also people going about their own business within their own society, and are fully capable of occupying themselves under the jurisdiction of their own code.' (Opie, 1969, p. v). In view of published work in these related fields, it seems reasonable to propose that, in the specifically moral context, children's behaviour should be interpreted in relation to the ethical problems and practices of their own society.

In general terms, the purpose of the present research is to establish the salient features of the moral culture in which children function. It is accordingly ideographic, or descriptive, rather than nomothetic or normative in intention and design. More specifically, the purpose is to differentiate aspects of the moral culture of children through consideration of situations reported by children. Accordingly, analysis of the moral situation of children is central in answering particular questions proposed in the research.

In detail the intention is to discover, from situations recalled by children:

5

1   The type and frequency of situations in which children were treated with consideration and with lack of consideration; also the type of situation in which they were not sure how to behave. (These different types of situation are described as themes and considered as Part III.)

2   The identity, and the frequency with which they appeared in situations, of those who treated children with consideration, and lack of consideration; also the identity of those who initiated situations in which children were not sure how to behave. (Those identified in this way are described as *others* and considered in Part IV.)

3   The type and frequency of children's reactions to considerate, inconsiderate and social problem posing treatment by others. (Reactions are considered in Part V.)

4   The identity, and the frequency with which they appeared, of those to whom children related in their reactions to considerate, inconsiderate and social problem posing treatment by others. (Others in reactions are considered in Part V.)

5   The degree of involvement shown by children in situations; the time when and the place where situations occurred. (These are considered in Part II.)

As well as the answers of pupils, certain social, educational and personal information concerning the sample was obtained during the survey. Interrelationships of such variables, and those discovered from children's answers are considered in the concluding part of the survey (Part VI).

3 Method of inquiry

GENERAL METHOD

Data from children were obtained by employing the critical incident technique. This method of inquiry was originated in Canada, and applied by Crawford and Signori (1961) in work with university students. McPhail (1967) developed the technique for use with adolescents and it has been employed in research with school pupils in the 13–16 age range both in England (McPhail et al, 1972) and in Northern Ireland (Ungoed-Thomas, 1972).

DEVELOPMENT OF PROCEDURES

Prior to the present work, however, the critical incident technique had not been employed with pre-adolescents. Two general problems therefore posed themselves.

First, procedures appropriate for administering questions to 8–13-year-old children had to be evolved; second, questions appropriate for use with this age range had to be formulated. Procedures and questions were developed in two pre-pilot, ten pilot and four post-pilot schools (see Appendix A – Participant schools). The programme employed was as follows:

1   Preliminary procedures and questions were formulated in discussion with headteachers of pre-pilot schools.
2   These questions and procedures were discussed with teachers partici-pating in the research in the pre-pilot schools, and modified in light of their comments.
3   Questions were administered in the pre-pilot schools.
4   Responses were analysed both to assess effectiveness of questions and procedures and to develop analytic instruments.
5   The findings of the analysis were discussed with the pre-pilot school teachers. (Since children's answers were anonymous, teachers were not

shown answers of pupils in their own schools to avoid possibility of
recognition.) Teachers also reported on the effectiveness of the administration procedures.

6   A preliminary session was held with participant teachers in pilot schools.
Questions and procedures which had resulted from pre-pilot work
were discussed, and modified.

7   A second session was held with research participant teachers in pilot
schools. Detailed plans were made for administration of questions in
pilot schools. (See Appendix B — Questions to pupils, pilot survey.)

8   The questions were administered, and an analysis of answers was made
to assess the effectiveness of the questions and the procedures, as well
as to develop analytic instruments.

9   Following this, a third session was held with research participant
teachers in pilot schools. Discussion with teachers was guided to cover
the following points: pupil reaction, pupil motivation, classroom
atmosphere, teacher role, pupil-teacher and pupil-pupil interaction,
classroom organization, organizational problems, reaction (if any)
from staff or pupils not involved in the administration of the
questionnaire, other factors which seemed significant. Opportunity
was also given to teachers to make written comments.

10   Questions and procedures were modified in the light of the analysis of
the answers and the teachers' comments.

11   Each of the four team members separately administered questions in
one of the four post-pilot schools, accompanied by an observer team
member.

12   The responses were analysed to assess the effectiveness of the
questions and procedures in relation to the analytic instruments. The
effectiveness of the administration procedures was discussed by the
team.

13   A final version of 'Questions' was produced for use in the National
Survey together with administrative instructions incorporated in
'Instructions to Pupils' and 'Guidelines for Teachers' (see
Appendix B).

The questions and the procedures for administering questions which were
eventually adopted were the outcome of a dialectic between initial research
policy and the interpretation of pupil answers together with teacher comment.
As far as the finalized administrative procedures are concerned, they may be
summarized, together with the considerations which led to their adoption, as
follows:

It was concluded that the questions should be given by teachers, but that in

specified control groups the questions should be given by team members. It
was initial project policy that teachers should give the questions, a procedure
which had been employed successfully in previous research by King (1973).
This policy of involving teachers in research was proposed first because it was
considered that it would encourage cooperation in schools with the research
team; second, that teachers, particularly in this age range, know their pupils
well personally and understand their needs and abilities, and would therefore
be more likely than research workers (unknown to children) to establish a
supportive atmosphere in which children could express themselves freely and
willingly; third, it would enable teachers' proposals, derived from operational
insights into the project's methods, to be built into the project's research
work from the beginning; and fourth, that by helping to develop understanding
of and identification with project aims and procedures by teachers, a firm
foundation for later dissemination of the project programme in schools would
be provided (Ungoed-Thomas, 1974).

In the event, project policy was endorsed and differentiated in the course
of the development programme. Independent observation by team members
led to the conclusion that the initial reserve expressed towards research work
by a majority of teachers involved in pre-pilot and pilot work changed to co-
operative attitudes in the case of all except one of these teachers; these attitudes
ranged from the passive to the enthusiastic. (In the pilot survey, participant
teachers were members of an area training organization course, not concerned
with moral or religious education however, this course had a minor research
component, the details of which were not specified to course members prior
to their joining the course. The 'minor research component' was the Schools
Council Moral Education Project 8–13 pilot survey. Accordingly, teachers in
the pilot study had not selected themselves to participate in the moral education research work, and so a possible cause of bias in favour of the moral
education research was removed.)

The atmosphere established by teacher administration of questions proved,
from teachers' reports and analysis of children's answers, to be satisfactory.
From an administrative point of view, teachers had little difficulty in giving
the questions according to procedures specified, and children answered freely.
Further, when subsequently children's answers in the pilot survey were compared with children's answers in the post-pilot survey in which team members
gave the questions, there was some evidence to suggest that children's answers
to teacher-administered questions were more satisfactory in terms of detail
and involvement than answers to team-administered questions. Teachers'
contribution to the development of questions and procedures was substantial,
and resulted in instruments which were valid in terms of the research objec-
tives, and relevant to and accepted by teachers. Had teachers not been involved

in the giving of questions, the research would have achieved a less comprehensive understanding of the needs of teachers and children in relation to the research. Finally, although the contribution of pilot schools to dissemination could only properly be evaluated after the publication of the project programme, it appeared from the views expressed by teachers in the pilot group that it was reasonable to conclude that teachers involved in the research would be willing to contribute to a dissemination programme, and would be more effective in doing so than teachers or others who had not enjoyed first hand experience of work with the project.

All the considerations which led to the adoption of teachers' administration of questions are highlighted by one account (which, although not isolated, was perhaps the most significant), given by a teacher in the pilot survey, who had initially been hostile to the idea of research. His school had once been visited, not by a research student, but by someone professionally occupied in research. This person required that a detailed pre-prepared questionnaire be administered to this teacher's class of 9-year-old children. It was a condition of administration that a set time be allowed, and that the teacher should give no assistance, apparently reasonable conditions. In fact, many of the children could not understand the questionnaire, and several broke down and cried. The teacher was not permitted to intervene. It was felt by the teacher concerned that, since the questionnaire had not been related to the developmental needs of his pupils and since it had been administered in an atmosphere which caused anxiety, the results would be of little relevance; he, and others present, were not prepared to participate in any research which was not, in their view, designed to meet the intellectual, emotional requirements of children in the classroom. It became clear that there could be a considerable divergence between the reports of researchers and the experience of teachers of the administration of research. It was initially, and became even more strongly, an aim of this research to diminish as far as possible the gap between teachers' experience and project reporting of research procedure.

A number of specific questions were raised in the pre-pilot and pilot surveys concerning the effect upon children's answers of the giving of questions by teachers. In particular it seemed possible that the administration of questions by teachers, rather than by outsiders to the school, could influence children; first, to mention school predisposed situations to be placed there more frequently — since the presence of the teacher might lead pupils to think to a greater extent than would otherwise be the case in terms of school; secondly, to mention teachers as others in situations more frequently — since the presence of the teacher might lead pupils to think in terms of teachers to a greater extent than would otherwise be the case; and thirdly, to show more frequently an intense degree of involvement in answers — since the presence of the teacher, a known figure, might put pupils more at their ease and so enable them to give answers with greater involvement as well as with greater freedom.

If such hypotheses were to be satisfactorily tested it was evident that it would be necessary to be in a position to compare children's answers to teacher-given questions with children's answers to non-teacher-given questions. Accordingly, it was decided to establish a control group, in which questions would be given by team members. In order to ensure that team members were familiar with, and able to put into practice, the standardized procedures of giving questions a post-pilot survey was carried out in which the questions were given in four schools by team members of the project. Details concerning the control group, the proposed hypotheses, and the findings are considered in Appendix E.

The team would have liked to obtain a second category of control, of children matched with groups in the National Survey, who answered questions given in their home environment. This possibility was investigated but proved impossible on both administrative and policy grounds. If such a group could have been obtained, the question of the extent to which children's answers were influenced by the environment in which the questions were given could have been answered. This emerged from the pilot surveys as an interesting problem.

The initial hypothesis of the team was that, since questions were being given in a school environment, responses would be more likely to concern school than other environments. Teachers in pre-pilot schools agreed with this hypothesis. Accordingly, in the pre-pilot 'Instructions to Pupils' it was explicitly stated that 'you can write and draw about things which have happened at home and in the neighbourhood as well as at school'. In the instructions the emphasis was placed on the significance of home and neighbourhood environment to counteract the influence of the school situation in which questions were being given. However, pre-pilot pupil responses showed a considerable majority of responses reported away from the school environment. This issue was discussed at length with teachers in the pilot survey, who felt — like the pre-pilot teachers — that the giving of the questions in the school would influence the children to report school situations, and that the wording of instructions in the pre-pilot survey should be repeated. The team concurred with this view, since it was possible that the comparatively small sample, and the necessarily trial conditions in which the pre-pilot questions had been administered could have combined to give a misleadingly low proportion of school based answers. However, analysis of pilot survey responses again showed a high proportion of non-school based responses. In view of this finding it was decided to rephrase the relevant instruction to remove the bias against school based situations. It then read, 'You can write and draw about things which have happened in school, or at home, or anywhere else.'

Further administrative procedures were intended to secure that questions were given under standardized conditions. This meant a set of conditions which — allowing for inevitable variations in curricular and classroom organization, in teacher and pupil skills and in attitudes from school to school — could be employed in all schools in such a way that pupil anxiety would not be generated unnecessarily and the ordinary classroom atmosphere not disrupted. These were the considerations which led to the conclusion that standardized 'Instructions to Pupils' should be read out, and that all teachers should be provided with a set of guidelines.

In order to ensure that pupils' answers were not explicitly influenced by the nature of pupils' relationships with their teachers, and further in order that pupils would not feel inhibited from expressing themselves freely by the fear that, when their answers were read by the project, they might be used in some way which might have undesired or unforeseen consequences for the child, it was decided that all pupils' answers should be anonymous. All pupils were therefore told that answers were private and that they should not put their names on their sheets.

Further, each pupil was provided with an envelope, in which to put his or her answer, to ensure that no other child or member of staff would read the answers. (In order to match pupil answers with data about their age, sex, class, etc., each pupil's envelope had his or her registration number on it. But arrangements were made to ensure that any envelopes which were in a teacher's charge had been sealed, or were placed in large sealed envelopes.) Teachers' comments, based upon pupils' informal comments, indicated that the envelopes and the privacy were motivating for many children; several teachers agreed that the privacy was a necessary precaution against their own interest in finding out what the children had written!

A corollary of the need for children's responses to be private was that they should not be influenced by ideas suggested either by other children or by teachers. Accordingly, in any one school where different classes were involved in the research, classes would answer the same questions at the same time. Within classes, children were not allowed to talk among themselves, and teachers were not allowed to suggest 'example' answers to children. This last point was important: teachers needed to prepare children to think about the questions in a short 'warm-up' session, since, with the age range in question, it appears that teachers were almost universally in the habit of preceding work undertaken by children with a preliminary discussion. Accordingly, it seemed unlikely that children would answer questions satisfactorily if they were introduced in an unfamiliarly abrupt style; teachers needed to be careful to avoid giving examples in such warm-up sessions. Further, in such a discussion, there was a danger that pupils might suggest examples. Teachers also had to prevent this happening.

Another standardization procedure involved organization of both class-room layout and classroom atmosphere. The pilot survey indicated a strong tendency amongst teachers to place a research exercise in the same general category as a school test; accordingly, a significant proportion of teachers, if not offered guidance, would encourage 'good' performance by pupils, expect pupils to give 'correct' answers, and — either through rearranging classroom layout, through what they said to pupils, through their general attitude, or through any or a combination of these factors — would transmit their attitude towards the research to the children.

Accordingly, procedures were laid down to counteract this tendency, and to ensure that a familiar, supportive, yet task-orientated atmosphere was created. Questions were given with a normal classroom layout (for example, pupils' desks if normally grouped were not to be rearranged in straight lines); teachers were told that no pressure to answer any question or questions should be brought to bear on children who did not wish to answer; children were told what the research was for, so that they would understand the task, and not identify it as either a sort of exam, or ordinary classwork. Teachers' reports suggested that many children were motivated to respond by the explanation of the task which was given.

Specific detailed administrative procedures were designed to ensure that children were not inhibited from taking as long, or short a time as they re-quired to answer questions; to ensure that children could obtain any help (in spelling, understanding questions, etc.) which they might require from the teacher, but in a way which would not distract other children; to ensure that if any children did want to discuss their answers with their teachers, they could do so after completing their answers. (In fact, no case like this arose in the pilot survey, but teachers felt it extremely important that a child who might wish to discuss, for example, a personal problem which they had written about should not be denied the opportunity of doing so.) Also, procedures were established to ensure that pupils' answers would be given, packaged and des-patched according to standardized arrangements, so as to facilitate analysis of data by the project team.

Finally, in control classes (where the questions were given by members of the team), procedures followed were modelled upon those used by teachers. Prior to giving the questions, the team member concerned would establish with the class teacher what the usual classroom arrangements were for the group concerned and would take as far as possible a 'visiting teacher' role, rather than an 'external examiner' role. Since all team members were experi-enced teachers, this policy caused no problems.

DEVELOPMENT OF QUESTIONS

The general context in which questions were developed has been discussed
above in relation to development of procedures. More specifically, development of questions was carried out with reference to three areas: first, the
content of the questions; second, the format in which questions were presented to pupils, and third, the media in which pupils answered the questions.

Problems of content, format and media were considered in relation to each
other. Questions in the pre-pilot survey were developed in discussion with pre-
pilot school teachers from questions used in the Northern Ireland Survey. It
was considered that the Northern Ireland questions, designed for use with
adolescents, were too abstract for children in the pre-pilot schools to grasp. In
order to verify this, the questions were put to a class of 10+ children, who
were indeed unable to understand them without considerable explanation.
Consequently, a simplified form of the questions was evolved. Teachers'
reports on administration and analysis of responses suggested the following
modifications of the pre-pilot questions: first, a number of pupils – particularly
younger pupils – described interactional situations in which the *other* was not
a person, but an animal, an inanimate object or, in a more generalized way,
associated with the environment (rain, lightning, etc.) It was considered that
such answers resulted, not from a misunderstanding of the question, but from
a view of the world in which the *other* interaction was not almost exclusively confined to people, but included, often in an animistic or personalized
way, non-personal phenomena in the environment. Research findings in
related fields tend to suggest that the young child's world is less person
orientated than the adolescent's or adult's world (Piaget, 1929). Consequently,
the questions were altered to omit the personalized word 'somebody' – so that,
for example, instead of 'Tell me of a time when somebody frightened you, or
made you angry. What did you do?' the first question asked, 'Write or draw
about a time when you were unhappy. What did you do?'

Other alterations concerning content were made, not because analysis of
pupils' responses showed that questions had been phrased in such a way
either that pupils failed to understand, or failed to provide the categories of
information the questions were designed to elicit, but because it was considered that alternative wording might further define and simplify what was
required. For example, the first question was altered from 'Tell me of a time
when somebody frightened you, or made you angry. What did you do?' to
'Write or draw about a time when you were unhappy. What did you do?' And
the third question was altered from 'Tell me of a time when you were with
somebody else (or other people) and you weren't sure what to do. What did

you do?' to 'Write or draw about a time when you needed to choose what to do. What did you do?'

In the event, teachers' reports and analysis of the pilot survey answers suggested that the simplifications and alterations resulted not in more precise, but in vaguer, more subjective, responses in which less relevant data were recorded than in the pre-pilot questions.

Consequently, the questions in the post-pilot schools, which were only slightly further modified to become the National Survey questions, restored the specific rather than the simplified form of question. So, the question designed to elicit a description of considerate treatment became not 'Write or draw about a time when you were happy. What did you do?' But 'Write and draw about a time when somebody made you feel pleased or happy. What did you do as a result?'

A change of substance, made as a result of pilot survey questions, involved question order. In the pre-pilot and pilot surveys, the question designed to elicit a description of inconsiderate treatment was placed first. Teachers' comment in particular, but also analysis of responses, suggested that pupils in the pilot survey were in some cases disturbed by having to answer the 'inconsiderate treatment' question first, and that this disturbance negatively influenced their attitude in answering the questions which followed. Accordingly, in the post-pilot survey, the 'considerate treatment' question replaced the 'inconsiderate treatment' question as the first question asked. This alteration appeared, from analysis of post-pilot school pupils' reaction and answers, to avoid the problem of negatively biasing pupils attitudes.

A further issue raised for discussion by pilot teachers was whether pupils at the older end of the age range, e.g. 11+, 12+ pupils, and particularly those who read and wrote with fluency, might prefer a more abstract form of question. However, since analysis of data required that a standardized questionnaire be used if the sample obtained was to be interpreted homogenously, it was considered that a different format of question should be introduced for older pupils only if analysis of answers showed that the 'childishness' of the wording of the questions resulted in antagonizing older pupils to the extent that they failed to answer the questions satisfactorily. However, analysis of answers showed that responses from older children tended to be more detailed and perceptive than those of younger children (which is what would have been expected, since as a general rule, maturation and longer education develop the abilities to perceive and to express perception). Consequently, although there was no evidence to suggest that more abstract questions might not have elicited more satisfactory answers from older children, there was equally no evidence to suggest that the questions as formulated were not satisfactory in relation to this group of children. Therefore, it was decided that the single set of standardized questions would be given to the full sample.

The format in which questions were presented to pupils proved to be almost as significant in enabling pupils to understand them, as the wording itself. As a result of the pre-pilot and pilot surveys it appeared that the most effective means of presenting questions to pupils was for them to be read out, and written on the blackboard by the teacher after general instructions had been given, but before detailed instructions concerning numbering of sheets, etc. Both in the reading and the writing of the questions, the second part of each question, 'Describe what you did as a result' was emphasized, in reading by tone of voice, in writing by capital letters (underlining and coloured chalks were tried to give visual emphasis as well, but capital letters proved the most effective). Until the second part was emphasized, pupils tended to overlook it.

The media in which pupils were required to answer, and which had proved most appropriate, were indicated in the wording of the questions themselves, and not detailed in separate instructions. It was discovered that this was both the most effective way of communicating to pupils how answers should be given; it also meant that teachers did not have to spend additional time in the 'Instructions to Pupils' explaining how answers should be given. Thus the phrasing 'Tell me of a time . . .' in the pre-pilot survey, which was intended to reflect the usual style of teacher—pupil interaction in a class of younger children, was replaced in the pilot survey by 'Write or draw . . .'.

The actual media decided upon in light of analysis of pilot survey results were writing and drawing. All pupils, including pupils from a 7+ group included for indicative and comparative purposes, an educationally subnormal unit, and classes from schools in socially deprived areas were able to express adequate answers to the questions asked in writing and drawing. In the pilot survey, pupils were offered the choice of writing or drawing, but those who drew only were required to write a short explanatory note on their drawings. Analysis of pilot survey answers indicated that, in some cases, pupils who drew only overlooked the requirement that they add an explanatory note. Further, nearly all younger pupils did in fact accompany their written text with a drawing, and these drawings frequently illuminated and extended the reader's understanding of the answer. Consequently, it was decided that younger children should be required to both write and draw, since, in the view of pilot survey teachers, nearly all children were happy to draw, and those who did not wish to, would not do so whatever they were told. Children over 11, however, were frequently reluctant to draw, one evident reason being that in many secondary schools at least there was a strong tradition in favour of writing only, rather than writing and drawing. So, although children up to and including those of 10+ were required to 'write and draw', children of 11+

and 12+ were required to 'write, and draw if you wish to . . . '.

All children up to 10+, before starting to answer questions, were provided with both lined and blank sheets. All children in 11+ and 12+ age range were provided with lined paper, and blank paper was available on request. Although for the majority of schools this was satisfactory, younger pupils in a few schools were accustomed to painting on large sheets, and not drawing. The possibility of offering painting as an option instead of drawing was considered, but it required so much extra time and created such problems in the despatching and analysis of answers that it was decided, reluctantly, to standardize the artistic media of answers to drawing.

Another medium for answering, proposed by a number of teachers, was recorded interview. This was seriously considered, because it was proposed that it might elicit more detailed and significant answers, and that it might offer an appropriate means of responding to pupils who, though capable of writing and drawing, did not find these activities congenial or easy. There were, however, considerations against tape recording as well. First, it would make it difficult, if not impossible, for pupils to give answers which they would have confidence were anonymous. Second, interviewing, since it is an acquired skill and one which would need to be standardized for this research, would have to be conducted by team members: consequently, the advantages of teacher administration, which the development of procedures had shown to be considerable, would have to be foregone. Finally, because of the time involved the number of pupils who could respond would be greatly restricted, and it was clear from the wealth of situational material in the pilot survey answers that a large sample would be necessary if an unrestricted view of the moral situation of children was to be revealed. Consequently, although the arguments for and against tape recording were relatively finely balanced, it was reluctantly decided to omit tape recording as an acceptable answering medium.

A concluding general issue concerning the development of questions relates to the style of language used. To begin with, members of the research team tended to use elaborated terminology, both because a significant point of reference in preliminary planning had been published research literature, and because in most research endeavours, problems are, at the start, seen as complex, and only simplify as work and familiarity reveal basic contours, and separate the essential from the inessential. However, in the pilot work it very quickly became clear not only that teachers had a strong professional preference for simple language, rather than what one described as 'researchese', but also that the research team thought a good deal more pertinently if subjected to the discipline of using plain English in place of plain jargon. So the team, instead of referring to 'administering questionnaires', started to talk about 'giving questions'; instead of referring to 'responding to questionnaires', they started to talk about 'answering questions'. Throughout the research, a consistent effort was made to ensure that simple words were used where possible to describe accurately what was meant. Not the least of the contributions of those members of the teaching profession who participated in the present research was that they have helped to ensure that its presentation at every stage has been clearer than might otherwise have been the case.

THE SAMPLE

Ideally a sample would have been obtained of maintained schools representative by size and type of the national (England and Wales) distribution of schools providing for the middle school age range. However, a number of factors made it very difficult to obtain such a sample. First, at the time when the sample was being planned (spring 1973) the numbers of the different types of schools in question were altering rapidly, and up-to-date statistics were not available. Thus, middle schools increased from 323 in 1972, to 544 in 1973; comprehensive schools increased from 1591 in 1972, to 1835 in 1973 (Department of Education and Science, 1974); but in spring 1973 the latest statistics available related to 1971 (Department of Education and Science, 1972). A further difficulty militated against obtaining a representative sample of schools. As discussed in Chapter 1, the project was previously committed to a set of working relationships with particular local education authorities, advisers and, to a lesser extent, individual teachers throughout the country. Inevitably the distribution of these contacts could not be made to coincide with the distribution of a representative sample. While it would have been possible — in the interests of the research design — to have ignored these professional contacts, to have done so would have forfeited for the project valuable goodwill and support and have seriously undermined the overall programme of curriculum development and dissemination. Another possibility would have been to supplement the existing sample. However, this would have required much greater resources in terms of time and personnel than were available to the project. Consequently, it appeared that there existed no viable possibility of obtaining a representative sample of schools. As an alternative it was decided to obtain, within the framework of pre-existing professional support, a sample which — although not representative — offered examples of all the different types of schools providing for the age range under consideration, with one exception. (This exception was selective secondary schools: since all children in the maintained sector up to 11 attended non-selective schools, and an increasing proportion of those up to 13 attended non-selective schools it appeared reasonable to restrict the research to pupils in non-selective schools.) Further, the sample offered examples of schools from the different regions of England and Wales and of differing sizes (see Table 1 and Appendix A).

Table 1   Participating schools by size and type

School type	School size — less than:							
	200	400	600	800	1000	1200	1400	TOTALS
First 5—8	1	2	1	0	0	0	0	4
Junior 7—11	2	6	4	0	0	0	0	12
Primary 5—11	4	0	0	0	0	0	0	4
Middle 8—12	0	4	1	0	0	0	0	5
Middle 9—13	0	3	4	2	0	0	0	9
Junior high 11—14	0	1	0	0	0	0	0	1
Comprehensive 11—16	0	0	1	2	1	0	0	4
Comprehensive 11—18	0	0	0	0	1	2	1	4
TOTALS	7	16	11	4	2	2	1	43

Various methods of obtaining a sample of pupils were considered, and discussed with teachers involved in pre-pilot and pilot surveys. The possibility of giving the questions to all the pupils in the relevant year groups of the schools in the sample was rejected on the grounds that the project team would not have had time to analyse the amount of data which would have been obtained; it was also extremely doubtful whether all the teachers of the year groups involved would have wished to take part in giving questions, and the disruption caused to schools would have been such that not all heads would have been willing to permit such research. Another possibility considered was that questions should be given to groups randomly selected from all classes in the relevant year groups. However, the following arguments emerged militating against this approach: first, picked groups might feel they had been specially selected, and so attempt to 'perform' and become overexcited; second, the normal classroom atmosphere and teacher—pupil relationship would inevitably be disrupted; and third, it would be administratively difficult in many schools to detach small groups from their classes for the time and under the conditions required. It was therefore decided that in each school one complete class from each of the relevant year groups would be given the questions. In all, 147 classes in the National sample were obtained. In all schools classes were chosen in consultation with the headteacher.

The total sample in the National Survey was 3475 pupils. For purposes discussed above (see Chapter 2), schools were asked to provide certain categories of social and personal information about pupils in the sample. Initially, and obviously, the sex of pupils answering was required, and their ages (see Table 2).

Table 2   Age and sex of pupils

Age	Boy	Girl	TOTALS
7+	18	17	35
8+	246	250	496
9+	414	430	844
10+	406	373	779
11+	347	351	698
12+	243	261	504
13+	64	51	115
Not given	3	1	4
TOTALS	1741	1734	3475

Statistically there was no significant difference between numbers of boys and girls in the sample. As far as age groups were concerned, the presence of 35 pupils in the 7+ age range is accounted for by some schools placing a few pupils, for academic or social reasons, in the year senior to their year group. Pupils in the 13+ age range were those in the 12+ year who had passed their thirteenth birthday: no third year classes (13+) were included in the sample, since this year lay outside the project's terms of reference. A breakdown of the number of pupils in the sample in each region is given in Table 3.

Table 3   Number of pupils by region

Region	Number
North east	537
North west	776
Central	565
South east	640
Wales	361
South west	596
TOTAL	3475

Schools were asked to provide results of reading tests, since these proved to be the only widely available measure of academic attainment. A wide variety of tests (nine in all) were employed by schools in the sample (see Table 4).

Table 4   Type and frequency of reading tests taken by pupils

Test	Frequency	%
Widespan	87	2·5
Schonell	1251	36·0
Burt	643	18·5
Holborn	463	13·3
Neal	92	2·6
Reading Lab	31	0·9
Daniels & Diack	99	2·8
NFER	126	3·6
Young	29	0·8
Not given	654	18·8
TOTAL	3475	100·0

Although the different tests are not strictly comparable, a general idea of the ability level in reading performance of pupils in the sample may be obtained by collating the reading quotients (see Table 5(a)). The distribution of the children's reading quotient groups is shown in Table 5(b). Teachers were also asked to provide paternal and maternal occupation. For a number of pupils however (23·1% of the full sample) teachers did not provide paternal occupation. In some instances this was because the information was not known. However, 18 teachers (8·2%) felt that they did not wish to provide such information to a research project, since they distrusted any type of research finding which might associate a child's moral development or perception with social class. After considerable discussion with the teachers concerned it was agreed that this viewpoint would be registered in the report. Of the children for whom paternal occupation was provided 6·6% were in social class 1, 23·6% in class 2, 52·0% in class 3, 14·0% in class 4, and 3·8% in class 5 (see Table 6). This compares with a national distribution of chief economic supporters of households in 1971 (Central Statistical Office, 1974) of 4·2% in class 1, 17·3% in class 2, 42·5% in class 3, 16·3% in class 4, and 6·6% in class 5 (13·0% not classified). Of the mothers 38·4% were given as in part or full time occupation (see Table 7).

Table 5(a)   Frequency of reading quotient groups

RQ groups	Frequency	%
less than 50	3	0·1
50– 59	12	0·3
60– 69	81	2·3
70– 79	234	6·7
80– 89	399	11·5
90– 99	561	16·1
100–109	638	18·4
110–119	476	13·7
120–129	297	8·5
130–139	165	4·7
140–149	44	1·3
More than 149	13	0·4
Not given	552	15·9
TOTAL	3475	100·0

Table 5 (b)   Histogram showing the distribution of reading quotient groups

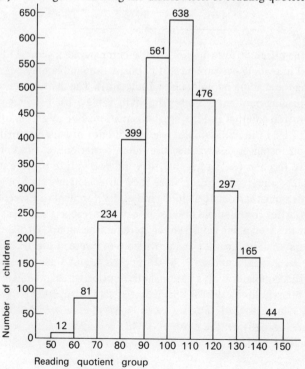

Table 6   Social class by father's
occupation

Social class	Frequency	%
1	169	6·6
2	606	23·6
3	1337	52·0
4	359	14·0
5	98	3·8
TOTAL	2569	100·0

Table 7   Social class by mother's part time and full time
occupation

Social class	Part time	Full time	Not indicated	TOTALS Frequency	%
1	5	0	2	7	0·5
2	165	27	50	242	18·1
3	268	69	161	498	37·3
4	147	86	77	310	23·2
5	43	153	83	279	20·9
TOTALS	628	335	373	1336	100·0

Of the remaining 2139 mothers, occupation was not given
in 1828 cases, 300 mothers were given as not working and
11 as absent

ADMINISTRATION OF NATIONAL SURVEY QUESTIONS

Project research centres were established in different regions of England and
Wales. Centre leaders, from authorities or individuals already in contact with
the project, were drawn from those with responsibilities for in-service training
(e.g. teacher centre wardens, local education authority advisers, and headteachers (see Appendix A)). Centre leaders, in conjunction with the project,
nominated schools in their areas which fulfilled the criteria established by the
project. Leaders approached these schools to establish the willingness of heads
to participate. Since the approach by advisers was informal and tentative there
was no record of schools which declined to participate at this stage.

Once a school had provisionally agreed to take part, a project member would visit the school at least twice. On the first occasion the project's needs were explained in detail to the head, and the school was formally asked to participate in the survey. Of the headteachers thus approached, one did not wish to participate. On the second visit by a project member the giving of the questions was discussed in detail with participant teachers who had been nominated, subject to their agreement, by discussion between project and headteachers (see p. 19). Finally in certain schools control groups were established (see Appendix E) by obtaining two matched classes of pupils in the same year. Team members visited the schools concerned to give questions to the control group at the same time as teachers gave the questions to the experimental groups.

EVALUATION OF ADMINISTRATION PROCEDURES

Following the giving of the questions, teachers concerned held meetings in each separate centre, usually organized by the centre leader; these meetings were attended by the project member responsible for schools at that particular centre. The purpose of these meetings was to discuss any future involvement of teachers in the project's curriculum development programme, and to evaluate the procedures employed in giving the questions. These discussions were guided to cover the points which had been investigated with teachers in pilot schools subsequent to their giving the questions (see p. 10). These discussions were taped. Teachers had also been offered the opportunity, immediately after giving the questions, of writing down their impressions on how the procedures had worked; these comments were sent to the project together with pupils' answers.

From the written comments and the taped discussions it was possible to establish whether or not the procedures developed in the pre-pilot and pilot surveys had proved satisfactory in the National Survey. The conclusion from both sources was that the procedures had worked well. In the discussions the concensus of teacher comment was that the giving of the questions had gone smoothly. Of the 122 teachers giving the questions, only 12 offered written comments, and these comments raised only minor points which had been covered in the discussions.

4 Rationale

The specific rationale of the questions as eventually formulated may be summarized in the following terms. The team members considered (in accordance with Piagetian and other generally accepted theories of child development) that children in the age range under consideration, with the possible exception of some of the older children, would not be able to grasp a presentation of those questions which required abstract thinking. Consultation with teachers in pre-pilot schools and the giving of questions formulated in abstract terms to a 10+ class confirmed the validity of the initial hypothesis. Accordingly, children's reports of considerate and inconsiderate treatment received were elicited not by asking a question phrased in abstract terms (e.g. 'Describe a situation in which someone treated you badly or made you angry'), but by asking a question phrased in concrete terms. Thus the children were asked to report situations in which they experienced those emotions and feelings which resulted from considerate or inconsiderate treatment (e.g. 'Write and draw about a time when somebody made you feel pleased or happy'). In other words, they were asked to indicate – through reporting interactions evoking positive emotional response – treatment perceived as considerate; and to indicate – through reporting interactions evoking negative emotional response – treatment perceived as inconsiderate. Similarly, children were asked to indicate – through reporting interactions in which they had been unsure about what to do – areas in which they were uncertain how to behave.

Although in one sense it can be argued that the questions asked are inductively derived, in so far as the specific form of question asked has arisen from operational research, it is also true that the general area being investigated was one decided upon prior to the inquiry by the research team. We consider that it is necessary for us, as an integral part of the description of our research method, to justify in general and philosophical terms the particular questions which we have formulated.

The questions we have asked are concerned primarily with the behaviour of the individual in relation to other individuals and with the happiness (or unhappiness) of the individual. Both these issues have long been considered important to moral philosophy, and their crucial significance is argued in a number of distinct traditions. Since moral behaviour almost necessarily involves others, moral philosophers have seldom considered the problem of morality exclusively from the point of view of a person in isolation from others. However, it is true to say that schools of moral philosophy have varied in the extent to which they have emphasized the role of the individual in relation to society. Kant (1948) and his followers, for example, with their emphasis upon the autonomy of the moral agent, and the duty of the moral agent to discover and obey a universal law, or set of precepts, or moral imperatives, belong to an individualist tradition of moral philosophy. Although evidently the actions upon which a moral agent decides will affect others, the emphasis in Kantian philosophy is nevertheless upon the freedom of the individual and the relationship of the individual with universal law, or the law of nature.

Other schools, however, are more specifically concerned with the social dimension of morality. In moral theology, for example, there has always been a tradition which has focused upon the interpersonal aspects of ethics. The friendship quality of love, *philia*, was accentuated in Christ's moral injunction 'Love thy neighbour', while contemporary theologians, including Buber (1958), have, as Tillich (1964, p. 31) has pointed out, 'strongly emphasised the person to person encounter as the experimental root of morality'. Non-transcendental moral philosophers, while in conflict with theologians over the motivation for moral behaviour, are not always in disagreement with them over the significance of the interpersonal context of morality. The Epicurean school perceived the moral norm of friendship as controlling the relationship of the individual to others. For Bentham, for J. S. Mill and for the Utilitarians, social wellbeing was one, if not the central, criterion for an individual in judging whether or not a particular action was moral. While, in twentieth century philosophy, G. E. Moore defined the right, or moral action as one which leads to achieving what is good. And the good he defines as 'the pleasures of human intercourse and the enjoyment of beautiful objects' (Moore, 1903).

A concern with the concept of happiness has characterized both ancient and contemporary moral philosophy; and, as with philosophers who discuss the question of the social context of morality, those for whom happiness is a crucial idea may, but do not necessarily, accept a transcendental element in the moral imperative. Most characteristically, discussion of happiness occurs in relation to the question of the moral aim.

Various schools of philosophy are agreed that it is the purpose of moral behaviour either to achieve a transcendental condition which is accompanied by a state of happiness or to achieve happiness directly, as an end in itself. In general, the more individualistic philosophers emphasize the importance of the achievement of personal happiness, while the more socially conscious philosophers underline the significance of happiness for other or others as well as for self.

For Aristotle, whose ethical works still remain influential, *eudaimonia*, or happiness, was primarily a personal rather than a social idea, and one which had a strongly spiritual aspect. *Eudaimonia* was a state of mind which accompanied the achievement of man's highest aim, participation in the eternal life through intuition of the divine. For Kant, too, although he argued that happiness was a somewhat indeterminate notion, happiness was a state of mind which, although not a moral aim in itself, was one which accompanied, albeit unsought, the fulfilment of duty, or the practice of virtue. Kant's thought was influenced both by Aristotelian philosophy, and Christian theology, which had developed and strengthened Aristotle's concept of *eudaimonia* so that it became the Augustinian and Thomist vision of the blessedness which accompanies the service and perception of God.

Philosophers who argue that the aim of moral behaviour is to secure happiness as an end itself, either for themselves or for others, do not specifically and necessarily exclude the transcendental from the moral imperative as do, for example, hedonistic philosophers for whom pleasure, not happiness, is the moral aim. Conversely, however, philosophers for whom happiness is the moral aim do not either in general explicitly admit the transcendental in the moral imperative. In classic philosophy, the Epicureans conceived of happiness as an end in itself, and laid emphasis on the achievement of personal happiness through the following of moral behaviour in establishing participation in a community of friends, and in shared cultural, cognitive and aesthetic values. The Utilitarians, on the other hand, although acknowledging the significance of personal happiness as a moral aim, placed greater emphasis upon the importance of happiness as a moral aim to be worked for in a social context. For them, what mattered was securing 'the greatest happiness for the greatest number'. Despite the sustained criticism to which this postulate has been subjected, it nevertheless continues to influence contemporary thinking in general and, in particular, that of the humanists. It has been pointed out, for example, by a critic of the Utilitarians that 'It is necessary to emphasise that the utilitarian advocacy of the criterion of public happiness is not only a mistake. That it seems so obviously the criterion to be considered in certain areas of life is something we owe to Bentham and Mill'. (Macintyre, 1967, p. 237)

An integral and necessary feature of any moral philosophy is the answer which it offers to the question, 'By what authority are people to instruct themselves, or others, to act according to the particular moral codes or commands which are recommended?' Both Aristotelian and Kantian ethics offer essentially the same response to this question: the individual is a free agent and must decide for himself what is, or is not, moral and act accordingly. However, since man is essentially rational, he is able, by use of his rational faculty, to perceive universal moral laws; for Aristotle, the laws are those commands obedience of which leads towards good, the practice of *theoria*, or intuitive, speculative reasoning upon the nature of unchanging truth; for Kant, the laws are those commands which it can be argued should be universally obeyed, both by the self faced by a moral problem, and by all other men. The existence of these external, universal laws, which may or may not be perceived and obeyed by individual free agents is simply an alleged fact; one either accepts the philosophers' argument that they exist, and one may perceive them, or one does not. The answer, therefore, to the question 'By what authority are people to instruct themselves or others to act according to Aristotelian or Kantian ethical codes?' is one's own authority, the authority of the philosopher, or the authority of universal reason.

More powerful sources of authority for moral action are offered both by Christian and by Utilitarian and humanitarian philosophies. The traditional view of moral theology has been summarized in contemporary terms as follows: '. . . the religious source of the moral demands is love under the domination of its *agape* quality, in unity with the imperative of justice to acknowledge every being with personal potential as a person, being guided by the divine-human wisdom embodied in the moral laws of the past, listening to the concrete situation, and acting courageously on the basis of these principles.' (Tillich, 1964, p. 41.) The Utilitarians and their followers question the logical possibility of a metaphysical theory of morals, and consequently in their view the authority which underpins their moral imperatives derives from an appeal to what are for them the self-evident facts of moral psychology. All men seek happiness and avoid unhappiness; accordingly individuals must necessarily — because of their nature — seek the greatest happiness for themselves and others. (It has been pointed out that seeking personal happiness is not necessarily consistent with seeking happiness for others. However, whether or not this is so, the psychological nature of the authority for morality which is proposed remains essentially unaffected.)

To conclude: it has been suggested that there are traditions in moral philosophy which argue that it is the aim of moral behaviour to achieve happiness, either as an end in itself, or as a state of mind which accompanies the practice of virtue or the reflection upon the eternal. It has also been proposed that there are traditions which lay emphasis in general upon the social context of moral behaviour and, in particular, upon the social context of moral behaviour which contributes to the achievement of happiness.

As far as the members of the research team are concerned, it has not been our purpose to elaborate or support a particular moral philosophy with which we all agree, and with which we consider others must agree if they are to accept our work. Rather, it has been our intention to indicate that our work derives from, and can be justified by, rich, complex and central traditions in the field of moral philosophy. Our differing personal viewpoints are contained within these traditions, and it is our hope that the general framework with which we have developed our work will prove acceptable to the majority of those who, like the research team, necessarily have their own particular moral standpoints, but who share standpoints within the traditions of moral philosophy which we have delineated.

Part II
Children's answers

5　Presentation and context

PRESENTATION

The questions to be investigated in the present study were defined in Chapter
2, and the way in which the questions, and the procedures for giving them
were developed has been considered in Chapter 3. The methods by which data
were analysed are discussed in Appendix C.

For the presentation of data obtained from children's answers the following
procedures have been adopted. One section of the study has been devoted to
each of the major areas of inquiry, thus Part III concerns *themes,* Part IV
others and Part V *reactions.* Within each part the same chapter structure has
been adopted. The second chapter, titled 'Happy situations' deals with
answers to the first question; the third chapter, titled 'Unhappy situations',
with answers to the second question, and the fourth chapter, titled 'Problem
situations' with answers to the third question. (The questions asked are given
in Appendix B.) The second, third and fourth chapters in each part consider
children's answers in relation to the area of inquiry which is the concern of
that part. The first chapter in each part discusses, for all three questions, the
way in which data from answers relevant to the area of inquiry considered in
that part are classified, tabulates the frequency with which specific categories
of data are found in each question, and compares the frequency with which
categories are found in each question.

In the second, third and fourth chapters for each part general problems are
discussed in relation to, and illustrated by, children's answers. Such answers
are nearly always given in full, rather than extracts from them. This was
decided upon first because it proved difficult, in some cases, to illustrate
meaningfully *themes,* or *reactions* or *others* described in answers without
giving the complete answer, and second because it was felt that readers should
have the maximum opportunity of reading and judging for themselves the
answers offered by children. It is, after all, on the nature and quality of these
answers that the value of this study ultimately depends. Accordingly, as a

general rule, in each of Parts III, IV and V, the second, third and fourth chapters consider issues in relation to children's complete answers, but attention is focused, for each answer, on the particular area of inquiry being considered in a specific chapter of a specific part.

Consideration was given to the question of how to present children's answers as regards spelling. It was appreciated that many readers might value the greater facility with which they could follow the text if misspellings were corrected. It was also realized that to publish children's writing without alteration might focus attention upon misspellings both unfavourably and unfairly.

Any strong criticism of children's spelling as presented in this study would be unjustified, since there are good reasons for supposing that their written performance for this research was of a lower standard than is normal in the classroom. This is because, while teachers usually — and rightly — strongly emphasize the importance of correct spelling, this inquiry evolved a research and not a teaching methodology which encouraged children to write freely about situations which mattered to them. It may well be that, in this age range where handwriting techniques have not yet become second nature, spontaneity is at times achieved at the expense of good presentation.

There were valid reasons in favour, at least in principle, of giving spellings in the original. In particular, such spelling raises interesting questions. For example, does children's writing have a natural rhythm in the interests of which spelling is on occasion distorted? Do children write phonetically in a way which reflects regional variations of speech? Do children sometimes reinforce their emotional understanding of a situation by misspelling? Are different methods and expectations appropriate in the classroom if children are involved in personal and creative writing?

It was therefore concluded that it would be preferable to present children's answers as written. However, it was recognized that, in a small minority of cases, misspelling does present a barrier to adult understanding. Consequently, in some answers, correct spellings have been placed in square brackets following misspellings. Also, in those few instances where named people were criticized, it was decided to omit real names to save possible embarrassment.

CONTEXT

Analysis of children's answers provided certain findings which, while not directly concerned with the main problems considered, nevertheless helped to provide a perspective and context for the situations reported. In particular these findings concerned answers which could not be classified — 'non-answers'; the type of environment in which situations occurred — 'place';

how long ago situations occurred — 'time'; and the depth of feeling shown by children in recalling situations — 'degree of involvement'.

As far as non-answers were concerned, the total numbers were relatively low. Out of the full sample of 3475 children 148 (4·31%) provided non-answers for the first question, 211 (6·1%) for the second question, and 542 (15·6%) for the third question. It was discovered in the pre-pilot and pilot surveys that some children found the last question more difficult to under-stand, and that a few were less willing to answer a third question, having expended their energy on the first two. These factors may account for an incidence of non-response which is greater for the last question than for the first two questions.

Non-answers consisted of various categories. There were, for example, blank sheets. There were also short notes to the project, explaining why a question was not being answered, or why it was inadequate. For example, a 10+ girl replied to question 3, 'I can not think of anything to write'. Another girl (aged 11+) wrote, also in question 3, 'I have never been in that situation'. Very briefly, a third girl (11+), again to question 3, simply replied, 'Sorry'. Poignantly, an 8+ boy replied to question 1, 'I am not happy'. A few other children gave similar answers. One child stated, 'P.S. sorry if it looks bad but 28 is staring at me. She is nosey.'

This answer, together with a number of others, indicated that many children took seriously the anonymity and privacy of their answers. In general, children's answers indicated a willingness to cooperate responsibly with the project, and even in certain cases almost an anxiety to communicate particular experiences. There were, however, a few interesting, and indeed welcome exceptions to this general rule. First, children appeared reluctant to report situations which they had found highly disturbing. For example, a girl from a broken family (as was made evident in question 3) answered question 2, 'I am sorry but I cant rember what has made me unhappy'. Another girl introduced an answer to question 2 by describing a pet rabbit she 'had had.' The answer continued '. . . one day my dad started to clean out her cage', and then stopped. An incidental reference in the girl's question 1 indicated that the rabbit had been taken by a fox. This reluctance to consider any personally profoundly upsetting matter doubtless helps to explain why no teacher in the entire survey was required by a child to discuss problems raised by answering the questions. It also interestingly suggests that children may have a well developed sense of what is, and is not, an appropriate response in sociopsycho-logical terms to given circumstances. Thus children apparently tend not to explicate in a classroom setting experiences which would be more fittingly considered privately in discussion with a responsible, experienced, and trusted adult. This awareness of the appropriate also appeared in the other main exception, the children's general willingness to answer the questions openly; children were reluctant to answer where a breach of trust was involved. For example, one 10+ girl wrote 'I felt unhappy when me and my freinds brocke freinds I gent tale you why because it is privete beetwean us.'

Other categories of non-answer were those which proved illegible, or incomprehensible, and those which failed to answer the question asked. Of the latter the most interesting were fantasy answers. Teachers in the pre-pilot and pilot surveys, and also to a lesser extent teachers in the National Survey, expressed some fears that numbers of children would make up answers. These fears proved, to a great extent, unfounded. Of all 3475 children answering, only 21 gave answers categorized as fantasy. Such answers were easy to identify, as for example the reply which started, 'When my freind and I were upon the moon', or 'When I was born I was very small I was pleased I could not talk . . .'; or the 9+ boy who wrote 'On last Monday somebody made me happily. and they made me happily by giveing me a motor bike and I started it up and I went round the sande common . . . and it went sevinty . . .' The possibility of course remains that numbers of children wrote fantasy answers with an essentially fictional nature not revealed by internal evidence. However, the arguments against this having happened are strong. For example, the great majority of answers showed, in a wealth of verisimilitudinous detail, preoccupations which were consistent from child to child, and not inconsistent with what is known of the child's world. Further, research indicates, and for the children in this survey teachers concerned confirmed, that boys and girls of 8–13 age range are with few exceptions authority orientated and willing to perform, to the best of their ability, reasonable tasks set by liked adults. However perhaps the strongest, yet the least easily supportable argument against children having written cryptofantasy answers is the realistic 'feel' of the answers; that, readers can judge for themselves in the answers printed in Parts III–V of this report. In the last resort however, any research which relies on questionnaire rather than observation must accept, subject to such checks as are possible, the good faith of the respondents.

The environments in which situations occurred were classified, from children's answers as: *home, school, neighbourhood, abroad, medical, seaside, multiple, elsewhere.* Except for the last two, these categories are self-explanatory. *Multiple* referred to those situations which took place in more than one environment – for example a situation which started at home and finished in the neighbourhood. *Elsewhere* usually in practice referred to happenings reported taking place on holidays or outings. The majority of situations (80·7%) were reported taking place in *home, school* or *neighbourhood.* About 10% of situations were reported taking place *elsewhere* and, of the remainder, *abroad, medical* and *seaside* were all reported in less than 4%

of situations. Usually it was clear from answers where situations had taken place. In the first question 271 (7·8%) were not classifiable; in the second question 400 (11·5%), and in the third question 712 (20·5%). If the frequencies of categories in the different questions are compared, the following findings emerge. Both happy (question 1) and unhappy (question 2) situations occurred more frequently at home than anywhere else. Happy (question 1), unhappy (question 2) and problem (question 3) situations occurred less frequently at school than either at home or in the neighbourhood.

Statistically, there was no significant difference between the frequencies with which different types of situation occurred in school surroundings. In other words, in school happy, unhappy and problem situations were equally liable to take place. If the place where problem situations occurred is considered, it is found that such situations took place very much more frequently in the neighbourhood than either in the home or the school. In fact 56·6% of problem situations were reported in the neighbourhood, over twice as many as were reported for home (13·7%) and school (10·8%) taken together. This indicates that, in contrast with happy and unhappy situations which occurred most frequently in the home, the neighbourhood was perceived by children as being the place where problems of a social moral nature were most liable to occur (see Table 8).

Table 8   Place where situations occurred

Place	Q1	%	Q2	%	Q3	%	TOTALS	%
Home	1475	47·2	1340	44·9	365	13·7	3180	36·2
School	290	9·3	326	10·9	288	10·8	904	10·3
Neighbourhood	604	19·3	894	29·9	1507	56·6	3005	34·2
Elsewhere	347	11·1	167	5·6	352	13·2	866	9·9
Multiple	135	4·3	78	2·6	35	1·3	248	2·8
Abroad	52	1·7	20	0·7	21	0·8	93	1·1
Medical	73	2·3	90	3·0	13	0·5	176	2·0
Seaside	150	4·8	72	2·4	80	3·0	302	3·4
TOTALS	3126	100·0	2987	100·0	2661	99·9	8774	99·9

Q1 = question 1, etc.

The time when situations occurred was classified: *very recent, fairly recent, distant* and *early childhood; very recent* was defined as within the last month, *fairly recent* within the last year, *distant* over a year, and *early childhood* 6 years old or younger. It proved possible to discover when situations occurred from just under half of answers given (47·8%). (The time when a situation occurred could be discovered because children specified their age, or stated previously when something happened, or provided internal evidence such as time of year, teacher concerned, etc.)

Of all answers given 9·7% occurred very recently, 22·3% recently, 11·2% at a distant time and 4·5% in early childhood (see Table 9). Accordingly 38·0% of

Table 9 Time when situations occurred

Time	Q1	%	Q2	%	Q3	%	TOTALS	%
Very recent	313	9·7	324	10·3	249	8·9	886	9·7
Fairly recent	869	27·0	614	19·5	563	20·2	2046	22·3
Distant	488	15·1	338	10·7	205	7·4	1031	11·2
Early childhood	189	5·8	159	5·0	68	2·4	416	4·5
Not specific	1371	42·4	1717	54·5	1700	61·0	4788	52·2
TOTALS	3230	100·0	3152	100·0	2785	99·9	9167	99·9

Q1 = question 1, etc.

all situations took place more than a week before the time of writing, compared with 9·7% which took place within a week of writing. This strongly suggests that a majority of children did not write indiscriminately about the most recent relevant occurrence in their lives, but chose a happening which had real meaning for them in terms of the question asked. It was of interest that just over half as many children recalled early childhood events (4·5%) as recalled very recent events (9·7%). It seems clear that for some children distant events could retain considerable clarity and significance. If the time when situations occurred is compared for different questions no very significant differences are discovered, although there was a tendency for distant and early childhood events to occur less frequently (9·8%) in question 3, than in question 1 (20·9%) and question 2 (15·7%).

The depth of feeling shown by children in recalling situations was classified *mild, medium, intense*. Classification of involvement posed problems both of standardization and interpretation. Particular attention was paid during standardization procedures (see Appendix C) to securing standardized classification of degrees of intensity.

As for interpretation, it was concluded that any particular degree of involvement should be seen as having its position on a continuum extending from very mild to very intense. This continuum should be seen as being arbitrarily divided into three broad, equivalent sections *mild, medium*, and *intense*. Thus, an answer classified as *low intense* would be close to, but separated from one classified *high medium.* The project concluded that, although in the final analysis any attempt to quantify degree of involvement must remain open to criticism on grounds both of lack of precision and of subjectivity, it was nevertheless preferable to provide, with the necessary qualifications, an indication of children's strength of feeling in recalling situations, rather than to offer no indication of findings in this area.

Of answers given and classified, over half (53·7%) were medium, while almost twice as many (29·5%) were intense as were mild (16·8%) (see Table 10). As with findings for time when situations occurred, these data appear to

Table 10   Degrees of involvement

Degree	Q1	%	Q2	%	Q3	%	TOTALS	%
Mild	414	12·8	225	7·1	904	32·5	1543	16·8
Medium	1673	51·8	1667	52·8	1586	57·0	4926	53·7
Intense	1145	35·4	1264	40·0	294	10·6	2703	29·5
TOTALS	3232	100·0	3156	99·9	2784	100·1	9172	100·0

Q1 = question 1, etc.

confirm that the majority of children did not treat answering the questions as a trivial exercise. If the degrees of intensity are compared for different questions one significant difference is discovered. While for question 1 and question 2 only 12·8% and 7·1% of answers were classified as mild, for question 3 32·5% were so classified ($p < 0.001$). Conversely, while for question 1 and question 2 35·4% and 40·0% were classified as intense, for question 3 only 10·6% were so classified ($p < 0.001$). Accordingly, as with time when and place where situations occurred, a different pattern appears to emerge for problem situations from that found for happy and unhappy situations. Typically, problem situations were more liable to occur recently, in the neighbourhood, and arouse mild degrees of involvement.

Although in the following Parts III—V many examples of children's answers are given, it is perhaps appropriate to conclude this section with two answers, where the place is self-evident, and which were classified as showing intense degrees of involvement. In the first answer the child, a girl, was 9 years old at the time of answering.

One day my parents said I phoned up the dentest, this was about four years ago. She said do you need the toliete. I said yes out I ran up the stairs in the dentest he the dentest man ran after me and he got me. He put me to sleep with gas, I had a tooth out and my mother said did you laugph with lauphing gas I said no, I had crying gas.

The second answer was written by an 11-year-old boy.

It was one cold morning and I was six years old and my mum was tacking me and my Brouther and my Sister to School and we had just got to the top of take Road and we stoped to wate for a petrol tanke to go past so we whent back a littel so it would get throw when sundley a car came whissing past and hit our car, our car was not to badly damidged but the other car was and when my mum got out of the car I was so angrey with the other man I starded to cry. but that is all I remember and I do not want to remember It.

Part III
Themes

Table 11   Classification of themes

Personal and home life
Siblings: trouble
Siblings: cooperation and concern
Grown-ups and home
Stairs
Food
Pets and animals
Moving home
Separation and reuniting

Other children
Peer groups and pressures
Boy/girl relationships
Friendship

Activities and pastimes
TV
Informal play and hobbies
Organized activities and sports
School work and activities
Shops and shopping
Vehicles

Special occasions and occurrences
Presents: giving and receiving
Christmas and birthdays
Social occasions
Public celebrations
Outings and visits
Staying away from home
Births and christenings
Engagements and marriages
Public appearances

Behaviour difficulties
Misbehaviour
Provocation
Drink, drugs and smoking
Law breaking and delinquent
    behaviour
Adult/child disagreement

Critical situations
Getting lost
Strangers
Fear and the dark
Fire hazard
Hostile supernatural occurrences
Accident and injury
Illness and operations
Death or disappearance

Problems
What do I do?
What do I choose?
How do I occupy myself?
How do I do it?
Losing, finding and forgetting

Expectations
Expected happenings
Unexpected happenings
Striving
Praise
Temptation
Unfairness
Taking responsibility
Concern for others

Miscellaneous

6 Classification and frequency—themes

CLASSIFICATION

The procedure by which themes were classified was inductive (see Appendix C). For the purposes of clear presentation themes have been grouped under eight major headings (see Table 11). These headings are: *Personal and home life, Other children, Activities and pastimes, Special occasions and occurrences, Behaviour difficulties, Critical situations, Problems* and *Expectations.* These headings indicate the major areas of concern shown by children in their answers. The placing of any particular theme under a given heading is not intended to be definitive. A number of themes are multifaceted, and have claims under different headings. For example the themes *siblings: trouble,* and *siblings: cooperation and concern* are placed under *Personal and home life;* they could however also be placed under *Other children.* Accordingly, the placing of any particular theme under any given heading is primarily indicative.

Titles of major headings and themes are descriptive and do not predicate the role played by a child in a situation with a given theme. Thus, an answer with the theme *misbehaviour* was not necessarily concerned with misbehaviour by the child; the misbehaviour in question might have been by other children or by adults, or animals. Further, titles do not predicate the nature of the situation reported, that is whether it was a happy, unhappy or problem situation. Thus, an answer with the theme *misbehaviour* was not necessarily associated with unhappiness. In fact 13 children gave answers with the theme *misbehaviour* to the happiness question, 203 to the unhappiness question, and 149 to the problem question.

A number of the titles given to themes are self-explanatory. Others however need more detailed consideration. Under the heading *Personal and home life,* the theme *grown-ups and home* refers to situations in which the children were primarily involved with adults, either through activities such as helping parents in house or garden, or through encounters with adult visitors and callers.

Stairs and *food* were included as themes because, despite their relatively low incidence, situations with stairs and food appeared significant to numbers particularly of younger children. *Separation and reuniting* refers to situations in which children were parted from, or reunited with those who were significant to them, particularly family members.

The themes under *Other children* are self-explanatory. Of the themes under *Activities and pastimes* two, *organized activities and sports,* and *school work and activities* referred to situations which took place in mainly adult controlled environments. However, in some of the situations referred to by these themes, children were actually in circumstances in which they were left very much to their own devices. For example, swimming pools, playgrounds, time immediately before and after team game events, although under the charge of adults, in fact frequently provided conditions in which children were allowed considerable freedom and related to each other rather than to adults. *Informal play and hobbies* referred to situations which involved non-supervised games and sports, board games, playing with toys, reading and, particularly with younger children, making jokes. *Vehicles* referred to situations in which a wide variety of machines appeared, for example cars, bikes, scooters, buses, lorries, boats, ships, planes, which children might have been controlling, or in which they might have been travelling, or in which they might have been experiencing breakdowns or crashes.

Of themes classified under *Special occasions and occurrences, parents: giving and receiving,* and *Christmas and birthdays* were perennial, intimate, well understood and well defined experiences for children. *Births and christenings,* and *engagements and marriages* were essentially concerned with family (but often the extended family), and could involve encounters with those relatively or totally unknown to children. *Outings and visits* referred to circumstances which were possibly new to a child; they did not require a night to be spent away from home. Visits could be to cinema, theatre, pantomime, zoo, relations; outings could be with family or school for the day; any treat or change of scene would probably require some outing or visit. *Staying away from home,* referred to lengthier excursions, and involved nights away, in the neighbourhood or on a family weekend on camps, or on holidays. *Social occasions* and *public celebrations* referred to activities which, from the child's point of view, often had an almost ritualistic aspect, and participation in which emphasized their independence of — rather than dependence on — adult support and initiative. *Social occasions* were, for example, parties and youth clubs; *public celebrations* were fairs, carnivals, bonfire night, halloween. Although the theme *public appearances,* like *public celebrations* had a ritualistic element, it was strongly adult orientated. It involved situations in which children received public awards or recognition for achievement, for example being singled out by name at school assembly, or being given a prize for winning a competition.

The group heading *Behaviour difficulties* contains, with the possible exception of *adult/child disagreement,* a number of closely related themes. *Adult/ child disagreement* refers to situations in which adult behaviour, particularly reprimands and prohibitions, were resented or disapproved of by children, when their feelings were either expressed openly through their behaviour, or covertly. *Misbehaviour* involved situations in which ill doing was accidental, alleged or actual; perpetrated by children, adults or animals; and included particularly breakages and lying. *Provocation* involved situations in which children either provoked, or were provoked by others; provocation might be by bullying, intimidation, argument, teasing, chasing, fighting. *Law breaking and delinquent behaviour* were distinguished from the themes of *misbehaviour* and *provocation* as involving only those situations in which behaviour by those concerned, whether children or adults, would be liable to lead to a court appearance. *Drink, drugs and smoking*, were categorized separately from *law breaking and delinquent behaviour,* so that an estimate could be made of the prevalence of such behaviour in the children's answers.

The meaning of the majority of themes under the heading *Critical situations,* is reasonably self-evident. *Strangers* referred to situations in which children were approached or chased, by adults unknown to them. *Fear and the dark* referred to situations in which children who were in the dark felt fear, not necessarily of the dark itself, but possibly of other phenomena such as strange noises, dreams, etc. *Hostile supernatural occurrences* referred to situations in which children encountered either, in their view, in actuality, or as a result of other people's tricks, ghosts, witches, haunted houses, skeletons. Ghost stories too were categorized under this theme. *Illness and operations* included visits to clinics and dentists. Disappearance was included with *death or disappearance* because children reported a number of situations in which animals in particular were missing, presumed dead. Adults also however on occasion vanished for ever without explanation.

Themes of *Problems* reported by children require careful definition. The theme *what do I do?* refers to situations in which children suffered uncertainty about following rules, codes or procedures because they were not known to the children; because they were known but not understood; or because there was a conflict between them. By 'rules' is meant orders officially laid down and enforced by those in authority, whether teachers, parents, other adults, or (very rarely) children. By 'codes' is meant regulations, not necessarily officially laid down or enforced, but being established by general agreement and having the sanction of social approval; codes might be features of either child or adult groups with which children found themselves in contact. By 'procedures' is meant guidelines to how to behave, not necessarily overtly explicated, but frequently informal and unformalized; these also might be features of either child or adult groups. The theme *what do I do?* could also refer to situations in which children had difficulty in understanding the nature of particular circumstances.

What do I choose? refers to situations in which children had a choice, or choices, within defined circumstances. *How do I occupy myself?* refers to situations in which children were faced with the problem of finding themselves something to do, whether it was informal play or any other activity, such as a visit to the cinema. *How do I do it?* refers to situations in which children either lacked a particular skill; or, although having the necessary expertise, lacked the ability required to deal with a difficult problem. For example, a child might be able to swim, but not be capable of swimming strongly or fast enough to rescue a ball being blown out to sea. These two aspects of this theme could well overlap. *Losing, finding and forgetting* refers to situations in which children lost, found or forgot the whereabouts of other people, animals or things. (Children losing themselves was separately categorized under *Critical situations* as *getting lost.*)

The major heading *Expectations* subsumed the themes of situations in which either children themselves enjoyed, or suffered the expected, or alternatively the unexpected; or in which children responded or failed to respond to the expectations of others, whether such expectations were personal (e.g. a mother expecting a daughter to babysit) or impersonal (e.g. rules such as 'stealing is bad' accepted, at least in theory, by a child). *Expected happenings* could refer to situations in which there was fulfilled anticipation of a pleasant event (typically in an answer to the happiness question); or to situations in which there was unfulfilled anticipation of a pleasant event (typically in answers to the happiness and unhappiness questions); or to situations in which there was unfulfilled anticipation of an unpleasant event (typically in answers to the happiness and unhappiness questions); or to situations in which there was fulfilled anticipation of an unpleasant event (typically in answer to the un-happiness question). *Unexpected happenings* refers to situations in which children had a pleasant surprise, or a fright caused, for example, by being jumped out on, or shut in. *Striving* refers to situations in which children exerted themselves, successfully or unsuccessfully, to attain valued goals, such as the award of a team place. *Praise*, refers to situations in which children were rewarded or encouraged by others for valued behaviour. *Unfairness* refers to situations in which children's expectations of how others should behave in circumstances requiring the interpretation of rules and codes were not fulfilled (*unfairness* as a theme was often linked with *adult/child disagreement*). *Temptation* refers to situations in which children's own expectations of how they themselves ought to behave were in danger of being unfulfilled. *Taking responsibility* refers to situations in which children were expected by themselves or others to play the part more usually taken by adults or other children; such situations included babysitting, looking after oneself or other children in the absence of adults and shopping for mothers. *Concern for others* refers to situations in which children responded both to others' expectation of how they ought to behave, and also to their own apparently more subjective and intuitive standards.

FREQUENCY

Because it was found that situations described by children frequently had two themes rather than one, it was decided that any single answer might be analysed in terms of one or two themes. Accordingly there is not a one-to-one relationship between answers given and themes recorded.

A view of the frequency of incidence of themes within major headings may be obtained by comparing the total number of themes occurring in each group, first within each type of situation, and secondly between the three types of situation (see Table 12). In the happy situations 45·2% of all themes occurred

Table 12 Theme groups: happy, unhappy, problem situations

Theme group	Situations Happy	%	Unhappy	%	Problem	%
Personal and home life	792	13·9	988	18·1	183	4·2
Other children	188	3·3	169	3·1	261	6·0
Activities and pastimes	832	14·6	698	12·8	1271	29·2
Special occasions and occurrences	2582	45·2	319	5·9	512	11·8
Behaviour difficulties	50	0·9	1047	19·2	350	8·0
Critical situations	171	3·0	1143	20·9	364	8·4
Problems	72	1·3	94	1·7	1805	25·0
Expectations	1001	17·5	990	18·1	310	7·1
Miscellaneous	20	0·3	12	0·2	9	0·2
TOTALS	5708	100·0	5460	100·0	5065	99·9

in the group *special occasions and occurrences,* while fewer than 20% of themes occurred in any other single group (17·5% in *expectations,* 14·6% in *activities and pastimes,* 13·9% in *personal and home life*). Fewer than 5% of themes occurred in the remaining individual groups — 3·3% in *other children,* 3·0% in *critical situations*, 1·6% in *problems,* 0·9% in *behaviour difficulties,* 0·3% in *miscellaneous.*

In unhappy situations a more even distribution was discovered. 20·9% of themes occurred in *critical situations,* 19·2% in *behaviour difficulties,* 18·1% in *expectations,* and 18·1% in *personal and home life.* 12·8% of themes occured in *activities and pastimes.* Fewer than 6% of themes occurred in the remaining individual groups (5·8% in *Special occasions and occurrences,* 3·1% in *other children,* 1·7% in *problems* and 0·2% in *miscellaneous*).

In problem situations two major heads predominated. *Activities and pastimes* included 25·1% of all themes (1271), and *problems* included 35·6% of all themes (1805). By comparison the group *special occasions and occurrences,* in which occurred the third highest frequency of themes mentioned had only 10·1% of all themes (512). Considering individual themes, 755 children gave answers with the theme *informal play and hobbies,* and exactly the same number gave answers with the theme *what do I do?* With the exception of the theme, *how do I occupy myself?,* which occurred in the answers of 441 children, fewer than half as many children gave answers with other themes. It appears therefore that the social moral problems with which children considered themselves to be confronted were concentrated in relatively few and clearly defined areas.

If the frequency of incidence of themes in individual groups is compared between questions the following findings emerge. The *personal and home life* group included 13·9% of all themes in the happy situation, 18·1% of all themes in unhappy situations and 4·2% of all themes in problem situations (statistically there was a significant difference between happy and unhappy situations, $p < 0.05$, and a very significant difference between unhappy and problem situations, $p < 0.001$). Themes for the three types of situation in the *other children* group were relatively evenly distributed showing no statistically significant variations (3·3% of all themes in happy situations, 3·1% in the unhappy situations and 6·0% in problem situations).

A very significantly higher frequency of themes under *activities and pastimes* was found in problem situations than was found in the other types of situation (14·6% of all themes in happy situations, 12·8% in the unhappy situations and 29·2% in problem situations, $p < 0.001$). A very significantly greater frequency of themes under *special occasions and occurrences* was found in happy situations than in the other types of situation (45·2% of all themes in happy situations, 5·9% in unhappy situations and 11·8% in problem situations, $p < 0.001$). Themes under *behaviour difficulties* occurred significantly more frequently in unhappy situations than in the other types of situation (19·2% of all themes in unhappy situations, 0·9% in happy situations and 8·0% in problem situations, $p < 0.001$). Themes under *critical situations* likewise occurred significantly more frequently in unhappy situations (20·9%

of all themes in unhappy situations, 3·0% in happy situations, and 8·4% in problem situations, $p < 0.001$). A very significantly greater frequency of themes under *problems* occurred in problem situations than in the other types of situation (25·0% of all themes in problem situations, 1·3% in happy situations and 1·7% in unhappy situations, $p < 0.001$). The low frequency of themes concerned with problems in unhappy situations suggests that children seldom found problems so intractable as to cause unhappiness.

Finally, themes under *expectations* occurred very significantly less frequently in problem situations than in the other types of situation (7·1% of all themes in problem situations, 17·5% in the happy situations and 18·1% in unhappy situations, $p < 0.001$).

7 Happy situations—themes

The answers which children gave to the happiness questions were apparently marked by considerable diversity, even within the separate groups of themes. It was nevertheless possible to discern a common pattern in much of what was written. From the children's point of view happiness and pleasure might frequently be experiences when they were treated with love and concern by others, or when circumstances enabled the children themselves to express feelings of kindness or compassion to others. Happiness therefore frequently arose in the context of a considerate life style, such a style being one in which children had the opportunity not only to be the recipients of good will, but also — either reciprocally, or of their own initiative — agents of loving behaviour.

For many of the children the family was the setting, if not always the immediate occasion, of much of their experience. The family's world was frequently perceived by children in vivid, truthful colours — a vision on occasion made possible by the unawareness of preoccupied adults that an observant child was very much, if uncharacteristically quietly, present, and made acute by natural curiosity, lack of learned inhibition, and the absence of adult rationalizations and interpretations.

Particularly for girls, events connected with the birth of babies were of considerable interest. A 12+ girl from a middle school described the scene and her insights and feelings when her older sister called with her husband to tell the family that, after a long wait, she was expecting a baby.

It was a late Thursday night. I was watching telly, when someone knocked at the door. I went to the door, to my surprise it was my sister and her husband. They walked in with a smile all over their face. I asked what was wrong, they said nothing. My sister walked into the kitchen, where my mum was. She was smiling but there were tears in her eyes. She put her hands round my mum and started to cry. She said something but I did not hear it.

I then went into the frount room, and whispered to my Auntie, 'I think

50

Ronnie's going to have a baby.' My Auntie smiled. Bobby, my sisters husband come in with his arms round Ronnie. Mum followed behined. My sister came up to me she put her arms round me. I was right she was going to have a baby. I was so pleased, I began to cry. Which made my sister cry. She had been married three years, and I had given up hoping that she would have a baby. Mum made a cup of coffee and we sat down to drink it. I asked what they were going to call it. My sister said 'give us a chance, there is plenty of time yet'. I got up and went in to my bedroom, where I found some baby wool and a small pair of needles. I started straight away making some bootees. After we had finished the coffee, Ronnie and Bobby had to go on to Bobby parents house to tell them the good news. The baby is in March near my birthday.

Another girl revealed not only concern about the birth of a baby brother, but a well informed knowledge about the details of childbirth which ensured that, in her case as in others, concern was not general but arose from a specific understanding of particular problems.

It made me happy to hear that my Mum had had the baby and it was a boy. I was happy that Grant the baby was O.K. because his cord was very tight tied around if my mum had not gone to the hospital to have him he would have died. As a result of this when mum and Grant came home I did my best to help her with the housework and cooking.

Girls are not alone either in concern or knowledge in the problems of childbirth. A boy in the first year of a Cardiff comprehensive school discussed the difficulties endured by his aunt and baby cousin.

The time that somebody made me happy was when my Aunt was having a baby because it came out feet first instead of head first and we were not shore weather it would life. The baby was born and he was all right but he was kept in the hospital in a special unit untill they were sure it would be all right. he could not breath propolly so when he went home he kept having to the hospital for injections. Then my Aunt phoned and said 'The baby is all right and we are calling him Paul.' That is what made me happy.

Connected with the problems of pregnancy were the wider difficulties of adult relationships. There were the stresses associated with older sisters who had babies but no husbands and the happiness felt when all seemed to turn out for the best. One girl in her first year at a comprehensive wrote about her delight when her sister returned home.

When my sister came back home after about 5 months from a place with my nephew (she didn't run off or anything) who had just been born. We went

Table 13   Frequency of themes: happy situations

Theme group	Individual theme		No.	% of themes
Personal & home life	Siblings: trouble		8	0·14
	Siblings: cooperation & concern		73	1·28
	Grown-ups and home		220	3·85
	Stairs		3	0·05
	Food		35	0·61
	Pets and animals		374	6·55
	Moving home		30	0·52
	Separation & reuniting		49	0·86
		TOTALS	792	13·87
Other children	Peer groups & pressures		14	0·24
	Boy/girl relationships		30	0·52
	Friendship		144	2·52
		TOTALS	188	3·29
Activities & pastimes	TV		34	0·6
	Informal play & hobbies		244	4·27
	Organized activities & sports		234	4·1
	School work & activities		151	2·64
	Shops & shopping		71	1·24
	Vehicles		98	1·72
		TOTALS	832	14·58
Special occasions & occurrences	Presents: giving & receiving		1009	17·68
	Christmas and birthdays		516	9·04
	Social occasions		106	1·86
	Public celebrations		59	1·03
	Outings and visits		404	7·08
	Staying away from home		302	5·29
	Births and christenings		67	1·17
	Engagements and marriages		47	0·82
	Public appearances		72	1·26
		TOTALS	2582	45·23
Behaviour difficulties	Misbehaviour		13	0·23
	Provocation		13	0·23
	Drink, drugs and smoking		4	0·07

Theme group	Individual theme	No.	% of themes
	Law breaking & delinquent behaviour	4	0·07
	Adult/child disagreement	16	0·28
	TOTALS	50	**0·88**
Critical situations	Getting lost	5	0·09
	Strangers	1	0·02
	Fear and the dark	1	0·02
	Fire hazard	3	0·05
	Hostile supernatural occurrences	3	0·05
	Accident and injury	64	1·12
	Illness and operations	89	1·56
	Death or disappearance	5	0·09
	TOTALS	171	**3·0**
Problems	What do I do?	2	0·03
	What do I choose?	9	0·16
	How do I occupy myself?	0	—
	How do I do it?	24	0·42
	Losing, finding & forgetting	37	0·65
	TOTALS	72	**1·26**
Expectations	Expected happenings	340	5·96
	Unexpected happenings	39	0·68
	Striving	264	4·62
	Praise	126	2·21
	Temptation	2	0·03
	Unfairness	4	0·07
	Taking responsibility	52	0·91
	Concern for others	174	3·05
	TOTALS	1001	**17·54**
Miscellaneous	TOTAL	20	**0·35**
	OVERALL TOTALS	5708	**100·0**

Percentages have been rounded.

up to see here every weekend and took here out on picnics. I was glad to see my sister home again and to see her baby. She lives with us now so I help her in bathing him and I sometimes take him out for walks now that he's a bit older. He's a beautiful little baby and I love him very much. Some how he doesn't seem like my nephew and I treat him like my brother I never think of saying something like 'Come to your auntie - -.' I'm very proud of my nephew and I love my sister very much.

There were also the more profound fears and joys associated with the dramas of parental married life. A 12+ girl in the last year of her middle school wrote simply

When someone made me happy was when my mother got married for the second time and my father accepted me for his child, with my sister.

Another girl of 9+, in the first year of a middle school, wrote of her similar feelings when she acquired, not a second father who loved and accepted her, but a second mother.

I wahs happy when I went to live with the pursun I am living with now. You may ask how that is well I will tell you it is my mum I always call her that because she is my mum now but I am stil living with my dad.

An 11+ boy not only showed pleasure for his own sake that this mother was remarried and no longer alone, but also appreciation of the qualities of kindness which the parents needed to reveal in their treatment of each other, and of their children, if they and the family were to be happy.

It was one Sunday evning and my brouther and my sister and I were coming home in our devorsted dads car becuse we allways sore him on a Sunday and mum was all alone at home. But we were allmost home. When we got home We seaid goodbye to dad, and when we opend the front door we heard talking in the loung so we whent in and there was mum talking to Bill. I had seen him ones befor and mum seaid meet bill children my haret feeted so hapey that I allmost kriyed bill had been marrid befor but I nyoow that he was gowing to be our new dad and I was glade and he is so undstanding and they have been marrid for all most two yeares and they have been kined to each uther and to us.

Sibling rivalry is a term made all too familiar by psychologists; and there would be few parents to deny its existence. However, it is perhaps easy to overlook the presence of its obverse, an active care and concern displaced by siblings for each other. Sibling cooperation after all does not often require adult intervention, or cause adult irritation; consequently it may too frequently be taken for granted. Nevertheless, to children in this sample it was on occasion a source of considerable satisfaction.

A girl aged 13 years 1 month, from a middle school wrote:

One of the times when somebody made me feel pleased and happy was when my sister told me I was a nice sister. So I told her she was a nice sister too and we both ment it. I felt warm and pleased inside.

A boy described his intense feelings when his brother, who had got lost in the woods, was found:

The day my heart nearly jumped out of my mouth with happieness was when Mum said we found him! Because what had happened was that, Andrew my older brother had gone out to the woods to pick some Bluebells out of it because it was Mums birthday, and he wanted to make her happy by picking her some flowers.
So he followed a trail of Bluebells, but he wasn't looking where he was going and he got lost.

It is noticeable how infrequently, in comparison with themes of *personal and home life*, themes of *other children* occur (this is a pattern repeated in unhappy situations, although not in problem situations). However, although *other children* may be the central theme of only relatively few answers, other children feature significantly in many situations with closely related themes, particularly themes in *activities and pastimes*, such as *informal play and hobbies, organized activities and sports*, and *school work and activities.*

The predominant theme (occurring 144 times) of answers concerned with *other children*, was that of friendship. A 10+ girl felt happy because she was able to help a friend whose family were not as well off as her own.

On Sunday 18th November it was comfomasion day whan people got comformed and my brother was geting comfermed and there was other People and my freind anglerjose was getting comfermed as well and I was Very happy to lend her my White shoes and after we had got home we had a comfermasion partey for my brother.
And angler in Returun for leting her borow my shoes gave me a Big Bar of choclete. I lent her my shoes becouse she did not have any and her mum could not afored to by any.
and I am happey because I have left the church choir.

A 9+ year old boy from a junior school in Swindon established a friendship with another boy when he paid for him to go to the cinema.

I payed aboy in the pitures because he lost his piture money a few weeks later I was invited to the boy's party who I payed into the pitures.

Of the themes concerned with *activities and pastimes,* the majority were associated with *informal play and hobbies,* and *organized activity and sports* (234). Interestingly, considering the popular impression that too many young children spend too much time in addictive television viewing, only 34 (0·6%) of the themes mentioned television as a source of pleasure or happiness. (This compares with 111 (2·0%) of the themes which mentioned it as a source of unhappiness, a very significant difference statistically ($p < 0·001$). It appears therefore that children in the sample were significantly more likely to consider television in the context of unhappy than of happy experience.

Even where television was mentioned in the context of happy experience the happiness was, on occasion, associated with emotions of aggression rather than consideration. One 9+ boy, for example, had been considerably elated by viewing the destruction of a German battleship.

I was watching a film about the sinking of the Bismark and the Bismark was coming down the Atlantic Ocean to get to Germany and join two other German ships, then put to sea with them and make the powerfullest fleet in the world. But before the Bismark could reach Germany she was badly damaged and later sunk this made me very happy. Later I started building the Bismark with my lego and I also played sinking the Bismark. I was happy because the Bismark had been sunk.

Another child, a 9+ girl from a London junior school, compared television unfavourably with a live show. 'The thing that most pleased me was that the show was live and not on TV. I went with my Mum, Siter and Aunt. I was pleased even after the show was finished because my mum said one day she might take me agian.'

Special occasions and occurrences were predominantly reported by children, not so much as isolated events significant in their own right, but rather as clearly focused and often deeply felt instances of situations or attitudes fundamental to and implicit in their everyday life. This was perhaps particularly true of answers concerned with the giving and receiving of presents and with Christmas and birthdays. These answers gave some, but not sub-stantial support to the view, expressed informally by some teachers in the survey, that numbers of parents lavished gifts on children, but gave them little real affection, with the consequence that children learned to become acquisi-tive and careless of their property, rather than discovering the real worth of gifts both as symbols of loving concern, and as objects needing to be well looked after.

Examples of children who were mercenary about presents did of course occur. There was the 10+ boy who spent the months preceding Christmas poring over catalogues, and eventually deciding on a cornucopia of expensive gifts, for which he showed no thanks or gratitude. And there was the 9+ girl from a middle school who was given money to buy considerable amounts of sweets.

My mum said to get £1.00 and spent it on sweets so I did I got two Big packets of steets that was 10p each and many more till I got it up to £1.00 and went home and than I had to go to a party I was full up all after that but I was very happy indeed and the next day I done It again.

On the other hand there were children who showed considerable insight into the problems and feelings of parents who, though finding it difficult to afford presents, nevertheless bought them. Such children displayed real and sensitive gratitude. There was the 10+ boy from a London junior school who wrote:

When my mother bought me a piano For Birthday result I behaved myself. She was just was able to buy it they are too expensive they shood be cheaper about £30 to 40.

There was also a 10+ junior school girl from Swindon who recalled a particular present given to her by her mother.

The day someone made me happy was about 3 years ago when my dad was in the navy. The person to make me happy was my mum. The day that she made me happy was on my birthday. We were rather short on money beacuase my dad could not send much money in and it some times got held up in the post. My mum worked full time but she did not earn very much money so we we short on money. I was not expeting a very big present. What made me cross and happy was mum had bought me a pair of expensive shoes they were lovely. She bought a lovely card and she gave me 25p to spend. What made me cross was I new she never had much money what made me really happy was my mum cared so much about me that she didnt care about money she cared about me.

This girl was not only quite explicit that the expensive shoes were important to her, because they showed that her mother loved her; she had also recalled the incident over a period of three years. Such relatively lengthy periods of recall were not uncommon. Another 9+ London boy for example remembered, 'When I was most happyest in my life was when it was my birthday. I was only five years old and my mum bought me a bycle and I didnt know what to say . . . And when my dad got home I was only too glad to thank him for

the four the four wheeler truck and everything.' That particular occasions
were often recalled, rather than simply the last birthday or Christmas sub-
stantiates the argument that for numbers of children individual events were
recalled as significant, not simply because they were the most recent, but for
specific reasons.

There was considerable evidence that many children viewed, and were
encouraged by adults to view, present giving and receiving as integral to the
successful functioning of considerate relationships. A 9+ girl from a Cardiff
school not only gave, but herself experienced considerable happiness from the
choosing and giving of a birthday present to her sister.

One day my sister told me it was her birthday next week. I was so pleazed
that I ran down stars and asked my mother what would she like my mother
said so many things but none of them were good wones. Then I thought of
some stamps towards her colletion and a bottle of hand cream so I saved up.
and went to town buy it then I saw a little contaner to put odds and ends in
it so I brought that aswell. when I got home my mother and father said that
it would be nice for a present so I went up stars and wrapped it up whith
paper and put some ribon on it. buy then the next day it was her Birthday.
next day at half past 5 all her freinds came and I gave her the present. She
opend it and said that it was the best presant she had I was pleased.

Another girl, in her first year at a comprehensive school described very clearly
her general pleasure in Christmas because of the atmosphere of loving kindness, her particular affection for her brothers, and her own joy at receiving a
longed for guitar.

Most Christmases I feel very happy because you know that your family,
reletions and friends are thinking about you by sending presents to you. One
Christmas well actually a few months before I was listening to a record it was
a gutarest. When I was listening to it, it really made me think how lovely it
was. From that night on I would have liked a gutair very much. Even when I
was listening to the record again it made me cry.

The months went by and it was drawing near to Christmas. Everybody
knew I would have liked a gutair but nobody hardly every said anything about
it.

On Christmas morning 1971 we were all opening our Christmas presents.
We soon had opened them all and were just going up stairs to get dressed when
my Mother said we had a present left, she then took us into the front room,
where there was two bikes. My mother said they were for my two brothers.
I did not look around to she what I had I was to pleased for my brothers.
Then I noticed a tringular box in the corner and I asked my mother what it
was, my mother said to go and have a look. I looked in the box I couldn't
belive my eyes it was a gutair.

Some parents were well aware of the dangers of children taking expensive items for granted, and so devaluing their worth both as symbols of love, and in simple cash terms. One father ensured that his son made a contribution towards the purchase of a costly bicycle — and his son worked with a will to raise the necessary capital.

it was March the 15th, 4 days away from my birthday and I was holding a jumble sale selling my toys and things which I did not think nessary to have as I was 11 years old. I did this in order to raise I hope five pounds towards my birthday present which was a 5-speed racer the first I had ever had and I could not face the fact that I was getting one but it was true I also gave my old bike to my sister as hers was to small and she sold hers to the bike shop then after the jumble sale I had rased something like three pounds which I gave to my father for safe keeping March 16th was here and to raise the extra two pounds to make five pounds I started doing errands like washing cars and at last I got the bike and to show my thanks I polished it as soon as I got home and a nice big thank you for mum and dad.

Other parents were not above using presents overtly to influence behaviour.

One day in March my Dad gave me a box of sweets and said that I was to behav I was so glad that I promist to be good for two weeks then my Dad said that I shoud keep my sweet for the next day so I did and I was glad for I did what my dad told me.

For some children presents were recalled as being important because they marked a change of status, or initiated a change of attitude. One 9+ girl at a middle school recalled the gift of a record player which was important to her, at least in part, because it marked a move towards more grown-up status.

At Christmas time last year when My Auntie & Uncle gave me my very first record player & it was a real one as well. That made me feel happy because it made me feel that I was having grown up's things & I was not having babies toys any more. But at that time I was eight years old.

A 10-year-old girl, from a junior school in Workington reflected on the ephemeral nature of happiness.

When I was eight years old I got a big bear and I was very happy with my bear and a very big doll too. It was good fun and then I went out to play out side with my bear and doll and after five weeks time I had put my nice big bear in a big padlin pool and I had to put my bear in the hash bag and I had put pen marces all over my dolls face and legs and armys I could not get the pen marces off my dolls face I could not wash the pen marces off my dolls face, and my big doll is one year old how I ham 10 years old and I do not play with dolls any more or I do not play with bears anymore.

There were occasions when presents were outcomes, not of familiar circumstances such as birthdays, or Christmases, but of unusual occasions which were themselves perhaps considerably more significant than any actual gift. There was for instance the 10-year-old girl from a London junior school who recalled the visit of her uncle from abroad, bringing with him West Indian delicacies.

I was happy when my uncle was coming to England for six weeks. When I went home My uncle was having dinner. He bought us some mangoes, fried fish and breadfruit we played rounders in the garden and my brother nearly broke the window. After that I showed my uncle round the house. My uncle could not wait to see my dad. My mum told me my uncles birthday is on the same day as her birthday.

And, on a less convivial note there was a child whose family was poverty stricken and was saved by a very welcome letter.

Once we had no money and there was no money to by petrol on wunday petrol we needed for the fire and we were very cold then there was a noke at the door and my dad went to the door and there was no one there but in the letter box there was a letter and my dad brung the letter in and we opened it up and it seid in it a check for a hundred ponds at Lloyds bank we all got in the car and went down to Lloyds bank and my dad and mum went in Lloyds bank and showd the people it and they looked at it and gave my dad it in new very new five pond notes and they came out with it and we all went home and they gave us some money and we put it in our money boxes.

Poverty, although an unwelcome aspect of children's experience was one which was undeniably present. In contrast to it some children valued possibly ostentations affluence. An 8+ girl from a London school described the happiness she experienced from visiting her wealthy aunt.

One day I was so glad becuse my mummy said that I could go up my antie and she had two phones and two teleusion one is a big coulour teleusion and the other one was a small tele it showes midlands and channel and ITV BBC1 BBC2 and she has an upstairs and down stairs and their are ten rooms 5 up stairs 5 down stairs and my antie is kind she let us make are own cup of tea and she gave us diner up their and when we were going home are cousin lesle gave us a lifit home because are daddy did go home all ready because he was hugry and when we reach home we had diner all together.

Other outings revealed the nature of children's attitudes towards their relations. The concern of the young for the old and the almost intimate understanding which could exist between grandchildren and grandparents was indicated, for example, by this answer.

One day somebody made me happy it was my mum and dad. I was happy because they said that we were going to see my great granma she was very old and when every I go up there to see her she allways gives us some money to buy sweets with. My great granmar said that wished that she was young and healthy like me and I said I wish she was to.

Outings could also highlight the nature of a child's daily existence, or the moral values implicitly held by a child. Bleakly, a 10+ year old from a school in an educational priority area reported 'The only time when I was happy was when I was chosen for the country dancing and we all got a free ticket to go to the circus.' By contrast an 8+ girl wrote about a visit to the seaside which had about it a golden, almost ideal quality.

I went to a place in barry that every one liked each other my mother said it was a day that people were very happy. One man came up to us and said would you like to play a game and it was a happy Joly game. And it made me so happy that I could not stop my self laughing. The game was a laughing game. And my sister was laughing so much I did not no why she was laughing so much she told us and when we got home I said to her I am so pleased.

Here was a world in which everyone loved every one else, and made each other happy, and it was good.

Second only in frequency to themes concerned with *special occasions and occurrences* (45·23% of all happy themes), were themes connected with *expectations* (17·54% of all happy themes). This group included explicit *concern for others* (reported 174 times), (as opposed to implicit concern for others which has been considered in relation to other themes); *expected* and *unexpected happenings* (reported 379 times in all), *striving* (reported by 264 children), *praise* (reported by 126) and *taking responsibility* (reported by 52). Worth comment was the relatively high frequency with which children reported that happiness was the outcome of anticipated happenings. On occasion the pleasure derived, as might be expected, from the fulfilment of hoped for events. But many children made it clear quite explicitly that pleasure for them lay primarily in the anticipation. One boy at a comprehensive school recalled the happiness with which, seven years previously, he had looked forward to going to school: but he specifically disassociated the pleasure derived from anticipation from the emotions actually experienced as a result of attending school.

I felt happy when I first heard I was to go to school. I felt as if I was bigg when I set of that morning, we had all our own classes and started on a long talk aboat the school. After a week I did not like and from thes day on I still don't.

Another boy, an 8-year-old, never in fact enjoyed an anticipated treat (seeing a football match), but he was still happy, because it was thinking about it that counted.

at my aunts my uncle was there I asked him if he could take me to a football match he said yes I could go and he made me happy, when the day came he never came to celloct me but the match was postponed for that day so the week after he came but he had no tickets or his wallet only his car keys. RESULT he never came but who cares, not me because I wern't allowed to go unless the ticket were shown to my mum and dad, but I was still happy. It was my thought that counted.

A third boy of 9+ from London, like may other children, wrote about a situation in which anticipation had been fulfilled, but in which the anticipation rather than the fulfilment was emphasized.

My father made me feel happy when he said that we were going to my cousins and and stay there till Sunday and I felt very happy when I heard that my other cousin was coming to stay there as well. I felt happy and pleased. I kept on looking out of the window and see that if my Uncle was coming. When he came we went in the car and stopped at my cousins house who was going to come with us. Then we had to change cars. The we went to my other cousins house where we were going to stay, in Palmers Green.

A theme which raised a number of interesting points was *taking responsibility*. There was in fact some evidence from the answers of either direct, or indirect adult hostility to children learning to take responsibility. It was perhaps because of this reluctance on the part of adults to initiate children into the adult world that this theme occurred relatively infrequently. One 11+ boy at a middle school recalled a time when he was given a garage job to do by his father, and finished it despite the mockery of his father's friends.

A few year's ago I went down to my dad's garage for something to do, but there wasn't any thing to do down there so after dinner I went down there again, and not long after I arrived dad gave me a job that I have alway's wanted to do but I never had any experience but dad still let me have a go at

it, he let me paint the back of a customer's van, the couler I had to paint with
was black. So a quarter of an hour dad's frend's came down and made fun of
me and about an hour later the job was finished and then I went home.

Another boy of 9+ conspired with his mother to keep secret the fact that he
had earned more than was officially allowed for a boy of his age — although
he believed he had worked hard and well for the money.

Once my manager at work, gave me £4 just for working a week. But one thing
is for sure, I work so hard for it, I am not old enough to get £4 pouds and my
mum said I must not tell nowone els about it. And then he went in his car.
When I got home I put 3 pounds in my saveings and spent 50p on a box of
choclates for my mum, because she kept me clean all thorw the week. and
2 fish and chips for my brothers and I. And on Sunday I went swimming.

What is also evident from these answers is that, for these children, the
chance of doing a serious job of work was important and significant. Another
aspect too, emerged from situations with this theme. The taking of responsibility could enable children to form a different, and potentially very rewarding
form of relationship with adults: a relationship formed not so much of
dependence, as of mutual respect. This point was well illustrated by the
answer of a farmer's daughter, aged 11+, who helped with the job of milking
cows.

Last year from June to November I was getting out of bed at 5 o'clock to help
the dairyman with the milking I made a cup of tea in the morning for mum and
dad and at half past 5 the dairyman knocked at the door for some hot water
because the hot water tap had broken down the farm when he knocked at the
door I knew that it was nearly time to leave so I made some coffee in a flask
and took it with two cups down the field to the milking Bail we get down there
by tractor and a crate what dad made when we are down there we both get
the cows in when we have been milking for half an hour we have milked about
15 cows so we have a cup of coffee there is four cup fulls in a flask so we can
have two cups each the dairy man moves the fence now and when he comes
back there is about 30 cows milked that means we have been milking for an
hour it is Monday so I only have about an hour left when it is 8 o'clock I go
back home and get ready for school the dairyman left at the end of November
(and) I was sad to see him go but for Christmas he gave me a stocking full of
sweets he left the sweets in our car because we had gone out in our grampys
car when I walked past the car I wished that it was mine in the front seat in
the car when dad took mum to shop they saw the stocking and found out that
it was for me their was a card as well. it was for helping him that he gave it to
me. He asked me down to dinner on June 3rd it was my Brothers birthday that

day but mum let me go he asked me whether I wanted to have tea as well and
mum said yes I helped him milk at the other farm as well.

The nature of these answers raises the question of whether the adult world
does not make it too difficult for children, even younger children, to begin to
learn to take a part in the adult world of work and to begin to understand the
pleasure both in work and relationships which can accompany the satisfactory
discharge of such responsibilities.

One facet of taking responsibility can be striving, an attempt to achieve a
given goal. The significance of achievement motivation for children has been
known for some time to psychologists, and is reflected in answers given by
children in the present survey. Striving and achievement enhanced for some
children a sense of their own individuality and capacity actively to control
circumstances, rather than be controlled by them — an experience frustrating
if at times inescapable for all children, particularly younger children. One 12-
year-old girl, from a Newcastle middle school, wrote about how she strove
successfully to achieve a situation in which she was able to raise the money to
go on a school trip abroad.

It was one day in March when mister McGeness said with all the 2 year stay
behind. We waited untill all the 3 year and 1st year went out then he said
right as you know there is a trip to spain and alot of people have droped out
so we want 7 people to take thier places. I said I would like to go so I got a
sheet about it. I took it home to my Mam and Dad I said mam I would like to
go it is only £33 pound my mam say's you'll have to see. I go to my Grans
every night and I told her about the trip and she said she would pay some
after I had my tea there I went round and told my mam she said all right then
you can go she singed the paper and I took it to school I was really. I was
pleased and happy and I thanked my mam and dad and gran. We went away
in april the 16th it was a monday.

The overwhelming majority of the answers indicated that children considered to be happy experiences those in which they were treated, or they
treated others with love and concern. There were however a small minority
of responses (that, certainly, in the context of the present research can be
described as abnormal) in which children obtained pleasure by destructive,
unsocial or aggressive behaviour. 50 themes altogether were concerned with
behaviour difficulties, 13 children reporting *misbehaviour,* 13 *provocation,*
4 *drink, drugs or smoking,* 4 *law breaking and delinquent behaviour,* and 16
adult/child disagreement as the themes of happy situations. Even in these
situations however it was on occasion possible to sympathize with, although
not condone, the actions of children. There was for example the 12+ girl who,
in her last year at middle school, became drunk at a pub.

The person that made me feel happy was my boyfriend. His name was Steve,
But most people called him Six Foot for the one reason that he was so small.
I first met him at Iyebridge, a river just out side our town. One night we went
round to the local pub. It was about 11 o'clock that we came out and I was
drunk. He had bought me load's of drinks and I could only just walk. That
night I had met all his friends he had made me very happy.
As a result the next night I bough all the drinks.

Socially unacceptable though this girl's behaviour was, it was motivated, at
least to some extent, by natural feelings of affection for her boy friend. Then
there was the case of the boy who derived pleasure from the bullying of a
younger child, and the successful evasion of a furiously pursuing father.

One day I was playing with my cousin and two of his friend's and one of his
friends started to play about in my cousin's garden and he started to hit us,
because we had been teasing him a bit, then my cousin got mad and hit him
this soon turned into a fight and my cousin came out on top.
The made my cousins friend mad as well and he ran home.
Me my cousin, Dick and his friend John went out on to a peice of waist
ground outside Dicks house and started to mess about. It was getting dark now
and we played a game of Hide and Seek, suddenly we heard a shout it was the
boy's dad we ran for cover, he got too close for comfort so we ran.
Then he got in his car and chased us half way round Eastwood, but we were
lucky there is a few jitties in Eastwood so we ran down those and we were
safe.
Then we walked back down to Dick's house.

In so far as this boy's happiness came from the excitement of the chase, and
the attendant adrenalin-provoking dangers, the pleasure he derived from it can
be interpreted in terms not totally negative. What is regrettable is that such a
child should have to gain excitement and happiness from the consequences of
delinquent behaviour. Finally, there was the 11+ middle school boy who
enjoyed himself in a French lesson because he scared his teacher into letting
him do little or nò work.

During every day of the week except Sat Sun and Friday we have french and
the teacher is Miss . . . I like it because I dont have to do any work I think the
french teacher is scared of me I just sit on a bench instead of a chair we had to
draw a picture of a man and a lady with clothes on and label them in french
and I drew a skinhead and the teacher never said nothing more about it as a
result I had to go to the Head and I nearly got the cane for that.

A number of happy situations were reported in which the themes related to

critical situations, particularly *accident and injury,* and *illness and operations.*
At first sight the appearance of such themes in connection with happiness
might appear unexpected. However, the happiness was usually associated with
a pleasant outcome of an unpleasant happening, rather than with the happening
itself. Thus, one 8+ girl from an inner-city school frankly acknowledged that
she had greatly enjoyed all the fun and excitement which had resulted from her
being run over by a car.

When I was little I got run over by a car I am glad it was not a lorry I would
be dead by now. So I had to be taken straight to hospital it was such a rush.
My mum made me pleased. It was my left knee that hurt a little but it's
alright now. It was such fun though.

Another 8+ girl was happy simply to be alive following a fire:

In 1971 I had a fire my brother knocked over the oil heater and it started a
fire. My brother managed to get but my two brothers and I were afriad and
so we never go out because we were afriad and my brother went up stairs to
get my dad, my dad got hold of the oil heater and we had to get water and
put out the fire. We could of been badly burnt or dead by now. But my dads
hand are rough and horble.

An 11+ boy, from a middle school in Chester, was happy because an injury
which he feared might be serious proved not to be so.

Ones not so long ago I went to my friends house and I nokced on my frends
door and his sister opened the door and I asked if my friend was coming out
and my other freind came out coud matin [called Martin] and my other freind
was not coming out so I asked him again and his sister shut the door on my
finger and I could not say anything so when my freind saw it he kicked the
door in and he said run home so I did and I ran home screming and my dad
came out of his friends house and toke me in his house, and then and then he
took me to the infermera and they put me arm under a ecray caberenet and
the said that my finger would be ouright and that made me very glad.

Another boy was happy because a broken bone meant that he did not have to
go to school.

When i was in the Garden one day my freind came and we was playing and I
had my dog on a lead and my friend trough a stone and my dog went after
it and he pulled my arm and he broke my coller bone and I had to go to
hospital and I was pleased because I did not have to go to school.

And a 9+ girl was happy, following a road accident and chicken-pox, because of all the letters she wrote and received.

One Saturday when I was at my nans. I got runover. I was crossing the road with my Auntie, and she ran across I could'ent run very fast at the time. Then! Suddenly a big ford car came. I just caught my arm. Id brocken my shoulder bone. the nures told me in hostpital. The next week I was ill I had chickenpots. every day a card came through the post addressed to me! When I was better I sat down writing thank you letters, that made me happy and I hope other people were happy too.

These answers, and others in a similar vein, all suggest that the outcomes of accidents and injuries may well have been more rewarding for some children than the original experiences were unpleasant. While on the one hand this indicates a welcome resilience and ability to look upon the bright side, it does on the other hand suggest that some children may be tempted to provoke accidents in order to benefit from resulting pleasant outcomes.

Answers which appeared to show that happiness was derived from accident or illness itself, rather than from associated effects, were very rare indeed. One 10+ boy did however produce such an answer. It is worth noting that the same boy was one of a very small minority who, in answer to the second question had Christmas as a theme related to unhappiness. This boy described a serious accident with an axe.

One sunney afternoon when I was in the forest with my brother and my uncle and we were chopping wood with a small axe and we chop one hunrder and 60 logs in to small ones the next day we went again with the small axe my uncle had a big one becoase he was strong my brother and I we had the giddles [giggles] and my brother was doing it all slopie and he did not hit it hard to make a mark and it came out of his hands and top in my back and blood was poring out my uncle took me home and my brother came to he took my brother in and then rushed me up to the hospitl and a doctor put me on a bed and took me down to X ray room to see if I and eney bonds brocken but no the I hard to have to sichis [two stitches] in it and I had blood all on my vest and driping down my back and then a blaster on it and I we home to my uncles house and a a hot drink I was in pain all on my back and I was crying all the time. The next day I had a phone call to say I had to go up there again and when I was there they told my uncle that I had pioson in my back so they got a niddle and put this stuff in my back it hurt a lot the I had to sit forward all the time and lay on my tumey for a for to days.

It is difficult not to interpret such an answer as that of a very disturbed child.

Sherlock Holmes once investigated a case in which the most significant clue was the dog which didn't bark. Of perhaps equal interest in the present investigation are the answers which were never, or only very rarely given. The pleasure and happiness of children occurred in a primarily restricted and domestic world. Events from outside school, home or neighbourhood seldom impinged. Public occasions were not sufficiently frequently mentioned in response to any of the three types of situation (happy, unhappy, problem) to be categorized separately. In happy situations only 12 answers in all were not separately categorized. Of these 3 were concerned with public occasions. One 10+ boy from a London school was made happy by a Chelsea football success.

I felt pleased when my dad come home with a paper which had football results on. I found out that Chelsea had won the European Cup Winners Cup. As a result I ran round talking about it.

Specific religious experiences likewise were never separately categorized. In happy situations they occurred in only 5 answers. One 10+ girl at a Church of England middle school wrote about Jesus.

On one sunday, when I went to sunday school, my teacher read to us out of the bible and it was about the crucifxion of Jesus, It made me feel sorry to him. when I got home I had nothing to do. so I went into my bedroom and booked at my book's I saw my bible. I rememberd about the crucifxion so I took by bible and looked up the right chapter. from that day I try to, every night but not always, I take my bible and read it. and I am verey pleased.

Another girl, in her first year at a Swindon comprehensive, wrote of the day she joined the Salvation Army.

The happiest day of my life was when I was made a junior soldoir in the Salvation army. I promised not to Steal, Swear, drink or Smoke. I promised to love the lord and follow him for the rest of my life I have not broken any of the rules. As a result I became a true follower of God his Son and the holy Spirit. And so now I am a true Christain.

But these girls were rare exceptions. For most children happiness was experienced in the context of an interpersonal morality of concern for others which would be acceptable to and encouraged by the followers of all the major world religions; but it was not experienced in the explicit framework of religious faith and practice.

8 Unhappy situations—themes

If the answers of individual children concerning unhappy situations are considered in relation to groups of themes, those themes which occur most frequently, and which perhaps merit closest consideration are *critical situations* and *behaviour difficulties*; not only did these occur marginally more frequently than the other groups, but individual themes from these groups were often (where two themes were noted in one answer) found associated with themes from the group of *expectations* and *personal and home life*. Thus, of the 169 times in which the theme *misbehaviour* was found paired with another theme, it occurred 69 times (38·5%) paired with themes from *expectations* or *personal and home life*. Of 213 times in which the theme *provocation* was paired, on 99 occasions (46·5%) it was paired with themes from *expectations* or *personal and home life*. Furthermore, the individual themes which were found most frequently in *personal and home life* (i.e. *siblings: trouble* (440) and *pets and animals* (309)) were found paired respectively 181 times (58·8%) and 224 times (74·2%) with themes from *critical situations* or *behaviour difficulties*.

There are those adults — whether parents, teachers or others — who in moments of particular exasperation almost believe that children can actually enjoy causing trouble. There is no strong support for such an hypothesis from the present survey. Not only did very few children cite *behaviour difficulties* as a theme of happiness, but *siblings: trouble,* and *provocation* were the two individual themes which were found most frequently in answers concerned with unhappiness; answers with these themes were typically concerned with being troubled or provoked, rather than troubling or provoking — at least in the first instance. Trouble with siblings happened in many different ways. There was the 9+ London girl cursed with an imaginative and malevolent sister.

when I want out in the Dark last night and my sister crept up on me and said winged monkeys of winky Do my will and I said to my sister its you. You canot scare me and she went back up the road with my Dad and I went back

Table 14   Frequency of themes: unhappy situations

Theme group	Individual theme	No.	% of themes
Personal & home life	Siblings: trouble	440	8·1
	Siblings: cooperation & concern	36	0·7
	Grown-ups and home	72	1·3
	Stairs	12	0·2
	Food	10	0·2
	Pets and animals	309	5·7
	Moving home	33	0·6
	Separation & reuniting	76	1·4
	TOTALS	988	18·1
Other children	Peer groups & pressures	27	0·5
	Boy/girl relationships	20	0·4
	Friendship	122	2·2
	TOTALS	169	3·1
Activities & pastimes	TV	111	2·0
	Informal play and hobbies	306	5·6
	Organized activities & sports	75	1·4
	School work & activities	92	1·7
	Shops and shopping	28	0·5
	Vehicles	86	1·6
	TOTALS	698	12·8
Special occasions & occurrences	Presents: giving & receiving	42	0·8
	Christmas and birthdays	22	0·4
	Social occasions	25	0·5
	Public celebrations	62	1·1
	Outings and visits	85	1·6
	Staying away from home	76	1·4
	Births and christenings	1	0·02
	Engagements and marriages	3	0·05
	Public appearances	3	0·05
	TOTALS	319	5·8

Theme group	Individual theme	No.	% of themes
Behaviour difficulties	Misbehaviour	203	3·7
	Provocation	550	10·1
	Drink, drugs and smoking	5	0·1
	Law breaking & delinquent behaviour	40	0·7
	Adult/child disagreement	249	4·6
	TOTALS	**1047**	**19·2**
Critical situations	Getting lost	31	0·6
	Strangers	63	1·1
	Fear and the dark	169	3·1
	Fire hazard	10	0·2
	Hostile supernatural occurrences	169	3·1
	Accident and injury	282	5·2
	Illness and operations	118	2·2
	Death or disappearance	301	5·5
	TOTALS	**1143**	**20·9**
Problems	What do I do?	25	0·5
	What do I choose?	4	0·1
	How do I occupy myself?	1	0·02
	How do I do it?	9	0·2
	Losing, finding & forgetting	55	1·0
	TOTALS	**94**	**1·7**
Expectations	Expected happenings	335	6·1
	Unexpected happenings	332	6·1
	Striving	24	0·4
	Praise	3	0·05
	Temptation	5	0·1
	Unfairness	140	2·6
	Taking responsibility	39	0·7
	Concern for others	112	2·0
	TOTALS	**990**	**18·1**
Miscellaneous	TOTALS	**12**	**0·2**
	OVERALL TOTALS	**5460**	**99·9**

Percentages have been rounded.

to my Dad and scared my sister and she scremed and my Dad said stop screming.

There was the boy in his third year at a middle school who suffered an unprovoked attack — which apparently broke the local Geneva Convention — from his brother.

The day somebody made angry was when, my brother pushed me down the stairs, it made me cross because it hurt me and he didn't give me a warning, also because I had just settled down to read a book in the landing, when I had got up and had treated my back I went up stairs and gave him a fight, because I had lost my temper it made me fight much wilder.

And thats most likely how I won, I enjoyed it but I had a 'shinner' and bloody nose, but my brother had a cut lip and bruised jaw, in the end we made friends and he hasn't done anything like that since.

However, this boy, like many others, both retaliated effectively, and bore no grudge. There was also the 10+ girl from a junior school in West Bromwich who was provoked into a fight by her brother. This particular girl however, not only, according to her report, tried to resist the provocation, but had no adult at hand to whom to turn for help; her parents were out at work.

Every night when I go home I read the note on the table and I go down the shops then when I come back home and my brother Gary is there. I take my coat off and then my brother keeps on saying do you wan a fight I say no and then a minute later he asks me again and he gets me angry and we start fighting then cames in my mom and we have to stop. Soon my mom goes out my brother askes me do you want a fight I say now don't start again and I start fighting with him and I beat him up but stephen comes and stops us so I start fighting on him then comes in my mom and I have to go to bed.

Parents, and other adults or older children who provided inadequate supervision were also to some extent responsible for situations in which fights between siblings broke out.

While siblings were frequently prepared to attack each other, they were also ready to defend each other. An unspoken code appeared to exist, whereby it was perfectly permissable for brothers and sisters to fight among themselves, but not acceptable for any outsider to maltreat a member of the family group. For example, a 9+ boy from a Chester middle school wrote, with succinct clarity, 'Last week a boy hit my brother and made my brother criey so I hit him.' Another boy, in his first year at a comprehensive, was outraged at the treatment of his brother by a babysitter. (Again, no adults were present when trouble broke out.)

It was when my mum and dad had gone out and we had a seater. It was my cosun and she kept telling my brother off and boseing him about. He started cryinging and ran off up stairs to his bedroom. She went up there and slaped him. This made me very angry and I told her to leave him alone. She left him alone all that night.

The view that girls, too, are increasingly becoming an easily defined group in relation to misbehaviour and provocation is supported by a number of the answers in the present study. An 8+ girl from a junior school in London was bullied and intimidated by two other girls.

Once Bridgit and Sharon where naughty so they stayed in our classroom. Bridget hit me with the ruler and I was frightened, that Bridget would hit me. Then Sharon frightened me more. Because Sharon said you are going to get bashed up. I said who by she, Sharon said by me and briget. I was frightened. But I fought not to be too frightened like a coward. Soon when they had bashed me up I went to tell my mum. And my mum said if they do it again, I will report then to the head-master.
Which, Yes! Which was lucky Yes! lucky for me. But I was still yes! still frightened of you know who, Briget and Sharon the trouble-makers! The trouble Maker's do you think they are? I do I hope you do too. please say yes! any·way Sharon and Briget did it such a long time ago. But now they still keep bothering me I do not know why! I hope they do not bother me any more and bother some one else, I think that bridget and sharon are trouble-maker's and I want them to bother somebody else. Then went back to my house.

A 9+ girl from a Cardiff junior school was the victim of verbal provocation.

My time when somebody made me unhappy was when Wendy made a remark a bough my mother and she said to the others who wants to meet her silly mother or something like silly or stupid and I didn't Wendy remark aboult that. And it made me very unhappy but I was pleased when Debra said that my mother was nice and because Wendy made that remark I wasn't her friend then but I was the next day but I have not forgotten that remark.

More serious violence, and older girls were also involved. One 10+ girl recorded an occasion when she had a tooth broken by a brick thrown by another girl.

About two years ago I was playing with my friend. We decided to play out in the lane. As it happened there was rather a nasty girl there who was playing also. She called us names said we couldn't skip properly and naturally we did the same back to her. We couldn't bear it any longer so we played in my friend's garden. We were looking at the rabbits. There hutch was near the garden gate leading out on to the lane. A few minutes later a large brick came hurdling over the garden door. It hit me deftly in the face. This was a frightening moment for me. Could it be my eye my nose all my head was aching. I just happened to run my tounge along my front teeth. I felt a rough space. I was my tooth! Half of it was missing! Would I look like a freak! Well my friend took me indoors and we went round the nasty girl's mother. She scolded the nasty girl. As a result I had a lot of trouble with the dentist!

An 11+ girl from a Chester middle school described vindictive verbal and physical aggression by a group of other girls.

One day my friend and I were walking down the road when a bunch of girls come up to my freind Julie and whisperd somethink in her ear I did not know what they said but as we got down the road we met beverley and rosie and I said Hello but they did not answer but they said Hello to julie. Julie, Beverley and Rosie said go on you we don't want you with us so I ran down the hill feeling very unhappy because my freinds had broke up with me I started walking up then I saw julie and her gang coming towards me so I ran but they caught up with me and every single one hit me then they all ran away and left me there crying then I got up and went home feeling very very unhappy.

Boys, naturally also got themselves into trouble. Usually, although not always, it was of a fairly straightforward nature of the sort familiar to readers of comics and stories for boys. A 12+ boy from a comprehensive in Nottingham had to endure and survive being chased by a gang who boasted that they were 'The best fighters around'.

In October 1973 there was a gange after me and my friend and we was being chased all around awsworth, and we was frightend because they was the best fighters around Awsworth, Kimberly, Ilkiston, and Eastwood. The gang was lomanhay.

Another boy, like others before him, was derided by those of, possibly a different class background and certainly an irreverent disposition, for his membership of the Scout movement.

In this incident I felt frightened, angry and unhappy. A few weeks ago, on a monday night, about 9.10 pm, I was cycling home from Scouts, it was nearly pitch black, except for the street lamps, and I heard some laughing, talking and shouting, about 80 yds. ahead of me, I saw a bunch of 'yobbos', or greasers, or whatever they label themselves. I though they'd try to do something so I went out into the middle of the road to avoid them. But this didn't stop them, as about 3 or 4 of them came out to me, and one of them punched me in the stomach, not very hard, but it hurt a bit. I just carried on riding, and they were all jeering and saying things like: 'I wish I went to scouts on a monday night', and 'Cor, I like your clown's hat',

People (or animals) like this must have something drastically wrong with their minds, because all day long they just go around spoiling peoples fun, and making a nuisance of themselves. On Saturday afternoon they are all up in the 'South End', the yob's end in the AFC Bournemouth's football ground, they dont go to watch the football but they have 'bundles' with themselves and Policemen. After the match they go into the car and smash up the away team's coach and supporters, and generally spoil other's enjoyment.

There was also a boy from a Chester middle school who was chased, by an understandably irate adult, for letting off a banger on the man's doorstep.

It was not so long [ago] me and my other two friends. We put a banger on a mans doorstep and we were just going to light the feuwes and the man ran around the coner and then we ran and I was at the bake and and I ran like the wind and then he shoted out if I catch you around here agian I will call the police and then he went back and the sliye buger came after us agian and I was at the back agian so we ran in to a feild and I was scared stiff. But he did not come in.

However, some boys found themselves faced with situations which were more serious, either because the protagonists exerted greater cunning and malevolence, or because the behaviour involved was more harmful either to people or property, and so was delinquent rather than merely troublesome. One boy of 10+ suffered from the jealousy of another boy who expressed his aggression by capturing the affections of a family cat and overfeeding it, a situation which led to the animal's eventual death.

A time when somebody made me unhappy was when another boy was jealous of me and always wanted to something to irritate me or make me unhappy. We had two cats one we had taken in as a stray the other was given to us from some relatives when she was a kitten and once when we left them with neighbours because we were going on holiday. and while we where were away the boy who only lived up the road about two houses away from the people who were looking after the cat, started feeding her to, and when we came back from our holiday the cat wouldnt come back to us it stayed with the boys family, as a result we tried to get her back but she would'nt come back, They overfeed her and she ran away and died.

A number of boys were involved in incidents with airguns. One reported, 'There was two boys with airguns they were shooting at me and my friend.' Another, similarly assaulted, counterattacked both physically and by invoking the power of the law.

When I got A shock by ane air gun pellet. It hit a stone then hit me in the ankle and made me angry. I got be hinde a hedge crept up on him and he heard me he started to run and I done a rugby takle he fell to the ground and I asked him if he had a lience for the gun, and he said 'no'.

Other boys found their behaviour leading them, potentially or actually, into conflict with the police. An 11+ boy in his third year at a middle school stole money from his mother, and showed no contrition — only anger that his friends reported his behaviour.

Someone made me angry and unhappy when I was talking with my freinds.
They said I wish I could go in that shop and take anythink I liked.
I said I now wot we can do My Mum ceeps old pennys.
I can steal some of thaws she wonet no.
So I did and when I had brought some sweets for them and me.
I went home soone they met my brother and they taled him wot I did.
So my Brother towlead my mum and she senet me to bed with no tea.
So I was unhappy and criging beacouse my freinds split on me.

A 9+ boy from a London junior school found himself in direct trouble with police for stealing and destroying dolls. He was very frightened by the results.

When I 9 year old, I was in trouable with the police, by taken dolls. I ever took one I saw my friends talking one, and one of my friend cut off one of the dolls head withe a pen knife. We that it was stole but it was a warehouse. Someone must of phone the police and we were cort and the police said did I talk one and I said no and it made me frightened and it was unhappy when the police hit one of my friend I ever got talk can [taken] to the police staiain, but my friends that run away agot could [all got caught]. One of my friends tood what the police dun at the stain and he said thay the police said what ever telephone numbers and were do you live and a your mum must come and get you I was frighted that every polices car I see would talk me to the police stainse and I will be in dead troubble withe the police and I thort that I would be sent to Jail.

Troublemaking and delinquency by children, although usually separate from similar behaviour by adults, did not take place entirely in isolation from the grown-up world. The answers of some children indicated that not only were they made frightened, angry or unhappy by children's misbehaviour, but also by that of adults. One 9+ boy from London reported, 'one day I was on the Harrow Road and I sow to man fighting and the big man hirt the other man in his eye and he punch him in his mouth.' Another 9-year-old from London saw a man deliberately, in his view, run over a cat.

At one time I visited my aunt's house and as I was looking out the window I saw a cat trying to get from one side of the road to the othere. Just then a man came along in his car and ran straight over the cat. This made me feel very angry because I am sure he saw the cat as he approached. Some boys saw what happened and went to get a policeman. A few minutes later the boys returned with a policeman. The policeman examined the cat's body but it was dead. So he layed it on the pavement and returned to his duty.

An 8+ boy returned home to discover that his house had been burgled.

One day I was at school and I was comeing home and suddenly I saw a hole in the window I open the door and the glass was on the floor what came out of the window and I went up stair and my mothers bed room was ruined I went in my bed room my money box broken and all my clothes was on the floor the sheet on the bed was on the floor and I was crying and then me and my sister saw our anutie coming and she start crying thus the poilce come then few month later mummy daddy anutie carrun went to court and they find the burger my mummy said his   was bad and I told mumy yes.

These three boys all came from schools in an educational priority area. By way of contrast, a 9+ Pakistani girl in a Cardiff junior school wrote about an adult crime which took place on a visit to Pakistan.

When I went to pakistan we was speeping and my Mother was praying on the pavement, and my mother sawn a robber coming throug the window he was in my mothers room he stoled 700 Shillings, and my cousins was all the time affording money to by things for Chrismas then we could [caught] the robber a Last we hit the robber then the police came and the police came and took him to Jail.

As well as the instances of observed adult delinquency, there were also a considerable number of children (249) who reported cases of *adult/child disagreement*. Many of such answers implied frustration at being prevented from doing something which the child wanted to do, rather than criticism of an adult for causing such frustration. There was, for example, the 10+ girl who was told to cut her nails by her mother, because of the danger they caused to her brother. On this occasion the mother had to intervene because the girl's aspiration to symbols of adult — or at least adolescent — status (long nails) conflicted with her inability to restrain herself from continuing childish behaviour (scratching her brother).

There was a time when somebody made me unhappy. It was when my mum told me off for scratching my brother with my long nails. I have not got them now because my mum told me to cut them. This happened quite a long time ago. I was unhappy because I had too cut my nails, but I wanted to let them grow longer.

On the other hand, some children were specifically critical of adult behaviour. A 10+ girl from a Newcastle middle school strongly objected to the obsessive cleanliness of an aunt: this child resented behaviour which, at least as she described it, seemed neurotic.

When I went to my anuty's she is very fussy. As we went in she said oh no. Pleas do not step on my new carpet. She went up stairs and got a white pillow case and said Here wipe your feet on this. I was very surprised. (and angry). When we eventually got in anuty . . . made some sandwiches. Please don't drop those crumbs on the Floor she said. As we were going she went and got a Flanell to wipe the doorstep with. I was really angry.

And, inevitably, there were children who were critical of adults because they felt they had been unfairly treated.

I was in the living room playing with my brothers called Johnathan and he scream just like all two year old children anyway mum said stop it and said to me why was he screaming I said because his bloon popped and Mum said don't tell lies and she sent me to bed, but I didn't do it i said and she still would not belive me as a result when I get to bed a began to swer at her and I was n't aloud to play for a week.

Those incidents in which children write about adult misbehaviour, or delinquency or, less dramatically, simple lack of concern for children's feelings were all reported by children as causing them distress; and, certain, as in the case of the boy who saw the cat run over, adults' actions could provoke a degree of overt disapproval. However, while children can no doubt have a positive moral perspective of their own, it seems over optimistic to expect it to be maintained if they are frequently in contact with adult self-centredness, or even criminality. It can be argued, further, that children are particularly liable to become demoralized if they see adult delinquency going unpunished: a child who observes that the world is unjust may be prone to adapt his behaviour to survive in that world, and to model himself upon the examples which it offers.

It is perhaps a temptation for adults both to romanticize the child's world, and to underestimate the extent to which many children, like their elders, are inescapably confronted by experiences involving hostile behaviour: fear of the dark, the inexplicable, even the supernatural, accidents, injuries, illness and death. In many of the answers in which these themes appeared, recurrent common features could be identified. Children grieved intensely and profoundly, but had an extraordinary resilience and capacity for quick recovery; children displayed a very pragmatic, at times almost stoical, attitude to the problems of suffering; children showed a capacity for an intuitive and personal apprehension of the paranormal, whether benevolent or hostile. It is possible, indeed, to hypothesize from the answers given in this research that children come closer to an experiential understanding of the supernatural through situations which evoked fear, anger or unhappiness, than through situations which evoked pleasure or happiness.

That the world which children described was on occasion perceived as hostile was due in part to the nature of individual adults and to characteristics of the world created by adults. In particular, manufactured machinery — and especially vehicles carelessly or aggressively controlled — were capable of a literally shattering impact on children. A 9+ boy described how his brother was run over by a lorry.

Last year when I went up to my nanners but she was there my brother hid under a box too surprise her. 'when a lorry came on to the curb and ran of the box and then I ran Into the house and told my mother she phoned the amblance when they got to the hospital they found had only got a broken arm.

Another 10+ boy wrote, 'One day about 2 years ago I saw a terrible accident and a man broke nealy every bone in his body. is all i did was walk over the road to my house.' A happier ending resulted for an 8+ girl who was run down on a crossing controlled by a lollipop man.

One day when I was walking my friend home when I cross the road first time I went across I was all-right. But when I was comeing across to go home the lolly-pop man came into the road and toled ma to go across and I did. But although he was in the road a min-car did-not stop, he dojjed and I got run-over. My mother was phoned at West Hendon Hospital. When the police-man phoned my mum he said, now don't panic please Mrs. Brown your daughter has just be nocked down and my mother fainted. But at Wilsden Genaral Hospital (thats were they took me) they said any-were hurt and I said my Leg any-were eles said the doctor and I said my thum and he laughed. Then they said were do you live and I said . . . whats your name I said . . . and what ward does your mother work I said ward 6. Then he puted me in a room and I had tea and bisciuts read a comic till my mum came for me. And my mum said . . . never ever frighten me again and I said all right mum. And when my dad came home he said weres . . .. And you would-not belive it but I even opened our front door for him.

Strange adults, even without the assistance of cars and lorries, could be threatening to children. Girls in particular were liable to endure unpleasant encounters. A city girl, aged 9+, was pursued by a man in a car.

When I was on holiday in the country once. I was chased by a man in a car. I was on my way back from seeing a friends horses, I was coming to the top of a lane and this man slowed his car down and tried to stop me I turned round ran half the way back to where the still [stile] was, but I did not go all of the way because he might not have been chasing me, but he was and he had caught up with me I ran past his car and got to the caravan site where I was staying. I did not do anything as a result.

A country boy and his friends were chased by a tramp whom they came upon in a deserted house.

There was a old cottage down the end of our land it didn't have windows, doors, and some of the floar board's were gone. One day Tony mein Wendy mein my sister and myself went in there to play we went up stairs there was a man up there we were frightened he came after us to get us out of there we all ran down stairs and out side he was not a very rich man well he didn't look rich because he was wearing old clothes with holes in a few days later we went in there again he was not in there but he had made a bed in a corner made out of braken leaves and he had a old sleeping bag as well as stayed out later that day and we sor him go back in about a week after he had to come out because they were going to bash it down to make more houses.

Another girl, 12+, from a comprehensive school in Workington, was approached, together with a friend by an old man who appeared from a street next to a graveyard.

One dark night about the middle of winter we were going to my Anties house, We had to go past a graveyard and there was a street next to it. We were passing by when an old man jumped out infront of us he was begging us to come with him we were terrified we ran down the street we told a woman she came up with us. When the old man saw her he ran away laughing. For about a week after I wouldnt go out after five oclock and I had nightmares nearly every night.

For some children, the line between the natural and the supernatural was not always easy to draw. Their common sense might tell them that ghosts and such phenomena did not exist: but emotionally they not infrequently revealed that they were capable of believing in spirits or apparitions. One girl freely admitted that she ran from what she thought was a ghost even though she did not believe in ghosts.

one night I was walking down the street and heard a horrible noise like a goast I ran for my life thinking that it was a real one even thoe I did not belive in goasts. Then I suddenly had a felling that it was not a real goast so I tearned round and found out it was only my freid I was so angry that I ran down the street and cought up whith her I asked her why she was making She said that it was not her. we were scared we started to go home then we both heard that noice. My freind started to panicke I told her not to if she did it would be worse. After a few minites it had stopped then it started again. Time after time it use to go on. When it stopped we found out that it was only the wind.

Children at play might be frightened by the possibilities that houses were haunted.

One day I went to my friends house his name was Gordon, his brothers name was Steven, and his sisters name was Lolly. That was her nek name. When we had finshed our dinner there was a knock on the door, my brother had come. Then Gordon said should we go out and play so we said all right so we went out and played on our we saw a house, then a boy game along and said that the house was haunted. Then to girls heared and they said they did not believe him so they went in the house and did not come out again so we ran away and did not go back to that house again I was rellay frightened.

Or children might be tempted to believe in convincing stories told by friends or acquaintances.

One day my friend sed to me That There was a little girl stade with her anti becaus her husbund was going to go to work in a difront country for three days. and one day the girl and her ante went to bed and they hered nousis like a houvering sound and some boude specing on the telephon so They went down stes to see how it was and they could not see enyone so they went back up stes and in the morning they got up and there breakfast was set out but they didunt eat it. and this day her uncl was coming home. and the girls ante was going to hang out the clous and when she was hanging out The clous she sour a hed with hands no boudy and The girls ante had a hartertac and she dide. and strat oufter that her husband came in. and I was frightened.

And frequently there were siblings, friends, even adult relatives, prepared to take advantage of a child's emotional readiness to believe in the supernatural.

I am very frightend of the dark and one night, when I in bed my sister came in with a white sheet over her head and she started making strange noises and it frightend the day lights out of me of course I did not know it was my sister. I screamed and my mum came up and told my sister off. And I could not get to sleep that night.

Occasionally children might make a more active and determined attempt to reach beyond the boundaries of the natural world. Such efforts could suggest the existence of forces unsuspected by and terrifying to children. One 11+ girl, in her third year at a Newcastle middle school, found herself involved in an amateurish séance, and determined never again to be involved in such an experience.

one Monday night our alan said lets play spirates. I said alright then so he made some letters on pices of paper and set them around the table then he got a glass and trurned it up side down and We put two fingers on and closed our eyes. and he started to say is anyone there and then the glass started to move so we opened our eyes and it went to p then e it went on until it spelt peter dixon I started to get frighend I said can I turn the lights but he said now I stared to cry because the table stared to move I said please stop it I am frightend stop it alan he said it's not me and so I koncked the glass over and turned the lights on and wiped my eyes and helped him clear the stuff up and put the table back. and We sat down and my thought We had been watching telvision all the time because she had been at ann's. and I have never played spirates agian.

For children, as for adults, death of those who were loved, not only resulted in the experience of deep personal emotions, but also at times raised questions, albeit formulated in simple terms, about the nature of after life and the presence of God. One girl, 12+, in her final year at a middle school recorded her emotions on passing the house of her grandfather, who had just died.

The time I was frighten was when my Grandad was dead and he was still in his house and I had to walk passed his house when it was just beginning to get dark and I though about grandad as I went passed his this frighten me cause I thought I saw him in the window. Even though I don't believe in ghost I just ran up the hill to our house.

Another girl, aged 9+, described the death of her mother.

My Daddy is lovely and a long time ago My Mummy died of a bad bug and I was very sad to see her go, and My daddy was very sad and he went down to wimborn and on her defe my daddy was very very sad aboat her and she was very beatyful. and we get flowers fole her.

The picture which accompanied this answer was of herself and her father at
the mother's grave, which was surmounted by a large cross, and across the top
of the picture were written the words, 'My daddy is lovely and my Mummy
has died.' A boy, 9+, described the death of his grandfather, and his reactions
to it.

Once last year, on Christmas Even my grandad died that night. He was over in
Iland at that time, when ward came throw my dad went over. When all my
frends' came in i was so unhappy I ran out of the room, they were all haveing
fun, when my grandad died.
As a result I pray for him every Sunday at church and light a candle for him.

There were other children who recorded the loss of parents. One girl wrote
only 'The unhappiest time of my life was when my Dad died.' A boy described how his father died in a car crash, and the family were too poor to have
him buried, and had to have him cremated instead.

I was once very unhappy. When I herd my dad had died. When he had a crash
going to . . . . I went upstairs and statred to cry. We could not aford to burie
him so we burnt him at the top of Penlyan hill. He was with a friend
called . . . .

One boy, in his first year at a comprehensive in Nottingham, wrote about how
he and his brother were left by his parents, who went for a car ride, and never
returned.

When some one made me unhappy is when I was four year old and we where
in a tent and my mother and father went for a rid in the car and I and my
brother were in a tent and some policeman come and then the policeman said
come with us and so we did and the policman put me and my brother in an
New home.

Some answers indicated the speed with which children could recover from
bereavement.

My mother made me unhappy one day. I came downstairs and went into the
front room, my brother, mum, uncle trev, and my nan was there. My mother
was comforting my brother and telling him to stop crying. I asked her what
was the matter with him, she then told me my father had died. As a result I
started to cry tears came rolling down my cheekes, I sat on her lap crying my
mother told my uncle to come and take me so that she could have my brother.
I then got 10p worth of sweets but i still cried a little bit.

When my Grandma and Grandad and Bamps and his dog deid I said to myself
I Will Never be happy again in my life I creid all day because I Knew that my
bamps had had a very bad illness but I was happy a week later, My Bamps dog
deid not long ago. On 22nd October My Grandad died of illness and my
Grandma deid of Sadness.

It was not always close family members whose death affected children. One
10+ girl showed great empathy and understanding of a neighbour who lost twins
in childbirth.

On October 21st the lady across the road babys died she had been carrying
them for about $6\frac{1}{2}$ months when she gave birth. She had been very ill since
she ever started. First of all the doctor said that they would die at this she was
very upset. Then about three weeks later he said their was a chance then she
was talking about them What she hoped them to be and what she was going to
buy. When she gave birth she had twins two boys the strongest one lived for 4
hours and the weakest lived for 36 hours. The funeral took place on the fort-
night Tuesday. The twins were about as heavy as a 1lb of sugar and the same
size of a sugar bag.

An 8+ year old boy from a London junior school had a friend who was killed
in a car crash.

A boy in class 7 was killed in a car crash. He was knocket down in the he was
rushed to hosptal but in the nigh he dighed this boy was 9 a was a very good
freind of mine has a result it made me sad when I herd in school it made me
sad for the rest of the day at school.

And an 11+ boy living in a rural and comparatively stable area was saddened
by the dramatic death from drugs of a cousin who had gone to the United
States.

There is one thing that made me very unhappy. It was when my coson diyed
he was a drugalick. He lived in America he was only 21 year old. I only saw
him three times. I was only very little but I can remebre him. He gave me
three pound befor he left. When he dived they found a gun in his draw loded.
This is the trouth.

Almost, perhaps even as intense for children as their feelings about the
death of people, were their reactions to the death of animals. Relationships
with animals appeared to play a significant part in the lives of many children.
Partly no doubt this was because the world of animals, like the world of play,

offered an opportunity to try out, learn about and experiment with behaviour and emotions which would eventually be needed as an adult in an adult milieu. But also relationships with animals could exist for children, not primarily, or even secondarily as a means (even if an unconscious one) to an end, but as having value in themselves, unique, cherished and deeply felt.

A boy, aged 10+, wrote about his friendship with a cat, how the cat died, and how he felt.

I was unhappey wene my cat diad. She was black and waet, and she was soft and frrey, with a nice face. he use to play and roll with me and we liked eachuthore. Me and my frends ate my sunday schole went to see a man ate the chars [pictures] in Bormoth. wen I got back are cat wood not come in. in the morning, my frend fond him dead on the parth. I was unhappy. I was misrpol all day.

Another boy, 12+, more briefly described the death of his cat.

I was unhappy when my cat Tiddles died and I was crying all day, I had found him frozen solid.

A girl, 10+, reported her intense grief following the death of her guinea pig. Another girl described, with the familiarity with processes of procreation and birth revealed by many children, the unfortunate circumstances leading up to the death of her ancient dog.

I was unhappy when my dog made love and got pregnant because she was old and nearly blind. When the first one came my mum was there late at night but it was dead they were all dead. So the vet said it was best to be put down because the tablets hadn't been any good. I was sad because she was the best dog we had. We've always had a dog since I was born that elven years ago.

Happenings less fundamental than death, but nevertheless a cause of considerable unhappiness in children occurred related to themes of *personal and home life, activities and pastimes,* and *other children.* Parents separated. One boy 10+ wrote,

I became unhappy when I heard my parents had divorced and when my mum had married again. I didn't do much but I was said.

A 10+ girl answered,

My father made me very unhappy when he told me he was going to leave just before last Christmas. When he had left after Christmas I found out that he had been decieving us. so I didn't care so much that he left. I am more free now. He obviously didn't care for us so it was best that he left.

Social problems, such as the difficulty of finding somewhere to live, impinged.

One day when I was at my anty Annes' place I came home from school and my mum said that she had to go out to look for a house with my brother while she was there me and my sister were unhappy but when my mum came back she said we have to go to state houseing cimeshen and they said we have to go in to a Hotel.

In the home particular circumstances causing distress arose. There was the problem of television; and particularly the everpresent threat posed by Dracula and his ilk. An 8+ boy from a junior school in Workington described his reactions to Dracula.

I was frightend wen I waced Frankinsteins Film it made me drem abowt it he cild a man in a big hontid casle and there were bats flinging in and out ov the casle windows.

Nor were siblings always averse to heightening the impression created by horror films.

My sister made me frightened when I watched a horror film called the time machine were there were children and some of the children every twenty four hours in the film were being eaten. When the film had finished my sister went upstairs and when I went she said the monsters were behind me.

For younger children in particular there was the strange, and frequently darkling no-man's-land between the well-lit bonhomie of kitchen and sitting room downstairs, and the safety of bed upstairs; on landings, and stairs danger in the form of horrible noises, nasty siblings, loose carpets lay in wait for the unwary. A 10+ boy from West Bromwich recalled the time when he first experienced real fear five years previously.

The first time I was realy frightened was when I was about five years old when I was going to bed before my mother or father would take me but this time they said I've got to learn to go up myself and I was scared of the dark and the doors was banging and it was cold. I slowly walked up the stairs. Then I stopped I could hear something rustling then I darted straight up the stairs and jumped into bed. In the night I could hear things It took me a long time to go to sleep but I've always been scared of the night.

The world outside the home had its dangers too. There were false friends, and unfamiliar places. There was the girl, 9+, who went to a friend's party, only to find that she was not wanted.

One day I went to my freinds house first. She invited me to her party all the things were done into her party there were ten people coming to her party and I was the eleventh girl then her Mum said come on everybody sit down then I said down and all the ten girls sat down then the girl who invited me saw me and said I didnt invited you She said I dont want you in my house them I went outside at my house and I told everything about it.

For numbers of children there was the first day at school, sometimes vividly recalled over a period of years, as in the case of a boy in his second year at a Nottingham comprehensive.

The first day I went to school was a day I will not forget because I was very nervous and unhappy about going to school. The school was a school called Southwark in Old Baseford Nottingham. When I got there I thought it was a huge place with buildings towering above me. I went to find out which class I was in, the headmistress told my mother that I would be in class 6a in the infants. When I got there I found a very tall ginger haired lady waiting for me. She said hello . . . and I sat on her knee she spoke to my mother for a few minuites then said to me that my mother was going home now and she would be back soon. I was very upset about this and jumped of her knee and ran for the door, the door was stuck and I got caught. My mother said 'that she would see me soon and was making for the door when I suddenly felt very frightened. I tried to get to the door but the teacher grabbed hold of my hand and pulled me back I burst into tears as my mother shut the door behind her. All that morning I was upset and would not speak to anyone but when my mother came back for me at 12.00 o'clock I knew I was alright at school.

School could be the setting for other unhappy experiences. A girl, 8+, described her dismay on discovering that she was very near the bottom of the class.

When somebody made me feel unhappy is when I was in the first year. When I heard that I came 24th out of 33st in my report which was very very bad so then in the 2nd year I tried my very very best to come more nearer to the 1st.

However, it is of interest that themes connected with *striving* occur only 24 times in question 2, as compared with 264 times in question 1, statistically a highly significant difference. Evidently the environment of children was more often arranged so that they could strive in hope, and with success, rather than pessimistically and with failure.

Finally, there were those themes which occurred too infrequently to be categorized. As in the first question, specific religious experiences occurred rarely, although (as has been discussed) more diverse intuitions of the super-natural were not uncommon. There were 3 children who reported public events which disturbed them. One child was upset by the Egyptian-Israeli war.

I was angry when I sor The war Between Israel and Egypt Becose I think that the hole world sood Be pessfull and evry time one stops anuther Begins and Egypt is always starting wars thay Been dowing it since mosses crossed the red sea. thar triying to tack Israel Becose it is a vary rich contry and Thay wont to have it all to ther oun. Egypt has lots of riches so I think that Egypt is gredy and if i wer thar Id soyom [show them] something thad never forget.

And there was a girl who suffered the peculiarly adult, even Proustian, emotion of nostalgia for time past.

When we had to come back from Canada, It was every so sad because we had great fun in Canada and we miss the swimming in the pool.
And we missed the lovely weather beacuse it gets in the 90s in Canada. And we allways had tea out side in the garden.
And we all had an evening swim.
Some times I think about it.

This girl however was indeed atypical. Although many children were willing and able to recall previous experience, few appeared anxious to reside in the past; for the majority of children no memories, whether unhappy or not, appeared capable of deflecting them from their steady inclination to cope with the demands of the ever arriving present time.

9 Problem situations—themes

In the answers of children concerning problem situations two themes were frequently associated. Of the 755 children whose answers revealed the theme *informal play and hobbies,* 441 linked it with the theme *how do I occupy myself?* (The latter theme, where it occurred, was always linked with the former.) The problem of why these two themes appeared with such relatively high frequency is perhaps most appropriately considered, at least initially, within a wider social context. With rare exceptions, society in England and Wales appears to be so structured that children are required to find occupation and amusement for themselves, by themselves, for hours every day and for very many hours every week. Furthermore, whereas increasing attention has been paid to the recreational needs of teenage children, particularly through provision of youth clubs, extra-mural school activities, etc., little has been done on a national basis, with the exception perhaps of the Cub and Brownie movements, to organize occupation for children in the middle school age range.

The consequences of this situation were evident in answers children gave in the present research. In general terms, the problems posed by, or arising out of lack of organized occupation loomed very large in their lives. Positively, the challenge to children to find something to do could lead to much serious discussion among themselves, with all that such an activity implied in terms of listening to others, working out worthwhile plans, and learning to evaluate practical possibilities. It could also result in absorbing and creative undertakings which led to great personal satisfaction. The solution which was worked out by one group of children to the problem *how shall we occupy ourselves?* was described by a 10+ boy from Swindon.

One day I went to call for some of my friends so that we could play a game. When I had called for them we were'nt sure what to do we wondered all over the place trying to think what we should do.

We kept coming up with suggestions but they were'nt very good then one of us said why dont we build a den. We got the wood from my uncle he has

Table 15   Frequency of themes: problem situations

Theme group	Individual themes		No.	% of themes
Personal & home life	Siblings: trouble		9	0·2
	Siblings: cooperation & concern		19	0·4
	Grown-ups and home		59	1·2
	Stairs		0	–
	Food		3	0·06
	Pets and animals		64	1·3
	Moving home		8	0·2
	Separation and reuniting		21	0·4
		TOTALS	**183**	**3·6**
Other children	Peer groups & pressures		128	2·5
	Boy/girl relationships		69	1·4
	Friendship		64	1·3
		TOTALS	**261**	**5·1**
Activities & pastimes	TV		11	0·2
	Informal play and hobbies		755	14·9
	Organized activities & sports		107	2·1
	School work & activities		189	3·7
	Shops and shopping		142	2·8
	Vehicles		67	1·3
		TOTALS	**1271**	**25·1**
Special occasions & occurrences	Presents: giving & receiving		27	0·5
	Christmas and birthdays		18	0·3
	Social occasions		87	1·7
	Public celebrations		35	0·7
	Outings and visits		215	4·2
	Staying away from home		99	1·9
	Births and christenings		0	–
	Engagements and marriages		13	0·2
	Public appearances		18	0·3
		TOTALS	**512**	**10·1**
Behaviour difficulties	Misbehaviour		149	2·9
	Provocation		96	1·9
	Drink, drugs and smoking		14	0·3

Theme group	Individual theme		No.	% of themes
Behaviour difficulties	Law breaking & delinquent behaviour		38	0·7
	Adult/child disagreement		53	1·0
		TOTALS	350	6·9
Critical situations	Getting lost		136	2·7
	Strangers		33	0·6
	Fear and the dark		7	0·1
	Fire hazard		16	0·3
	Hostile supernatural occurrences		3	0·06
	Accident and injury		137	2·7
	Illness and operations		17	0·3
	Death or disappearance		15	0·3
		TOTALS	364	7·2
Problems	What do I do?		755	14·9
	What do I choose?		338	6·7
	How do I occupy myself?		441	8·7
	How do I do it?		179	3·5
	Losing, finding & forgetting		92	1·8
		TOTALS	1805	35·6
Expectations	Expected happenings		68	1·3
	Unexpected happenings		38	0·7
	Striving		22	0·4
	Praise		7	0·1
	Temptation		54	1·1
	Unfairness		1	0·02
	Taking responsibility		49	1·0
	Concern for others		71	1·4
		TOTALS	310	6·1
Miscellaneous		TOTALS	9	0·2
		OVERALL TOTALS	5065	99·9

Percentages have been rounded.

lots of wood because he is a carpenter. We built the den at the back of my house. It took us all day to build it, when we had finished it ther was room for us to stand up in it and room to put bikes in so we put ours in it. When it

was time to go in we camouflage it with leaves because there were alot of trees
were we built it.

Other children, such as two girls from West Bromwich contrasted unfavourably the situation at home, where they had to find themselves occupation, with the more structured environment of school where work was provided.
Nevertheless, the girls concerned did find themselves something to do, and in
the process no doubt began to learn something about the necessary skills of
choosing in unstructured situations.

Last Sunday I woke up and got dressed I went downstairs and went out to
call for my friend Sharon I said what shall we do she said I do not know I
said I wished we were at school doing work. I said lets go on a picnic Sharon
said OK and we went on the coman. We lay the blanket out and put the food
on the blanket, but when we had finish the food we had nothing to do so we
serjested to play hide an seek.

In some circumstances the discussion of what to do took place, not
between familiar groups of friends, but between children who had just met
for the first time. Since there seem to be few children who have not faced the
problem of deciding how to pass the time, the discussion of a type of difficulty
familiar to all present could be a useful initial method of getting to know and
understand each other. One boy described how he established, in accordance
with his mother's firm wishes, friendship with 'my mums friends grandchildren'.

One day when I went to my mums friends caravan, on a caravan site there
were my mums friends grandchildren. My mum told me to make friends with
these children. So I did. I made friends with them quite easily. I went into
there small bedroom. We sat there for a long time but we could not think of
any-thing to do. After about 15 minutes we came up with an idea. We went
outside and played chase.

But there were children who failed to rise to the challenge of providing
occupation for themselves. For some, if they were lucky as one group from
Swindon was, there might be organized facilities available for them.

One day I went out with my friends we soon got bored because we didnt
have any thing to do a boy said that he knew a place were we could go so we
said that we would go with him but his mum called him in so we were back were
we started we just sat down and hoped that some one would come up with
something then our mate said go to the boys' club so we did we played football snooker and we did gymnasticks and we started going 5 days a weak.

However, very few of the answers indicated that such facilities were regularly and easily found and where they were it was usually the older children who were provided for. More commonly children without occupation would simply sit around, bored, and sooner or later they might get into minor trouble, or at least fear such a possibility. One girl described how she and her friends accidentally broke a mirror off a broken down car. They used to sit on the car.

Around our street we have got a car a red one, that belongs to a man across the road. The car does not work. Me and three of my friends always sit on it. One-day when we were sitting on it and me and my friend were arguing about where we were sitting, we both went to sit down and we sat on the mirror and it broke off. We did'nt know what to do so we chucked it under the car and walked away from it. The man still does'nt know but the car is in more of a state.

A boy, aged 9+, wrote about how, for want of anything better to do he and others intentionally caused damage.

on the way to the holy well we did not no what to do so we smashed the lanp and we rust like the wind.

It was unusual, nevertheless, for the difficulties of finding a pastime to end in disaster. Perhaps the adult assumption, implicit in many of the answers, that children were quite capable of playing by themselves and should learn to do so, was justified. On the other hand, there were some answers which clearly indicated adult negligence. There was one child (whose mother was a supply teacher and who therefore presumably had a professional knowledge of how to organize children), who was simply left at his birthday party to find amusement for himself and his friends. Perhaps naturally, he arranged things so that he got up to an activity which possibly would not have found favour in his mother's eyes.

When it was my Birthday I did not no what to do so we made up games and watched tele while everybody was doing that I was doing something else with my girl freind (kissing).

The most frequently mentioned theme in the general category of *Problems,* was *what do I do?* which appeared in the answers of 755 children. This theme was connected with a variety of related issues. The question *what do I do?* arose as a result of uncertainty as to how to follow social guidelines which were not fully understood; or because of uncertainty as to which of particular guidelines to follow; or because of difficulty in correctly interpreting specific circumstances. Of the 755 answers in which the theme occurred, it appeared 105 times on its own; 173 times with themes involving comparatively unfamiliar social circumstances (*outings and visits* — 77, *social occasions* — 38, *staying away from home* — 30, and *grown-ups and home* — 28); 117 times with *school work and activities*; 55 times with *informal play and hobbies*; and 50 times with *organized activities and sports*. With all other themes with which it was paired it occurred fewer than 20 times.

A problem which appeared, in a variety of forms, in many of the answers, was concerned with the difficulty of discovering and practising social techniques appropriate to establishing satisfactory relationships with unknown or little known people, whether other children or adults. In earlier generations such difficulties might have been characterized as being concerned with etiquette. However, because of the overenthusiasm which the Victorians once brought to the cult of etiquette, to this day a faintly disreputable aura can be associated with a concern for social decorum, and even the concept of good manners. But perhaps the pendulum has swung too far; for, if members of a society are to understand each other, to relate to each other in a civilized way, and to express concern for each other, it helps if there is an established way of doing these things, particularly between people who are not very familiar to each other.

Many children in the present survey faced difficulties which could, but for the prejudice against the word, be described as associated with etiquette. It is possible that the relatively high incidence of such problems arose, on occasion, from adult reluctance to recognize both that difficulties of etiquette could seem significant to children, and that a concern with such matters might be helpful in the good upbringing of children. This is not to claim that adults consciously neglected children's needs; indeed they were frequently kindly. It was simply that there were times when they seemed to lack insight in this particular area.

A number of the etiquette difficulties experienced by children arose in the home, and were connected with the appearance of visitors, or at least outsiders to the family group. A girl from West Bromwich was left alone to entertain her grandmother, who had arrived on an unexpected visit, and found the going heavy.

A time when I was with somebody and I did not know what to do was when my mother and sister had gone to town and I was left with my father. I got out a book and began to read it. All at once there was a knock on the door window, my Grandmother and Grandfather had come to see us. My father

asked my Grandfather if he would like some apples so they went out in the
garden to get some. I was left alone with my Grandmother and I had not got
the faintest idea what to do. I tried showing her old Christmas and Birthday
cards that were stuck in my scrap book. Then we got talking about birthday
cards and my birthday but I was not very good company. Eventual Eventually
my mother and sister came home and they were better than I was a talking.

Another girl, of 12+, found herself in a dilemma when she went into the sitting
room to find that her father had someone with him. The father at least gave
his daughter a pretext to leave the room, although he did not appear to have
made any particular effort to help the girl deal with her social difficulty
constructively.

I wasent sure what to do when I went into the sitting room without knowing
that my dad had somebody in with him talking I dident know wether to go
out or to shake hands, or just to sit down and go red. In the end I went out
going red after shaking hand with him. I went out because my dad had told
me to put the kettel on.

The answer of a third girl showed how the most progressive and concerned
family relationships were not necessarily a guarantee that etiquette problems
would be avoided. The parents in question had gone to watch their son in a
pop group. The son's girl friend had come to babysit and a difficulty arose:
girl friend and sister did not know how to relate to each other.

I was with my brothers girl friend as she had come to baby sit while my mum
was out with dad because my brother had joined a pop group (son of igor) and
they had gone to see them at last she asked me wether I had scrabble and I
said yes and so we played scrabble and watched TV.

More difficult problems arose when children, as the visitors and not the
visited, left the familiar terrain of their home ground, and ventured into alien
fields. Sometimes they returned with a sense of wonderment reporting that,
out in unexplored territories, strange customs were to be found. A child from
a London school described what she had discovered on venturing for a holiday
to deepest Somerset.

There was a time when I was was with other people, they live in Somerset I
went there for a holiday with my brother. We had a good time there! They had
many different ways of doing things. I did'nt know all about there ways, so I
just tryed to get used to them. It was funny being away from home, with all
our ways.

Children also reported that not only people in different regions, but in different classes had unusual mores which required careful observation if successful contact was to be established. One child, aged 12+, was amazed at the laughter and numbers of cakes enjoyed by a family in a private house. Should she put her hands on the table?

My sister and I were showing two people round a Mently handycaped home one day. This is where my sister used to work. The peoples names were Louis and Angela. Angela was staying with Louis in her house. They lived in a privat house, down a very posh road. Louis asked Ronnie and me to come in and have tea and cream cakes, after we had looked round the home. I was at my best behaviour. When we sat down at the table I noticed about 20 cakes on the table. I was amaized, the cups were very wide. I just looked at everone and whated for them to start to drink and eat. Although they were in a privat house and they talked posh, they were very nice. Laughing and joking at the table. I was not to sure on wether I could put my hand on the table or not. When everone else laught, I laught. They said I was a very nice girl, which made me proud.

Meals in other people's houses presented difficulties of the sort familiar not only to earlier generations, but possibly to many of today's adults. Visits to houses of friends, although eagerly anticipated, could raise problems.

I was invited to tea by my friend called Susan. All day at school I was getting a little excited about going to tea with her. When school finished I walked home with her and her sister called Maureen. When we got to there house I said hello to there mum. I went upstairs and played with Susan in her bedroom. We looked at pictures of pop-stars till it was time for tea. We went downstairs and sat at the table. There were two sets of knifes and one fork. I wondered which fork to use so when we had our dinner given I used the wrong knife. I wondered what to do next. I changed the knifes round and ate my. I wondered whether I was doing the right things. I used all my table manner's and when I was asked what I want to drink I said it in shyness. Well I was glad when dinner was over.
    After that we listned to records and played leap frog till I was to be taken home.

Visits to other houses, where the inmates were less well known, might cause similar dilemmas.

I was at somebodies house who I did not know very well and it was dinner time. The first thing that worryed me was that I was not sure whether they said grase or no.

The second was that there were lots of little knives and forkes and I didn't know which to use.

In the end I said I wasn't very hungry.

Apparently simple tasks could provoke situations which proved difficult to deal with, and which were sometimes recalled over a period of time. One 12+ girl remembered an incident, some years previously, when she first encountered the mother of a friend.

Well it was a few years ago when I had first me my friend Sandra and i was going down her house and her mum was there and i did'nt no what to do so i said hellow and i got to know her mum better and her dad.

A 10+ boy visited a cinema with a friend and his parents. Placement presented a difficulty. Where was it correct to sit?

One Day on one of my freinds birthdays we went to see two James Bond Films. I was not sure wether to sit by my freinds mum and dad or not. But in the end I did.

Occasionally there were more subtle and at times even bizarre problems of etiquette, connected with choosing an appropriate style of response to unexpected social situations. One child, for example was worried about how he should react to a sick joke.

It happened about a year ago. I was with my friend. His name is Anthony. I was at his house. We were on a coal bunker. Anthony's cousin came. We started to talk together. Wille we were talking Anthony's cousin told us a story. It was a story a teacher had told her. It went like this. Once there was a couple. They found a majic stone. Every time you rubbed it you could have a wish. But you could only rub it three times. The first time they wished they wished to be rich. The second wish the wife had. She wished that her son would come back to life. The son had fallen into a mangling machine. But the husband wished him not to come because he would be all horrible. I didn't know wether to laugh or be serious. I decided to be serious.

The theme *what do I do?* involved, as well as difficulties of social mores, comparatively straightforward problems which arose from a lack of knowledge of established rules or procedures. Such problems could be found, for example, in those answers in which the theme *what do I do?* occurred associated with the themes *school work and activities* (associated in 117 answers) and *organized activity and sports* (associated in 50 answers). That the theme *what do I do?* was found in 167 answers in which problems occurred in primarily adult controlled environments indicated that such environments by no means necessarily offered a milieu in which children were confident as to how to behave. Indeed, although as discussed, children frequently had difficulty when on their own in deciding how to occupy themselves, they were less often unsure how to behave in child controlled than in adult controlled environments. *What do I do?* was associated only 55 times with *informal play and hobbies.*

A number of explanations for these findings may be offered. First, adult controlled environments typically offered a greater multiplicity of rules and regulations than child environments, and lack of familiarity with school, club, sport, etc., or lack of emotional or intellectual capacity to comprehend what was required, could lead to confusion. Second, within most adult controlled environments areas existed in which children were left to their own devices, but in which child developed rules were not always as clear as in the perhaps more familiar setting of house or even neighbourhood. Third, the informal methods of organization, prevalent in particular in many schools, intentionally created situations in which children were expected to contribute to the definition of, and themselves find answers to, particular problems.

More complex problems relating to the theme *what do I do?* were those which arose as a result of having to interpret ambiguous circumstances. Where there were difficulties of recognition a child not only had to decide which of various possible interpretations of a given set of circumstances was correct, but also to decide upon the correct reaction to make to the situation as interpreted. Further, the reactions to the various possible interpretations needed to be considered in making an interpretation, since one line of reaction might be so far preferable to another that it might be better to decide on the particular interpretation which predicated the preferable reaction, even if some data suggested that the interpretation chosen was not necessarily the most likely to be correct.

An example of such a difficulty was given in the answer of an 11+ girl who, with a friend, saw a man lying on the grass. It was possible that he was just having a sleep, but the reaction predicated by that interpretation was just to leave him. He might however have been ill; the reaction to that interpretation was to warn an adult. It was preferable to take the risk of being wrong that the man was ill, and get unnecessary help, than to ignore him and leave him in perhaps serious trouble. The girl in fact took the most sensible course.

There was one time when me and my friends were not sure what to do. We were walking home from school and there was a man lying on the grass, we didn't know what to do, we didn't know if he was just laying there or if he had fainted. I plucked up my courage and walked over to him, I saw he hadn't fainted and he wasn't just lying on the grass. I ran over to the telephone box and was just about to dial 999, when the policeman who lived in one of the houses came out. He phoned a doctor who came straight away, the man lived next-door to my friend. She told the man that this man kept on having fit's. Then an ambulance came along and took him away.

Another problem of recognition, and one of practical importance to children, involved the correct interpretation of the nature and intentions of unknown or little known children. Failure correctly to diagnose whether new arrivals were likely to prove hostile or amiable could have regrettable conse-quences. One girl on holiday stood her ground although she estimated that some strange children were trouble makers. Luckily for her, the diagnosis proved wrong, the action correct.

I was on holiday at the time I was alone because the others had gone out shopping. I saw there was some campers who I made friend easily with then I saw some children comeing towards me they didn't look very friendly they looked like trouble makers. I didn't know wether to run or stay. I stayed and acted usual, I said hello to them and they said hello to me I made friends easily with them. They were not as as bad as they looked.

Conflicts between mutually incompatible, though clearly understood proce-dures, could also give rise to difficulties. An 8+ girl from London was baby-sitting for a friend of her mother's, who was late in returning home. Should she go home, so as to be in time for dinner? Or should she stay and look after the children?

i was round my mums friends house and I was looking after her children so I wanted to go hom and I thought I should go home and I thought no I should stay and wait till her friend comes and I did not now what to do I was in a temper and I was skeard so I wondered and I dident think of her children I was just wishing her friend would hurry up I just hopped and hopped her friend would hurry up so I just said by Margy Ive got to go home for dinner and just as I opened her street door I saw her friend was unlocking the door so I went home.

338 children gave answers in which the theme *what do I choose?* (involving choice within a defined area) occurred. Of the 338 times the theme appeared, it was unpaired 91 times (26·9% of all answers in theme); of the 247 times (73·1%) in which it was paired, it occurred in association with *outings and visits* 45 times (18·2% of paired themes), in association with *staying away from home* 27 times (10·9% of paired themes), and 20 times in association

with *shops and shopping* (8·1% of paired themes). No other theme was found paired more frequently than 16 times. Accordingly, the theme *what do I choose?* was associated with a relatively high number of other themes, with no single theme or group of themes massively predominating.

The problems which occurred in this theme were, as is predicated by the nature of the theme, of a comparatively straightforward nature. There were for example choices to be made between two alternatives, such as were offered by her mother to a 10+ middle school girl in Chester.

Once I was with my eldest sister and my mum said, 'do you want to come to the river Dee or stay at home with your friend'. I said, I would stay with my friend and play with Nicola (My doll) and Ian (My teddy). So me and my sister stayed at home and we played with my friend.

There were also choices, which could cause protracted consideration among a variety of options, albeit of a pleasant nature, as in the case of one 10+ boy.

The day when I didn't know what to do, was a couple of weeks ago, I was deciding what to have for Christmas. I was with my mum deciding out of her catalogue. First I wanted a cassette tape recorder then I saw a good punchball and boxing gloves, or would I have a record player, I just could'nt decide. My mum got out her friend's catalogue. I had the same problem with each article. I saw a good battery operated stunt cycle then I saw a game called Flight Deck, then Striker, then Super Striker. At last I decided to have about three games.

However, more difficult or serious problems did occur. One girl, sent shopping by her mother, found herself in a situation in which she could not do what she had been asked to do, so that the choice before her was between two alternatives, both of which were unsatisfactory, and one of which might prove – in her mother's eyes – more unsatisfactory. But, in her mother's absence, the girl could not easily judge which was the less unsatisfactory alternative.

I was with my mum and my mum told me to pop into Mase to get some Soap powder but she told my to get the small box I went in and asked for a small box of Soap powder but they dident have any I dident know weather to take a medeam box or nothing at all in the End I got the medeam box.

Another problem, also caused by a mother, was posed to a boy who returned with a cousin to his house, only to find the house locked. Should they wait, or break in? Either way they might get into trouble; as it happened the cousin nearly had an accident.

My cousin and I were trying to get into his house we did not know whether to wait until his mum got back or to climb in the window in the end we decided to climb through the the window since my cousin was smaller than me we decided that he should go through the window but he had to jump a long way down, he jumped and nearly broke his ankle.

The theme *how do I do it?* occurred in the answers of 179 children. The theme was concerned with situations in which children lacked a particular skill, or had the skill but lacked the ability to put it into practice. An 11+ boy from a middle school in Chester found himself, in circumstances upon which he did not elaborate, lacking the skill to deal satisfactorily with a dumper.

I hat to Drive a Dumper and I was not sure how to revers it.

A girl had similar difficulties of manoeuvring, albeit with an animal, not a vehicle.

When I was with my mum and dad, and brother and sister, Once when we was going to christ Church park and we saw horse rides for five pence a go. We was allowed to have a go each. First of all my brother had a go, then my sister had a go, then it was my turn. First of all I stood by the horse, then I got up onto the saddle, and sat there and wondered what to do, then I kicked the horse and got hold of the raiens, the horse walked. then I kicked it again not noing what to do, and the horse started to trot, It was all bumpy and horrable, when I got up to the part where I had to turn round and go back I, wondered what to do first of all I turnt it the wrong way, but the second time I got it write.

Lack of ability to cope with a difficult problem was illustrated by the answer of a 9+ girl caught with her mother in a crowd of men who were waiting for the pub to open. Presumably the only skill required was to push and shout effectively, but the girl and her mother were without the necessary weight and voice.

I was in town with my mother and we ran into a little road place. As it happened a pub was to be opened at a certain time. There were a lot of men waiting outside singing and going mad. I was terribly scared and my mum, who was holding my hand tightly lost grip almost. That was another frighteining moment. We just couldn't get through the crowd and it was getting very dark. At last the pub opened and we were able to get through but it was a frightenin experience.

For some children there were problems in which lack of skill and lack of ability overlapped. An 8+ girl had to measure a tree trunk, as part of a class exercise at school: she had difficulty over the perspective.

When I went to the park with the class I went in my desk group so there was three of us. So we had to do this old tree trunk one of the boys counted how old it was and thats were I got my problem I could not draw it it was the size that that made me frustrated so I looked at it in a diffrent way from far back that was a bit better I finished it but that was rotten the other one was better.

The skills children were expected to acquire were occasionally unconventional. One 9+ boy had a problem associated with etiquette. His knowledge of deaf language failed him at a crucial moment.

When I went to My Grannys She took Me to a deaf Club They were all talking to Me in deaf language. I was talking Back but I forgot how to say thanck you in deaf language.

Besides the groups of themes (*problems, activities and pastimes, special occasions and occurrences*) which appeared most frequently in answers, other groups of themes, particularly *other children, behaviour difficulties,* and *critical situations*, raised points of interest. Difficulties could occur in the context of peer group activity. An 8+ girl found that her desire to lead or impress her friends put her in a situation in which she was by no means sure whether she was prepared to risk the displeasure of the headmaster.

A time when I didn't know what to do was when my friends wanted to go toilet at school. You see because we are not allowed to go toilet at playtime. So one of my friend's said who is going to be the brave person to lead us. And I said 'I will.' But as I was going upstairs I thought that the headmaster would catch us so I ran downstairs. And then I said 'We might as well not go'.

Friendship could also entail difficult responsibilities, as another girl, aged 9+, discovered.

One day I was walking home from school when I saw on of my friands comeing toward me. She said will you walk me home becase some boy are after me so I said yes by all means I was walking her home when I saw two big boys from . . . school in London they wanted my freid but 'I' said they can not have I felt a fool and we ran away from them we whent into the park and there we had lost them.

Behaviour difficulties gave rise to dilemmas, not only when children themselves were directly involved, but also when they observed such difficulties.
Misbehaviour or delinquency by others, whether contemporary or adult, was
liable to cause difficult moral problems for children. An 8+ girl saw a man
whom she and her friend thought was trying to trap a cat.

One day me and friend went out to play with little reta we were crossing the
road and we saw this man trying to catch the cat so we hide around a wall and
watch want he was doing but reta was keeping laugh and kay said stop laughing
then we still watching the man trying to get the cat then kay and Jill and zoe
and Dawn reta and me we all said shall we call the policeman but Jill said no
we might get in a trouble then siddy the dog came barking in and we said shut
up siddy. but Siddy kept on barking so we took siddy out to play.

A 10+ boy from a middle school stated simply the problem he faced when a
game between himself, his brother and two girls went too far, and his brother
started assaulting the girl.

Me and my brother was in the field at the back of our house went to girls came
up along the road. We started to creep up on them but they saw us and dash
off to hide. We can after them going in and out of the houses that were being
built up.
At last we got them. We all then played a game hide and seek. Me and my
brother dash off to some pipes and hid. They came along and found us. then
we got hold of the girls arms and legs ('called' crossed out) and My brother
started to ('take of her dress to do to' crossed out) do some thing dirty.

Behaviour difficulties on the part of others could also cause very practical
problems. One 11+ boy found himself involved in hooliganism at a football
match.

Once when I was up the back at football and there were lots of skinheads
around me I didnt quite know what to do there was lots of people everywhere
there was lots of fights I just stayed there and there was bangers going off and
bottles being thrown on to the pitch the people were shoving and pushing
and people were falling over and getting troden on in the end I worked my way
to the back and just walked out.

Behaviour difficulties in which children themselves actively participated
not infrequently led to situations the outcome of which could only be
awaited, at times in fear. A girl from a middle school had a fight with another
girl.

One day when I was coming home for my deiner I had a fith with this gril and she said that she going to get her mouther up to the school when I came to school I was't sure what to do so when the wille weat [whistle went] I went to my casse room and did my work and than Mr. Robie came and said go up to my room so I did and the gril came up and than Mr Robis came up and told me and the gril of for fithing and than he said go back to your casse room and no more fithing.

Conflict between children and adults also caused worry. An 11+ girl from a comprehensive in Workington found that her mother had promised her services for babysitting, while the girl herself had already decided on other arrangements for Saturday night's entertainment. This was an occasion when a child was provoked by an adult's not treating her as a person to be considered as an independent individual.

It was a saturday night and I wanted to go to the disco with my freinds and my mams freing wanted me to watch he little girl and my mouther said I would when my mothers freind had gon I was arguing withe my mother the I wasent going to watch her and my mother said you will watche he or you wont go out tomorow.

Themes of *critical situations* in children's answers predominantly concerned *accident and injury,* and *getting lost.* Situations involving accidents were typically of the sort in which a child was hurt, and another child or other children went for help. Children showed a considerable capacity for losing themselves, especially when shopping, or on outings and visits. A 12+ girl, in an answer which was very unusual in that it showed a self-conscious attempt at literary style, described her experience of getting lost in a large department store.

Woolco, a big department store can be very frightening if you happen to lose a parent whilst looking at the bright fancy things on the shelves. In fact terrifiying.

About two years ago, when Woolco had just opened, Mum took me to do some shopping. Mum wanted to buy tonights dinner and I wanted to look at the toys and books. So I said I'd meet her at four o'clock. I could sense that Mum was worried about leaving me, so I reasured her I would be perfectly alright and would be by the doors on the dot at four o'clock.

After a browse around the various counters I noticed that it was nearly four. I scampered round to the big set of metal cast doors narrowly missing women with shopping baskets and trolleys.

I waited ten minutes she still did not come. By now I was getting worried.

I shuffled my feet uncomfortably. Butterflies were beginning to form in my stomach. I stood on the chair that was by me to see if there was any sight of her. I was on the verge of tears. There was no sign. Just then the attendant came along. Hurriedly I hopped of the chair and ran outside to the car hoping she might be there. It was no use. No sign of Mum anywhere.

Solemly I went back into Woolco. I had decided to tell the attendant. Suddenly it occured to me that there was another set of doors. As quick as a flash I ran to the other doors bumping into trolleys and sending them flying. My stomach was tense my legs ached and my heart was pounding but a glimmer of hope rushed through my body. 'Mum' I shreiked 'Mam I've found you.' Throwing my arms around her I gave her a relieved kiss. Nothing like that had ever happened to me before.

A boy in his second year at a Nottingham comprehensive school recalled his first visit to the school, an almost Kafkaesque occasion and one in which, unusually, a child managed to lose himself in the company of his parents.

The first every time I came to West Bridgford Comp was with my parents. None of us had been to this school before so we were not sure what to do or where to go. I said that we must follow the people but there were no people about. We walked straight on until we came to some swing doors, we went through them and found ourselves three different choices, straight to the left or to the right we stood waiting thinking what to do when ahead of us we saw some people but up the stairs to the left I heard a noise. I ran up the stairs and just turned the corner when I bumped into a teacher. I said sorry but he did not seem to pleased and said what do you think you are doing up here, for a second this question froze me, I did not know what to say eventually I mumled that I wanted to know where I was to go because I was knew and I did not know he told me the way and we finally got there. On the way out we also found difficulty when again we lost the way but finally we got out.

Part IV
Others

107

Table 16   Classification of others

Family
Parents
Siblings
Special close relations
Other relations

Children not close family members
Friends
Known children and cousins
Unknown children

Adults not family members
Teachers
Other adults in authority
Friends and neighbours
Unkown adults

Creatures, objects, environment
Living creatures
Objects
Environment and surroundings

Supernatural, fictitious and well known figures
God
Religious figures
Public figures
Fictitious figures
Spirits, ghosts

Miscellaneous
Somebody
Myself (no-one)
Activity group

10 Classification and frequency—others

CLASSIFICATION

The classification of significant *others* was reached inductively (see Appendix C). The answers of children in both pre-pilot and pilot surveys had raised an immediate problem. From Chapter 3, p. 14 it was evident that a number of children interpreted 'somebody' in the questions asked as referring to anybody human or non-human, animate or inanimate, rather than as exclusively referring to another person. It was decided to admit as valid (rather than rejecting as non-responses) those answers in which the somebody mentioned was non-human, or non-animate. The reasons for this decision were twofold. First, from the point of view of defined meaning, body can mean 'an entity; an agent or cause of phenomena' (O.E.D.). The Oxford English Dictionary quotes Mill, 'a body may be defined, the external cause to which we ascribe our sensations.' It was in this sense that some children used the concept 'body', and it seemed as if it might be an acceptable use, even though 'body' prefixed by some is generally taken to refer to another person.

The second, more compelling, reason for admitting answers which used somebody in the broad sense of the term was that a number of children evidently considered themselves to live in a world in which they formed relationships with, and interacted with bodies which were not necessarily people. For many children animals, for some children objects such as vehicles, or environments such as schools, or hospitals, were the perceived cause of particular emotions and reactions. The child's world, as described in the present research, was more primitive, more animistic than the adult's world. To have disallowed those answers which indicated this would have been to impose on the interpretation of the children's writing an adult view of their world; this would not only have been distorting, but directly contrary to the aims of the research.

Another problem which arose was that a small minority of children answered the questions by describing the other not as a body external to themselves, but internal. A child might write, for example, 'I hurt myself'. The

109

operational reality of circumstances in which the self can be split into active and passive (the agent and the acted upon) components is acknowledged in language by the reflexive construction. Accordingly it was decided to admit those answers in which the agent was the self. In general the intention was to admit the answers of children who had clearly understood the questions, even if they had interpreted it in their own terms rather than terms which an adult might have used or expected. On the other hand, obviously answers were not admitted where children had evidently misunderstood the question, and failed to mention any *other*.

The general principle employed in constructing the classification of *others* was to use categories which reflected the terms used by children. Thus, children might refer to their mothers as *others,* or their fathers, or both parents, or (very occasionally) a parent without making clear which. Accordingly, the general category of *parents* included the appropriate sub-categories.

A number of the terms used in the classification are self-explanatory; others however require comment. *Mother, father, parents* included natural, step-, foster and adoptive parents. Under the general category *relations* special close relations was included to differentiate visiting or visited relations, from those who actually were, or were close to being, *in loco parentis. Relations* could include 'uncles' or 'aunts' who were in fact individuals living with single parents. *Family group* was included to classify others in those situations where children referred to a collection of relations (possibly, but not necessarily, including members of their immediate family circle) whom they did not differentiate individually, or whom, despite such differentiation, they described primarily in group terms. Such groups might be written about in the context of festive occasions, family visits, etc.

In the general category of *adults not close family members, unknown* (unspecified) *adults* could include hostile strangers, friendly strangers, or adults not sufficiently familiar to be named or described in a personal context. *Adults in authority* could include any adult (except teachers) whose relationship with a child was formulated primarily in terms of the adult's professional role. Thus doctors, youth leaders, nurses, farmers, dentists, Cub, Brownie, Scout leaders were all adults in authority. *Friends and neighbours* included adults who were friends of the family, or whom children saw as their own friends.

In the general category *children not close family members* the use of the term 'cousin' caused difficulties. Cousins were clearly distinguished from friends, however friendly the relationship might be. But sometimes named children, not described as friends, appeared from other evidence in an answer to be perhaps cousins as well; accordingly *cousins* were classified with *known children.*

Table 17   '*Other*' groups: happy, unhappy, problem situations

Other group	Situations Happy	%	Unhappy	%	Problem	%
Parents	1244	38·8	439	14·0	195	7·1
Siblings	129	4·0	519	16·5	128	4·6
Relations	471	14·7	186	5·9	254	9·2
Adults not close family members	416	13·0	335	10·7	288	10·4
Children not close family members	390	12·1	822	26·2	1348	48·8
Supernatural, fictitious and well known figures	60	1·9	86	2·7	4	0·1
Creatures, objects and environment	291	9·1	517	16·5	180	6·5
Miscellaneous	207	6·4	237	7·5	366	13·2
TOTALS	3208	100·0	3141	100·0	2763	99·9

Under the general category *supernatural, fictitions and well known figures, fictitious figures* could include figures read about, seen on television, imagined, or heard of: Father Christmas, Dracula, monsters of all shapes and sizes, and Dr. Who were fictitious figures who featured. Under the general heading *Creatures, objects and environment, environment and surroundings* could include fire, treacherous conditions, storms, the dark, etc. *Objects* might be food, fireworks, toys, dolls, footballs, etc. 'Something' was any defined body, often simply referred to as something; or perhaps the unknown origin of a noise of any other phenomenon. Under the general category *miscellaneous,* 'somebody' or some people, were usually those referred to by children as such; and it was often unclear whether somebody or some people were known or unknown, adult or child. *Activity groups* were groups of others, usually but not always children organized formally or informally for activities. Football teams, cubs, dancing lessons, were examples of activity groups.

FREQUENCY

The frequency of individual categories, within general categories of *other* may be considered first, by comparing frequency of categories within each type of situation; and second, by comparing frequency of categories between each type of situation (see Table 17).

Of the children who described happy situations and mentioned *others,* 38·8% wrote about *parents,* 4·0% *siblings* and 14·7% *relations.* Consequently 57·5% of children, or more than half, mentioned members of their family as

making them pleased or happy. Of the remaining *others* written about by
children 13·0% were *adults not close family members,* and this group included
5·6% of children answering who wrote about teachers, and 4·1% who wrote
about *adults in authority. Children not close family members* were mentioned
by 12·1% of children, and this group included 9·2% of children who wrote
about their *friends.* Of the remaining groups of *others,* 9·1% of children mentioned *creatures, objects and environment,* 6·4% *somebody, activity groups*
and no-one or *myself (miscellaneous)* and 1·9% *supernatural, fictitious or well
known figures.*

Of the children who described unhappy situations and mentioned others
almost twice as many mentioned *children not close family members* (26·2%,
822) as mentioned the next most frequent category, *siblings* (16·5%, 519).
Altogether therefore 42·7% of children wrote about other children. 10·7%
mentioned *adults not close family members,* 14·0% *parents,* and 5·9% *relations;* thus 30·6% of children mentioned adults (excluding the 0·5% who wrote
about public figures), 12·1% fewer than those who mentioned children. Apart
from the predominance among *others* of *children not close family members,*
and the comparatively low representation of *relations* and *supernatural, fictitious and well known figures* (mentioned by 2·7%), *others* written about were
fairly evenly distributed among categories (including *creatures, objects and
environment* by 16·5%).

Of the children who described problem situations and mentioned *others,*
almost half mentioned *children not close family members* (48·8%) and, as
4·6% mentioned *siblings,* over half mentioned other children. Apart from the
miscellaneous category (which itself probably contained a number of children)
– mentioned by 13·2%, no other group was mentioned by more than 11·0%
of children. *Parents* occurred in 7·1% of answers, *relations* in 9·2% and *adults
not close family members* in 10·4%. Adults, therefore (other than public
figures and those occurring in the miscellaneous group) were mentioned by
26·9% of children. Of the remaining groups, *creatures, objects and environment* were mentioned by 6·5% of children, and *supernatural, fictitious and
well known figures* by 0·1%. It appears therefore that the situations in which
children were not sure what to do were almost twice as likely to occur in a
social milieu in which other children were described as one in which adults
were described.

If the frequency of incidence of categories of *others* is compared between
questions the following findings emerge. Parents were statistically very significantly more likely to be mentioned in happy situations, by 38·8% of children,
than in unhappy situations (14·0%), $p < 0.001$. They were significantly less
likely to be mentioned in problem situations than in unhappy situations,
$0.05 > p > 0.01$. In each question mothers were mentioned more frequently

than fathers (in happy situations by 14·9% compared with 13·3%; in unhappy situations by 6·5% compared with 5·8%; in problem situations by 3·7% compared with 2·3%).

Siblings were mentioned very significantly more frequently in unhappy situations (16·5%) than either in happy situations (4·0%) or problem situations (4·6%), $p < 0.001$. In each type of situation siblings of the same sex were mentioned more frequently than siblings of the opposite sex. Relations were mentioned by 14·7% of children in happy situations, 5·9% in unhappy situations and 9·2% in problem situations. They accordingly feature very significantly more frequently in happy situations than in unhappy situations, $p < 0.001$. There was no statistically significant difference between the frequency of mention in unhappy and problem situations.

The distribution of *others* in the group *adults not close family members* was relatively even among the types of situation, mentioned by 13·0% children in happy situations, 10·7% in unhappy situations and 10·4% in problem situations. No statistically significant differences were found. However, there were variations as far as individual categories within the group were concerned. Teachers were mentioned by 5·6% of children in happy situations and, excepting members of the family (parents, siblings, relations), were the most frequently mentioned individual category in any group after friends (child). In unhappy situations, on the other hand, teachers were mentioned by 2·6% of children, and in all groups were mentioned less frequently than any single category of *children not close family members,* than any single category of *creatures, objects and environment* (with the exception of objects), and less frequently than adults in authority (3·3%) and unknown or unspecified adults (3·9%).

Children not close family members were mentioned by 12·1% of children in happy situations, by over twice as many in unhappy situations (26·2%), and by over three times as many in problem situations (48·8%). Significantly more *children not close family members* were mentioned in problem situations, and fewer in happy situations, $p < 0.001$.

Of the remaining groups of categories there was no statistically significant difference between numbers of children who mentioned *supernatural, fictitious and well known figures* (in problem situations (0·1%) than in happy situations (1·9%) and unhappy situations (2·7%)). *Creatures, objects and environment* were mentioned significantly more frequently in unhappy than problem situations, $p < 0.001$, and in unhappy than happy situations, $p < 0.01$.

11 Happy situations—others

In answers concerning happy situations children mentioned parents most frequently as making them pleased or happy. Although individual children wrote about a wide variety and complexity of circumstances the situations reported were typically ones in which adults by their actions showed sympathetic understanding of children's needs, or even wants, and if necessary gave support to children and took their side. For example, the father of a boy in his first year at a Nottingham comprehensive, by his timely presentation of an Airfix model, contributed to the child's recovery from an illness and earned his gratitude.

One day in the summer holidays I woke up and I had stumach ache and I was sick and I was not able to go out to play so I just sat in bed all day I was very boring and every time I had some thing to eat I was sick at night time I went down stairs to watch the television and have my tea after tea I was not sick so I felt a bit better while I was having a drink my farther walked in the door and gave me a presant it was an airfix modle of an airoplane I was very happy so I thanked my farther and started to make my modle when I had made it, it was time for bed so I went upstairs put my pygarmers on and climbed in to in the morning I felt a lot better so I went out to play with my airoplane with my friende.

The mother of a 10+ girl intervened on her behalf against a neighbour who was determined to keep children off grass which in any case did not belong to him.

When I had just moved into our new house, My sister and I went outside to go around and advestigate. When we was walking round theses blocks of houses we saw this man coming out of his front door with a walking stick in his hand, In front of this man we saw this little girl running away. She looked about four years old. By the side of their house there was a streath of grass which didnt, belong to him, He alway kept on being bossy, and telling us to get of the grass which was ment for the children to play on. One day my sister and I went to play on the grass, and this man came out and told us to get off because he said it will be all spoillet, so we got off and went in doors to have our dinner. When we had had our dinner, my brother, my sister and I played on the grass. The man that kept telling us off was watering his garden. When he had finished watering his garden he said to us, get off the grass because I want to water it, but that was just said to us because he wanted us to keep off of the grass. So my sister and I just got off the edge of the grass and my brother stayed on there. The man turnt on his hose pipe and started putting water all over our brother, so we went and told our mum, and she came out and started to tell the man off. In the end the man gave up and went in. When he had gone in we all started to laugh and we played on the grass again.

Another mother, of an 8+ London girl, attempted to improve the girl's school performance by the offer of a prize, duly won.

Here is a story of how I got my bike. When last year when we first got our reports my mum was not quite pleased because eight children had beaten my in class work also in the test. so my mum bought a comperttition between my and my brother. The comperttition was to see whether we could come first second or third. And could you belive it I came third, anyway because of that my mum bought me a bike: its name is a Tomahalk.

The parents of a boy from West Bromwich finally, after (one infers) considerable pressure, took him on a much desired outing.

When I went on holiday up New Castle on Tyne I wanted to go to hadrians wall and walk along it but my mum and dad said it was too far. Near the end of our holiday. We didn't know where to go. So we set of and after about an hours drive we come to hadrians. This pleased me very much. I didn't know how to say thank you. We started to walk along till we come to one of the ruined forts here I found 50p. I got some stone from the wall and I bought a booklit with the 50p and some pictures of the wall and a booklit about all the armour a weapons. Then we went on from there to a roman fort. It had signs telling you what the rooms was. It had the kitchen, larder, Leader head quarters, and the soldiers sleeping quaters among with other rooms.

Siblings, although more frequently a source of displeasure, could also by flashes of consideration cause happiness, as a girl in her first year at a Cardiff comprehensive reported.

I have been made very happy, when I was Ill with chest infection my little brouther came up to me and said I like you and gave me an apple. My little brother was only 1½ years old at the time. I then almost cried and give him a hug and kiss.

Table 18   Frequency of others: happy situations

Other group	Others		No.	% of others
Parents	Mother		479	14·9
	Father		426	13·3
	Mother and father		334	10·4
	Parent		5	0·2
		TOTALS	**1244**	**38·8**
Siblings	Sibling(s) same sex		90	2·8
	Sibling(s) other sex		37	1·1
	Siblings, both sexes		2	0·06
		TOTALS	**129**	**4·0**
Relations	Relation(s)		266	8·3
	Special close relation(s)		14	0·4
	Family group		191	5·9
		TOTALS	**471**	**14·7**
Adults not close family members	Teacher(s)		179	5·6
	Unknown, unspecified adult(s)		40	1·2
	Adult(s) in authority		131	4·1
	Friend(s), neighbour(s)		66	2·1
		TOTALS	**416**	**13·0**
Children not close family members	Known child(ren) or cousin(s)		81	2·5
	Friend(s)		295	9·2
	Unkown, unspecified child(ren)		14	0·4
		TOTALS	**390**	**12·2**
Supernatural, fictitious & well known figures	Fictitious figure		16	0·5
	Public figure		38	1·2
	Religious figure, God		5	0·2
	Spirits, ghosts		1	0·03
		TOTALS	**60**	**1·9**
Creatures, objects & environment	Object(s)		137	4·3
	Living creature(s)		103	3·2
	Something		0	0·0

	Environment	51	1·6
	TOTALS	291	9·1
Miscellaneous	Somebody (s & pl)	80	2·5
	Myself (no-one)	53	1·6
	Activity group	74	2·3
	TOTALS	207	6·4
	OVERALL TOTALS	3208	100·1

Percentages have been rounded.

Relations, and particularly grandparents, could show great insight into the minds of children.

My Grandma came down to stay, and she slept in my bedroom while I slept up in the sitting room on the soffa, it was very uncoftable and I didn't get much sleep. However in the morning I felt tied and a bit cross. I slept on the soffa for a hole week, and on Saterday when Grandma when back home, just before she got on the train she gave me a five pound note for sleeping on the soffa and not being to cross. I was so glad that I couldn't say anything, just then the guard blew his whistle and Grandma went. Afterwards I felt that I could sleep on the soffa for years for nothing at all. My sister got five pounds as well but it wasn't for the reason I got it.

Of *others* outside the family teachers were mentioned most frequently. Children showed the ability of experienced and perceptive consumers to discriminate good professional work, and to acknowledge a caring and human approach. A boy in his third year at a middle school recalled a good teacher from his time in the primary (first) school.

When i was in the primery schoole. One of my techers called mis Davise was very nice. When i yosed to get fed up she wouled let me do craft or needel work or weving and when i could not do a paragraph of maths she would let me turn over and go onto the next page or she would let me do english i yoused to like english and she yoused to think i could do better if i sat on my own single desk i did do better as well.

Another 11+ boy, also from a middle school, likewise commended a teacher for his work.

I felt very pleased and happy when we had Mr. Bird as a teacher in 2w.

He was a very good teacher and our class frequently had 'discussions'. We chose any thing to talk about. e.g. Someone had been naughty and we had to 'discuss' how to punish him. In the end he got the usual: an essay. Because he was an art teacher we did a lot of art. He preferred us to do unusual shapes, rather than proper objects, which I like better as well.

Everyone thought he was an excellent teacher.

A 9+ girl was simply grateful and relieved that she did not have to confront the terror of a man teacher.

I was happy when I left my other school and came up to this school. It was a bit frighting at first but know it is all right. I am glad we have a lady teacher. I worked as hard as I could as a result. I am pleased that I did not have a man teacher.

An 8+ girl from a London school was very pleased when her teacher agreed to walk home with her.

One sunny day when it was home time I asked my teacher if she would go down my way she said yes and I was so pleased.

Numbers of children wrote about *adults in authority,* other than teachers. A 9+ girl was reassured during a visit to a hospital by a nurse.

The Last time I was Happy was when I went to hospital to have a heart test at first I was frightened but then a nurse had to come around with me. She was very nice and very funny and made my Happy when I went in for my test I wasent scared any more because the nurse Had made me Happy.

Other children showed similar gratitude to doctors, youth club organizers, etc.

The pleasures of friendship were enjoyed by children in many forms. A young junior school child from Workington felt happy because his friend pretended to be a clown and made him laugh.

my friends name is Simon and he made me very happy by being funnuy because he was trying to be a clown he always slipped over when he got up he went down again.

A girl in her last year at a middle school recalled the time when she met her pen friend.

I felt very happy when I first met Christa my pen pal. she was telling me all about kenya and India and other places around the world. And other things about her bording school in Torkey. At the end of our talk I asked some qustions about the places she had been to and her school life.

Other experiences between friends, such as the lending of toys, inviting on outings, although less exotic, caused similar satisfaction.

Figures outside the everyday experience of children, whether mythical (like Father Christmas) or real (like the Prime Minister) or transcendent (like God) seldom featured as agents of children's happiness. Occasionally there might be a treasured encounter with a being from another world, as when a boy had his autograph book signed by a famous footballer.

I felt.most happy when somebody else did something when Ted Mac Dougall, my favourite footballer signed my autograph book and my football. As a result I have supported both him and the teams he has played for ever since.

Or the knowledge of results of public sporting events might provoke elation: I was happy when Arsenal the football team I support won Man. city on Satuardy they won 2 - 1. I jumed in the air and was so happy. ·

On occasion personalities seen on television were mentioned.

Less infrequently reported than situations in which contact was established with unfamiliar persons were circumstances in which children enjoyed relationships with non-human entites, whether animate or inanimate. *Objects,* such as bikes or dolls could give happiness, and so could animals whether they were pets, well known and loved; or more exotic beasts. An 8+ girl reported on an encounter with a gorilla.

At Britol zoo two years ago in the summer There was a gorilla there, me and my family went to see him. When we got there he was jumping up and down (by the way we had ice-creams) and he saw our ice-creams and spat on my ice-cream. I said to my Mother, Mum the Gorilla spat on my ice-cream (she thought I said I don't want it) and she eat it (egh) I taped her on her shoulder she said yes and I said Mum the gorilla spat on that ice-cream. She said why din't you tell, i said I did.

Another 8+ girl, on a walk in the forest of Dene was made happy by the environment, the sunshine in the trees.

Last Sunday I went up my Nans to see her. My nana lives in monmouth she lives with my Antei carole. every summer we went camping up monmouth in the forest of Dene. When were up the forest of Dene my uncle Daivid and my cousin garthe came too up the forest on a sunday morning the sun was shining. After we had our breafast my mum and Dad went shopping why me and my uncle and my garthe and my sister helen went into the forest it was nice the trees glittered down the path. When we got back to the camp I told my mum and I picked some flowers.

Some children wrote about an internal relationship, not involving others, which made them happy. An 8+ London girl put it very explicitly.

When I was going to Greece on a boat. We mist our boat so we had to get another one. And as we were going we saw the ship that we should have been on and it was burnt. I made myself happy because we mist the boat that got burned.

12 Unhappy situations—others

Parents, as might be expected, were considerably less often a source of unhappiness than of happiness to children. In those situations which children did give where parents were involved the circumstances extended from parental insistence, if necessary backed by sanctions, upon the observation of rules to the exhibition by parents of vicious and perhaps emotionally damaging attitudes. Typically, however, children reported as causing unhappiness uncaring or unfeeling behaviour, rather than just, but stern behaviour. There were of course some children, like a 10+ girl, who were cross at being punished apparently reasonably, or at not being allowed to get their own way.

Someone made me angry when I asked for a animal pet and I couldn't have one, I was very angry.
    As a result I kept asking for one but mum said: sharply 'NO', I was unhappy and very angry.

There were other cases in which children were similarly frustrated, but in which parents perhaps were felt by the child to be displaying some vindictiveness; a 10+ middle school girl wrote about such a situation:

I was very angry with my mum, because everything I asked for, for Christmas she said I couldn't have it. First I wanted a riding jacket, but she said I'd grow out of it. Then I asked if I could have some riding boots, but she said the same thing as the jacket. After that I asked for an action girl, but dad said it was the same with all my dolls, I get them and then just throw them in my cupboard.

Collectively, parents sometimes created circumstances in which children felt worried. For example, parents who left children alone at night and returned late and could cause distress. A 10+ girl wrote,

Once when it was about 9 a clock in the night our mum and dad said they will go to the pub for a drink, so they said they wouldnt be long. when they had

Table 19   Frequency of others: unhappy situations

Other group	Others		No.	% of others
Parents	Mother		203	6·5
	Father		181	5·8
	Mother and father		51	1·6
	Parent		4	0·1
		TOTALS	**439**	**14·0**
Siblings	Sibling(s) same sex		312	9·9
	Sibling(s) other sex		205	6·5
	Siblings, both sexes		2	0·06
		TOTALS	**519**	**16·5**
Relations	Relation(s)		112	3·6
	Special close relation(s)		8	0·2
	Family group		66	2·1
		TOTALS	**186**	**5·9**
Adults not close family members	Teacher(s)		82	2·6
	Unknown, unspecified adult(s)		124	3·9
	Adult(s) in authority		103	3·3
	Friend(s), neighbour(s)		26	0·8
		TOTALS	**335**	**10·7**
Children not close family members	Known child(ren) or cousin(s)		305	9·7
	Friend(s)		367	11·7
	Unknown, unspecified child(ren)		150	4·8
		TOTALS	**822**	**26·2**
Supernatural, fictitious & well known figures	Fictitious figure		41	1·3
	Public figure		17	0·5
	Religious figure, God		0	0·0
	Spirits, ghosts		28	0·9
		TOTALS	**86**	**2·7**
Creatures, objects & environment	Object(s)		116	3·7
	Living creature(s)		211	6·7
	Something		81	2·6

			109	3·5
		TOTALS	517	**16·5**
Miscellaneous	Somebody (s & pl)		117	3·7
	Myself (no-one)		72	2·3
	Activity group		46	1·5
	Unclassified		2	0·06
		TOTALS	237	**7·5**
	OVERALL TOTALS		3141	100·0

Environment appears in the first row.

Percentages have been rounded.

gone valerie and I went to bed. My brother went to bed at 10 o clock. Before my brother went to bed he locked the door, then he went to bed. When all of us was in bed we heard this noise banging on the bedroom window then some-one banging on the door, we was to scared to go down and open the door, so our brother went down and opened the door, it was only our mum and dad trying to get in when the door was locked.

Mothers caused unhappiness by interfering with matters which children regarded as personal to themselves. A 10+ girl complained because her mother cut her hair short.

My Mum made me unhappy when she cut my hair when it was very long and she cut it in to a pag boy, and I was very unhappy.

A 10+ boy resented a toy being thrown away.

The time when some one made me argry, was when mum pot my Aerxe plane in the bustbine.

Children also reacted, not unnaturally, by feeling distressed when their mothers undermined their confidence. An 8+ boy was not helped to face an apparently dangerous situation on holiday.

Once when I was on holiday at Haverfordwest we got tapped by the sea and my mum made me feel scared because she said that the cliffs round this part of Pembroke were very crumbley and I was suddenly very scared.

A 10+ girl found the task of settling into a new school made considerably more difficult by her mother's prophecy.

When we moved over to Eldene my Mum said that she did not think that I would have nice frieds and that made me unhappy I was frightened to come to Shcool the first day I was unhappy I had no one to play with.

The failure of a mother to love a child could be clearly perceived, and profoundly felt. A 12+ girl at a comprehensive in Workington described her own relationship with her mother.

I will always remember when my mam told me she liked my brother better than me. I knew she did because I always get the blame for everything.
I asked my mam if she would be sad if I got run over and she relieped 'I don't knaw.'
I really like my mam but she is always petting my little brother up. She never seems to find time for me. If I ask her advice she never seems to give it to me. I always think these thaughts when I get told off. Then I just forget them.
But the feeling of not being wanted always makes me unhappy.

At a less profound level children could be distressed by quarrelsome or noisy adult behaviour. This was clearly illustrated in the answer of an 8+ girl, who, rather than suffer the argument caused by her mother sticking up for her rights, slipped away from the scene with her friend — the cause of all the trouble in the first place.

My frend hit my hid sow I went to tel my mummy and my mummy went to sey my frend's mummy and that had a fit and my and me frend wend awt sud [outside] Becas we did not like the noys and the sgwobling so we went owt siyd.

More simply an 11+ boy from a Chester middle school objected to his parents' 'banging'.

If theres one thing I hate thats continual banging and loud noises. Sometimes say when farther or mother bangs the it (might) make me angry, frustate, some people at some time of the day when nothing goes right, this sometimes happens to me.

Fathers on occasion distressed children through simple thoughtlessness. A A girl from a Nottingham comprehensive described how she lost her father at a fair.

The day I was frightend was when I got lost at the goose fair. Itwas about severn oclock and my father and I were at the fair. We went on many things such as the paratrooper, the clown of laughter and the clyclone. Then as I went on the horses, my father told me he was going on the machines. Well when the horses stopped I went to the machines. But my father was not there. Then I went up to the cyclone and he was'nt there. I looked all over for my father But I couldnt find him. In the end I found him eating hot dogs at the hot dog stall. This was a frightening night for me and I have never forgot it.

Fathers could show aggression, progressing from teasing almost to savagery at times, particularly with daughters. A girl in her first year at a Swindon comprehensive recalled what her father had once told her about footballs.

When I was small my dad toled me that when you play football they cut your head off take the eyes out and cover it with plastic and kick it around. I was frightened because I thought it was true. I thought somebody would come and take my head off and kick it around. So when I was out with my friend I said some one will come and take your head off and kick it around. She said pardan and I said someone will come and take your head off take the eyes out and cover it with plastic and play football with it. She said it is not true they blow something up and kick it. Or if it went on a pice of glass it would not burst and the stuff you blow up can burst.

Another girl, 10+, described how her father had threatened her.

There was a time when I was unhappy it was when my farther shouted at me and he threatened to burn my brownie suit and I started crying and my mother told me not to cry and then he told me to go to bed.

Unhappy situations initiated by siblings included many in which children felt, rightly or not, that they had been provoked. A 9+ girl from London wrote about circumstances caused by her brother.

The times when I am angry my brother is mostly at fault, he picks up our little kittens while they are having milk from their mother, they start to sgeal and it make me feel sick so as a result I hit him and my mother tells me off.

Siblings could also be the reason for unhappiness through no fault of their own, by for example being taken ill. One child's distress when a sister was taken ill was due, not by any concern for the sister, but by annoyance at the likelihood of missing a treat.

A time when someone made me unhappy was when my sister was ill. We were going to go out to dinner and after go the Aristocats. And because she was ill we could not go. As a result my mothers cousin took me to town and bought me a poster. On the poster there was a dog and a cat. When I got home I put it on my bedroom wall.

An 11+ girl whose sister likewise was taken ill, although much more seriously, while probably worried about her sister, was deeply fearful for herself.

A few years ago my sister noticed she had a curved spine. She told my mum. They booked an apointment with the doctor. He sent the to the hospital. She had many checkaups and exrays. Then he sent her to a sighciatress and he told my mother father and sister she would have to go to hospital for three months and have a operation on her back or go in a plastic jacket for the same amount of time.
    Months went by and then she went in hospital in Oxfordshire. Every day my dad mum and I went up to see her. After two weeks she had to be put into a plaster jacket to keep her straight. A week later she had her operation. After I once again went to see her. It was horrid. She had tubes in her arms. Pumping blood into her. When she got well again we were all told she would have to stay in hospital in a plaster jacket for six months. That made us all very unhappy. I saw many horrible cases in the Ward. I got very frightened about my back incase I had a bad back but no. THANK- Goodness.

Adult relations demonstrated that they could evoke distress in children in much the same way as parents. A 12+ girl was frightened by her grandfather telling ghost stories.

Well one Saturday my gramps and nan came over and he was telling me about Some ghosts he said he had seen and when it came to be time to go to bed i was terrified so thats when i was frightened.

A 9+ girl was distressed by a grandmother's selfishness.

Once granny was eating an ice-cream, I felt so unhappy as she ate eat. Anyway she said she was sorry that I could have not one. Then I just went out of the room.

Of *adults not close family members* teachers, although the type of adult most often encountered by children, were relatively infrequently mentioned. Where teachers did provoke distress it was typically through thoughtlessness, unfeeling or aggressive behaviour. A 9+ girl was told by her teacher of a murder.

A few monthes ago we were having a lesson whith Mr . . . and he toled us about 15 years ago in coady peggy chiles there was a Murder by a Man the murder happned like this where we live now there was a woods and there were black-brries growing a lady was picking black berries and a man came and got a rope and killed her.

An 11+ middle school girl was upset when a teacher changed his plans, possibly inadvertently, for an Assembly reading.

One day our class were going to do something about our parents. Some of us were going to read in Assembley but Mr . . . choose Someone else to Read My part I felt so unhappy that I began to cry. On the day Mr . . . gave me something to read then I felt frighted to Read but I did it.

Shouting and hitting were much resented. Two children from the same school reported on different teachers.

The only time when I feel frightenes is when Mr . . . shots at us and when he shots some times he looks like a Tiger and he is very unkind to some of us in our class But that is worse than any thing else and I wish that he was not in the school.

When miss . . . put me out of the Door and made me write lines and she Banged my head on the ground.

Unknown or unspecified adults occurred more frequently than other types of adult in the category of *adults not close family members,* (probably much more frequently as the majority of those described as 'somebody' were in all likelihood unknown or unspecified adults). Unknown or unspecified adults caused distress through cruelty to animals, particularly where it appeared accompanied by more generalized uncaring or immoral behaviour. A 9+ boy was saddened by seeing birds being shot for sport.

It was when we went out to the moors in Plymouth and we saw some people shooting birds and when they had killed it a dog would go and fetch it in his mouth and it felt very unhappy to me to think that happens.

A 12+ girl in a middle school had her dog run over by a woman who left it, and refused to acknowledge responsibility.

The time when I was made to feel unhappy was when my dog was run over by a car and the lady who ran her over just drove on and left pip to die in the road.

When I went to see her she denied she even went near our house when my brother had seen the whole thing happening.

Strange men were feared by girls, not always perhaps with much justification.

I had gone to stay with my Granny and she didnt feel well so I went to some shops down the road for her while I was walking I saw an old man staring at me and I began to feel frightend so I began to walk fast he was still looking at me so I began to run, then he said 'Its all right dear I won't hurt you'.

Adults who stereotyped children as bad, and refused to listen when there were difficulties apparently (but not necessarily) caused by children, were often considerably resented. A 12+ boy from a Workington comprehensive, was completely alienated by a woman who blamed him for the non-delivery of a newspaper.

The last time somebody made me unhappy was on my star round, it was the last house on my round and the star office had sent me one star short, well I didnt know this and by the time I had got to the last house there were no stars left. I had to miss them out so I went to buy a star from the garage meaning to charge the star office for it when I took the money down. There were no stars left in the garage so I went home. The next night I delivered that house's star and they played war with me and wouldn't believe that I tried to get them one. They said they would cancell it if it happened again. I said I wasnt bothered. That Old bag makes me sick.

Adults in authority caused unhappiness because, on occasion, like some teachers, they shouted and bullied. A 10+ boy from a Dorset middle school took a strong dislike to his Cub mistress.

When I joined the Cubs I was very unhappy and angry because of the noise when she shouts she gets on my nerves she also is very fat and tuby she has got a very big mouth. Even her to sons and he husband are fed up with her.

Medical figures could be the source of distress, through inept handling of children, or simply because what they had to do or say to children in the course of duty was unwelcome. A 9+ girl wrote that a doctor made her unhappy, because he it was who had to put her broken arm in plaster, so preventing her from doing P.E.

One day when I was doing p.e. I fell and hurt my arm. The teacher who was taking me for p.e. rang my mother to tell her that I had heart my arm.

I was fealing frighterned because I did not want my arm to be broken because I was getting on well in p.e.

A little later mummy came to take me to the hospital to see if I had broken my arm or if I had not broken my arm.

I'M a fraid to say I had broken my arm so I had to have it in plaster and I was unhappy becase I could not do p.e. so the doctor made me unhappy.

Friends and neighbours figured relatively infrequently; at times they were resented for harsh behaviour, but more typically they misjudged children's reactions to behaviour which was basically intended to be good natured. A boy, staying the night with a friend, found himself confronted by a curious monster.

I was down at my friends to sleep for a night we gone upstairs I nor my friend knew what was going on downstairs we came back down. My friend was first to open the door but to my surprise he shut it again very quickly. Then he said to me in a harsh voice dont go in yet. Then the door opened slowly what I saw was a large figure dressed in a brown coat with a mask on. inside it was his dad and sister. His sister was on his back so it looked like a hunch back.

Children not close family members were mentioned more frequently than individuals in any other category. Typically the reason was provocation, as for example reported by an 8+ child from a London school.

Some one pushed me over. when I went to get my coat. it was a boy a big boy he did not say sorry to me. he just laughed at me. And he made me unhappy.

Sometimes, although the immediate source of trouble was another child, there were in fact underlying circumstances, reported by the child which were likely to lead to difficulties. One girl was teased by another because the teacher had given her a severe reprimand.

1 group o 5 is 5 2 groups of 5 is 18. 'Jane what on earth are you saying dont you know your tables yet.' was what Miss . . . said. She was very angry with me. Out in the playground Jenny and I were talking. Miss . . . really 'Blew her top' with you dident she said Jenny. I heard a voice behind me. It was Liza 'Who dosent know there tabels then' she said. Oh no all I need now is that smirky smug twit. I thought. Get los Liza I shouted. She punched me and I said 'do that again and youll know it.' She did do it again. So I hit her 'hard' soon we were having a real 'rough and tumble'. Then the teacher came up and stopped us. On the way home Liza triyd to Beat me up but I beat her up. She never tryd to touch me again.

Another girl, 12+, from a Nottingham comprehensive, got involved in an argument at school, having learned in the lunch interval that her grandfather had died.

This was a time when a friend, well she was a friend then, made me angrey and unhappy.
 I was playing french skipping with some other friends. I had just come home from dinner. When I was at home my dad broke the news to me that my grandad had died. I felt alful, and I had to go to school.
 At school I felt very depressed. I took my elastic I didn't tell any one. I chose to be first I put this girl in the end. She went made, but we made her go in. The other girl in the end didn't mind. I started with side, side. I got right up to gives then when I had finished, this girl said I was out. All the others said I wasn't so I didn't take an end. After a while I began to cry becouse she made me go in the end. She called me baby. Then I told them. She was all, 'Oh I am so sorry' But she wasn't I know. Then she went and told the dinner lady. And for that I will neaver forgive her. I hate her.

Some children reported circumstances which it appeared possible they had themselves provoked in the first place.

What makes me angry is when other children ask me to play whith them when I have got sweets and when I have'nt they walk pass me. If I refuse to give them any they call me names or hit me.
As a result I wont give anything to any body unless I offer them.

 Of *supernatural, fictitious and well known figures* the most frequently reported by children were the fictitious. Typically these were beings seen on television, such as Dracula or a horrible undersea monster viewed by an 8+ girl.

One day when I was watcking telly I saw a horribol monster it had scalle and big eye and long legs it was uder the sea it was the most horriboles thing I had every seen under wate I was very scared after I saw the film I went to bed and I dreamped about it. I tried to get it out of my mind but I coulded I couldnt slep becus of it I trid to I dreamed that the monster was holding my and trieing to eat me I was treble frigted I neary drowed becuase he wouldnt let me go I scearemed and I sceamed I saw all kinds of sea creathes there were lots of them surouding me then I noticed it had 10 or 8 legs I thort it was a Octipus they were dancing along in the sea it was very ugly had a large round head and great big eyes then a sea mun came to save me and the monter was afraid of the sea man he recused [rescued] me he was very kind he took me to his house in the sea and gave me food and gave me fish to eat and gave me a nice warm bed to slep in then that was mornig and I woke up.

In the category of *creatures, objects and the environment* numbers of children reported that they were saddened by the illness or death of pets; others were scared by animals, like an 11+ girl from a Nottingham comprehensive.

When I went upstairs I saw a cat so I ran downstairs and shut the door. That made me feel very frightned because I hate cats.
Well has a result my daddy chased him and then put him out the door and then shut it.

The environment, for imaginative children, could at times take on an active and malevolent aspect, as an 8+ boy at a Cardiff junior school discovered.

Onc I went in the cichin and the cetul was on and it went off I was frightened and scked and it went on a gane the lite off. and on my nese was shackine the wind was blowinge it was a windy nite it was terubul and I did not like it it was ckreapy ther was a spideru it was big and rownd and fat this wos tow much for me I jumt owt of my shows I was scked I sed to my self I not a frade I sed I was terufid I wos so scked that I nely jumt owt of my sckin I didnt licke it and I thort tha I sor a gost.

13   Problem situations—others

Parents figured relatively infrequently as the cause of problems written about by children. When they did it could be through failure to provide expected support for a child, or through an obliviousness to the effect of their actions upon a child. There was little evidence of parents intentionally structuring problems for children.

A 9+ girl found that her mother, who should have collected her from school, failed to appear.

The time when I was with someone else and I wasnt sure what to do was when I was my friend and my mother said that she would wait for us by the school and take us into town but my mother forgot to come up the school so my friend and myself waited for about 10 minutes and then we ran home to my house, and as we were ringing the front door bell my mother said that she had forgotten to come up to the school; my mother was minding my friends money and my money because we were going into town to get our Brownie outfits.

The father of a 9+ boy from Dorset took him fishing, but refused to allow him to do anything.

I went fishing with my dad and when we had takled up my dad went and carst. My dad just wold not let me fish. So I got some bread and magets to the minows.

Another 9+ boy, from a Cardiff junior school also had a fishing problem. His mother told him to go fishing, but he was worried about the main road.

one day my mouther said go fishing up the lake I was not shur to go becuse of the main roads. But I went with my friend.

Relations (9·2%) and *adults not close family members* (10·5%) were both

132

mentioned by children more frequently than *parents* (7·1%). Adults, other than parents, often featured in answers concerned with etiquette *what do I do?* themes (see Chapter 9, p. 94). Relations, and parents of friends, could also cause difficulties either by assuming that rules accepted in their houses and families were also practised in the houses of visiting children — when in fact this might not be so, or by assuming that visiting children would know about their particular rules, procedures or domestic arrangements when they might well not.

A 10+ girl from a Newcastle middle school found herself in a quandary when, on a visit to a friend, the friend's mother told the two girls that they could go down into the town; the trouble was that the visiting girl was not allowed into the town without a grown-up.

One day my freind Nicol rang me up and said would you like to come to my house in Westerhope. I whent and said my mam said I could. Nicols mam said if you want after dinner you can go to the town at the time I was just 9 and she was 11 and my mam had never let me go to town I said I didnot know weather to our not I said yes but I was very woried because my mam works in Marks & Speansers so if she came out I would have got rong so when we got home I was glad I did not tell my mam that I had been to the town whith Nicol.

Another 10+ girl, from Nottingham, did not know whether to accept a last minute invitation to lunch from a friend's mother. The mother appeared to assume that there would be no problem for the girl; but the girl did not know what her own mother's attitude would be, and appeared to baulk at having to ask for permission to telephone.

One day I was at Harrys house, we were lying on the grass behind the house reading comics. It was about 10 to 1 now and I was getting ready to go when Harrys mum asked me if I would like to stay to dinner. I wasn't really sure what to say, if I said yes I would have to ring mum up and tell her that I would not be coming home for dinner. I made up my mind and said no thankyou to Harrys mum may be another time. When I got back home I asked mum what she would have said if I stayed at Harrys for dinner. Mum said that she would not have minded at all. Now I think I should have said yes to Harrys Mum.

An aunt caused a difficulty for a visiting niece, simply by forgetting that the girl might not know where things were kept in the house.

Table 20   Frequency of others: problem situations

Other group	Others		No.	% of others
Parents	Mother		102	3·7
	Father		63	2·3
	Mother and father		30	1·1
	Parent		0	0·0
		TOTALS	**195**	**7·1**
Siblings	Sibling(s) same sex		77	2·8
	Sibling(s) other sex		49	1·8
	Siblings, both sexes		2	0·07
		TOTALS	**128**	**4·6**
Relations	Relation(s)		128	4·6
	Special close relation(s)		7	0·2
	Family group		119	4·3
		TOTALS	**254**	**9·2**
Adults not close family members	Teacher(s)		84	3·0
	Unknown, unspecified adult(s)		90	3·3
	Adult(s) in authority		51	1·8
	Friend(s), neighbour(s)		63	2·3
		TOTALS	**288**	**10·5**
Children not close family members	Known child(ren) or cousin(s)		205	7·4
	Friend(s)		1067	38·6
	Unknown, unspecified child(ren)		76	2·7
		TOTALS	**1348**	**48·8**
Supernatural fictitious & well known figures	Fictitious figure		1	0·04
	Public figure		2	0·07
	Religious figure, God		0	0·0
	Spirits, ghosts		1	0·04
		TOTALS	**4**	**0·1**
Creatures, objects & environment	Object(s)		63	2·3
	Living creature(s)		44	1·6
	Something		2	0·07

	Environment		71	2·6
		TOTALS	180	6·5
Miscellaneous	Somebody (s & pl)		87	3·1
	Myself (no-one)		100	3·6
	Activity group		179	6·5
		TOTALS	366	13·2
		OVERALL TOTALS	2763	100·0

Percentages have been rounded.

One day I went to my uncles house. I stayed there Saturday and Sunday. My aunty was washing some dishes. My aunty gave me some rice she didnt say anything to me she just gave the boul of rice to me. I didnt know anything what to do with that boul of rice. I asked my aunty what to do my aunty said throw that rice away.

Teachers were inevitably involved with problems of school work, particularly where the themes *what do I do?* and *how do I do it?* occurred. Teachers' expertise in maintaining discipline could cause nice problems for children, as a boy from Swindon in his first year at a comprehensive recalled.

It was at my junior school and we were having a lesson. This boy seating next to me had some sweats. I asked him for one. He gave me one but the teacher (saw) him but he did not say anything. Then I was not sure to eat it in case he was wating me. Then finally when he turned away I put it in my mouth. But just as I bit it he saw me and I got in trouble.

Teachers, like other adults, also made difficulties for children by failure to display insight. An 8+ girl from London was asked to help by her teacher, and did so, only to be late home and find her mother very worried.

Once I was at school and miss sed will you help me to put they's up on the wall and I was not sure so I had to think then I sed yes I helped miss then when I come home it was about 5 o'clock my mum was looking every were and then I was coming down the mues and my dad saw me and when got home my mum told me off.

Adults in authority could pose similar problems. For children who lived in, or near the countryside, or who spent holidays there, farmers could be a particular threat (the feelings were often reciprocated). A boy in his first year at a comprehensive played on the property of a farmer, without permission. The boy showed an awareness of the legal situation, but like others before him, displayed a willingness to disregard it (possibly feeling that children have a natural right to play in woods and enjoy the countryside). The farmer in question, having spied the boy and his friends, showed no hestitation in exerting his legal rights.

One day I was in the wood near our house with my two cousin's, Dick and Tub and my sister, Vicki climbing trees. We were really tresspassing because the land belongs to the farmer.
After a while we went home through the farmers field, but the farmer was there and he sent his dogs after us we had to decide weather to run or stay we stayed and got told off and sent home by the farmer.

Another farmer appeared to go beyond action he was entitled to take in defending his property. Adults determined, by whatever means, to defend their interests against the encroachments of children could pose considerable difficulties.

The time when I did not know what to do is when me and my friend had our bikes stolen by a farmer who thought that we had been trespasing on his land we saw him put the bikes into his car and we went up to him and shouted at them and he pushed my friend in the nettles and drove off we did not know what to do so in the end we ran $2\frac{1}{2}$ milles home crying In the end we did get our bikes back again but I would not like it to happen again!

On the fringes of a child's world, peopled with familiar, if not always well loved adults, there lurked *unknown figures* who, as well as being threatening could also be sinister. Apart from the strangers who frightened girls in early adolescence, other children also could be at risk. At times danger to a child seemed obvious, at others more difficult to gauge. What, for example, were the intentions of the woman who told a London girl to address her as 'mummy'? And should the girl tell her mother, though warned by the stranger not to do so?

I was with a lady And she told me to call her mumy And I did not know what to do And then I called her mumy after And on our way Back home she told me not TO TELL my mum so I did not tell.

Children's problems were more frequently caused by, (or faced in the company of), other children whether siblings or others, than by adults. Often answers showed that the sources of such difficulties were lack of occupation, and the need to find something to do. Some problems were caused either by direct pressure on children by peers, or by children's ideas of what peers would expect; further problems could arise from conflicts between the requirements of the peer group, and either a child's own individual desires or the behaviour expected by adults. Clashes between adult and peer standards appeared to be particularly acute with some of the older children.

A 12+ girl from a Workington comprehensive felt that her friend expected her to join them on a particular contraption at the fair; the girl however decided to stay on the ground.

It was fair day me and some friend went to the fair. It was a very miserable day I only had a small jacket on.

When we arrived it was pouring with rain, very, dark, and cold. We were a bit disapointed because there was only three things to go on the bomers, walsers and optopus.

First we all had a ride on the walsers. I enjoyed it very much. Then we wandered round.

If Gillian hadn't went to the fair I woudn't of either because I knew it was a complete waste of money, and besides I was saving up for Xmas presents.

Anyway Julie, Gillian and Val decided to go on the bomers that went up in the sky at top speed. I said 'I didn't want to go on them. But I knew that Julie, Gill, and Val would say they were great and make me feel as if I was missing out on something.

They all queured up while I watched I was thinking if I should join them or not. I was wet and miserable. I longed to be at home. 'No' I wouldn't go on the bombers why should I waste my money.

When they came off I asked them if they had enjoyed them, they all looked a bit pale and vowed never to go on again.

Another child from a Workington comprehensive, a boy just aged 13, found he had to face a direct conflict between what his friends and what his father expected of him. He calculated that it would pay him in the long run to obey his father, so he did.

It was up at the Scout Hut on the New Years Eve party. I was playing cards for money with some other boys and girls, I was winning about 20p and then went and got something to eat and drink, after that I played darts and sat around for a bit. Then I started playing cards again I was still winning at 9.45 and my dad said I had to be in for 10.00 my mates tried to persuade me to stay and play for a bit longer. I was undecided but then I made my mind up.

I went home because if I was in late he might not have let me out to partys again and it was better to be aloud out than to haved about 15 minutes more time playing cards and not aloud out to something like that again.

A boy from a Cardiff comprehensive, in his first year, had a similar but more difficult problem to face. Although he too followed adult rather than peer expectations, he nevertheless found himself in trouble. An adult tendency to find young adolescents guilty until proved innocent was a feature of a number of situations described by children.

I was with freinds and we were not sure well at least i was not sure weather we could go down to the little town because we were with a party of children i went and asked and when i came back with the answer which was NO! but they were gone i followed a little road to try and find them to tell them to come back i found them we went back and we were told off and i releiced i should not have followed.

There were occasions when some children found themselves tempted into trouble by others. At such times there might be a direct reference, mental or actual, to adult standards or adults, for help in keeping to the paths of virtue. Or, a child might apparently rely primarily on his or her own sense (whether learned or innate) of correct behaviour in the circumstances. And sometimes children surrendered to temptation.

A 10+ boy in a London junior school encountered a particularly boastful delinquent. He decided to play safe, and avoid the proposed entertainment of Indian baiting.

When I was at the park and I was with a boy that I just met and he told me he likes getting into trouble all the time because he said that he was driving a car round Kensal Rise and the coppers came after him and he crashed. He said shall we start calling the indians over there names but just saw my friend and I went to play with him.

Non-human *others* caused a number of problems. One child, a 9+ boy, had an encounter with a rabbit.

One day I was walking in the woods and I saw a little rabbit and it (crept) up behind me so I had to keep still and I tried to think of something to play when I thought to play catching eachother but when I turned round it had gone.

An 8+ girl from a Newcastle middle school was faced with a difficulty, due to the need of plants for water.

A Holiday was to come in a day and I am in charge ov all the plants some were going to frends housess but some were left, I go home for dinner so I asket my grandmorr and so I did wate she did I put them I the sink and when I got back from the holiday the sink was dry I did not no wate to do so I watered them and they were alright.

   Numbers of children caused their own difficulties (or at least ascribed them to nobody or nothing else). A 9+ boy tripped, and fell into the sea; from first to last he was on his own, and did not blame anyone or anything for his predicament.

One summer day on my holloday I was ran along the harboor and I triged [tripped] ofer the sied of a jetty and I shouted but nowbody herd me I swam a shore and rane to the hotell and I did not now what to do.

Part V
Reactions

Table 21   Classification of reactions

Non-active
Adult referent
Peer referent
Aggressive
Avoidance
Positive
Autonomous
Reflective
Emotional

14 Classification and frequency—reactions

CLASSIFICATION

The reactions of children to happy, unhappy and problem situations were written in response to the second part of each question (in questions 1 and 2 'Describe what you did as a result'; in question 3 'What did you do?'). Classification of reactions was primarily by inductive procedures, but reference was made to the categories used by McPhail (1967, 1972). However, these were of limited value in that they had been developed from work with adolescent children and incorporated measures of intensity which have been assessed by other procedures in the present research, and in so far as they employed categories of experimental behaviour which were not found feasible in the present study.

The words employed to describe reactions are intended to be descriptive, neutral and free of value judgement. It became clear from children's answers that any particular type of behavioural reaction of a child was not necessarily indicative in itself of 'goodness' or 'badness'. For example an aggressive reaction, although it might be inconsiderate or bullying, might also be brave and concerned. Thus, a child who saw his smaller brother being bullied by an older child might threaten the aggressor and tell him to go away. Such a reaction behaviourally is aggressive: but it is not necessarily immoral. It is suggested therefore, as a result of this research, that the morality of a child's behavioural reactions can perhaps be most appropriately assessed in the context of the particular situation. A possible consequence of this is that those concerned with the education and upbringing of children may not be able to rely on the simplistic method of interpreting the morality of children's behaviour by categorizing particular types of behaviour as morally acceptable or unacceptable What needs to be considered as well is the intention of a child in behaving in a particular way, in particular circumstances. The morality of children's actions accordingly has to be considered as much by intention (which is often difficult to discriminate) as by overt behaviour.

143

The categories of behavioural reaction which were defined as a result of the research were as follows: first, *non-active*. A non-active response was one in which a child did not make an overt behavioural response. A non-active response might be due to passivity, to lack of knowledge of the behavioural reaction appropriate to a particular situation, or to the intentional refraining from an overt behavioural reaction in order to avoid exacerbating a particular situation. An *adult referent* reaction was one in which a child turned to an adult or adults for assistance or for help in achieving a particular objective. As an example, a child who was not certain whether he should go and play football with his friends and asked his mother would be making an adult referent reaction. For a child to refer to an adult was often not a sign of immaturity — rather, an appropriate response in the circumstances in which a child found himself. For a small child, in a world of bigger children, to ignore adult assistance might be misguided. A *peer referent* reaction was one in which a child turned to a peer or peers for assistance or help in achieving a particular objective. In the course of analysing the children's responses we found that this definition of referent response had been too restricted, and that sharing an experience by telling about it should also be considered as a referent reaction (see p. 162).

An *aggressive* reaction included not only physically or verbally aggressive reactions, but also psychological aggression. Examples of psychological aggression were aggression against people displaced onto objects (a child not daring to hit an offending father, tearing up his newspaper), and fantasy aggression (a child planning an imaginary revenge, swearing silently at someone who made him unhappy). An *avoidance* reaction was one in which a child reacted by distancing himself, physically or psychologically (or both) from a situation. Avoidance might include running away, going up to one's bedroom, refusing to listen, or to look, etc.

A *positive* reaction was one in which a child followed the social and moral norms as he or she perceived them. For younger children such norms tended to be those of the adult world. However, older children on occasion were influenced by peer group norms. One source of moral conflict for older children could be in situations in which they had to choose between norms approved by adults and norms approved by peer groups. It would be possible to describe a reaction as positive, in the child's view, which followed either peer group or adult norms. However, the group whose values were rejected by the child would be unlikely to view his behaviour as positive. A group tends to regard its own values as absolute, whereas an individual having to choose between the conflicting values of groups is prone to see them as relative. When children are put in this position they find themselves on the threshold of the adult world with its recurring dilemma of whether to identify with particular groups, or whether to pursue an individualistic path, justifying their actions by reference not to groups, but to reason, revelation, their own desires, or a combination of all three.

An *autonomous* reaction was one in which a child, on his own, decided upon a reaction not predicated by convention. Autonomous reactions had in common an element of originality. As with other reactions, autonomous reactions were not necessarily either morally acceptable or reprehensible. Imaginative, deceitful, questioning behaviour might all, in context, be autonomous. A *reflective* reaction was one in which a child considered what to do, either as an individual or in discussion with others, before taking action, or in which a child simply pondered upon events. An *emotional* reaction was one in which a child reacted physiologically — through screams, tears, laughter; psychologically — through dreams, nightmares; or physically — through running about, jumping up and down, kissing or hugging, etc.

There were in addition two sub-categories of reaction, examples of which were only discovered in the complete sample after the random sample had been anlaysed and the classification of reactions finalized. Logically these sub-categories probably would justify discrete classification, but the low incidence of answers classified within them and the exigencies of the classificatory procedure both militated against such separate classification. The subcategories concerned were *psychosomatic* and *animal referent*. Psychosomatic reactions were classified under non-active reactions, and animal referent reactions under positive reactions. Finally, it is worth emphasizing that all categories were derived, not from the observed behaviour of children, but from childrens' descriptions of their own behaviour. Thus, for example, a reflective reaction was one which a child was sufficiently aware of, and which was to a child of such significance that the child wrote about it: therefore it was classifiable. But many other children may have actually reflected, but done so without self-awareness, or without considering it sufficiently significant to describe.

A number of children described more than one reaction to particular situations. Such multiple reactions were of two differing types. In the first type of multiple reaction more than one response was described immediately following a particular situation: for example, a child was given a present and reacted by saying 'thank you' (first reaction, *positive*) and by kissing the donor (second reaction, *emotional*). In the second type of multiple reaction responses represented a sequence of attempts to modify a particular situation. For example, a child had a toy taken from him by another child and wished to get it back: he reacted by telling the child to give it back (first reaction, *positive*), but that did not work so he hit the child (second reaction, *aggressive*) and that did not work either, so he told an adult (third reaction, *adult referent*) — and that worked.

It had been hoped to incorporate a measure of the extent to which children's reactions were experimental: this however proved to be difficult. This was because, although the second type of multiple response might be classifiable as experimental, it was not possible to tell, from one described situation, whether or not any single reaction, not occurring as part of a multiple reaction, was experimental. The reason for this was that the situation ▪ described might have been one of a type which the child had not encountered before, so any reaction was likely to be experimental; or one which a child had encountered before, but to which he or she was trying out a new reaction. However, in order to discover whether or not reactions were experimental, the team would have had to have had available a long sequence of related situations. This the research design did not provide. It was concluded that to obtain such a series of situations behaviour would need to be observed rather than recorded. However, one tentative conclusion was drawn, and that was that no discrete category of experimental reaction could be satisfactorily defined. Thus there could not be such a category as 'experimental' within the framework of the research design. On the other hand any reaction, whether *adult referent, autonomous,* etc., might have an experimental element. Thus there could be *experimental adult referent, experimental autonomous* reactions etc. In fact, this research suggests that children's reactions can be divided into two broad classifications, *experimental* and *non-experimental,* each classification being subdivided to offer the same categories. The present study, while not making such a distinction, indicates that it could be an interesting field for further investigation.

FREQUENCY

If the frequency of reactions is considered, the first question to be answered concerns the number of reactions reported by pupils in the sample. For example, how many pupils recorded no reaction to a described situation, how many one reaction, how many two reactions, and so on? (See Table 22.) For each type of situation the pattern of number of reactions is similar. 'No reactions' was relatively uncommon (10·8% happy, 8·9% unhappy, 4·4% problem situations). For all types of situation 'no reactions' was less frequent than three reactions, although more frequent than four or more reactions. One reaction only occurred for about 50% of all pupils answering, in each type of situation (54·6% happy, 45·4% unhappy, 48·4% problem situations). For all types of situation two reactions were reported about half as frequently as one reaction only (22·0% happy, 26·0% unhappy, 28·9% problem situations). Again, for all types of situation three reactions were reported about half as frequently as two reactions (11·0% happy, 16·1% unhappy, 16·3% problem situations). Four reactions or more were reported relatively infrequently. If, within this general pattern, differences are sought through comparing numbers of reactions for different types of situation one interesting finding emerges. Children were statistically significantly less likely to record no reaction to a problem situation than to a happy situation ($0.05 > p > 0.01$). This does seem to indicate that children were more liable to react to problem situations than to happy situations.

If the frequency of categories of reaction for first reactions is considered (see Table 23), the following findings emerge (For second and third reactions, see Tables 25, 27, 29; findings concerning frequency of categories of reactions are not dissimilar to findings for first reactions.): 56.0% of reactions to happy situations were *positive.* All other reactions to happy situations were reported in 11% of cases, or less. Of these reactions, 11.0% were *emotional,* and 10.5% adult *referent.* A very small minority of reactions (0.4% *aggressive,* 0.3% *avoidance*) were behaviourlly unacceptable in conventional social terms. It would seem from the present study that the great majority of children, at least in their own eyes, react to considerate treatment in ways liable to be approved by adults and others.

The frequency of categories of reaction to unhappy situations was more evenly distributed than to happy situations. No category occurred in more than 23.0% of cases. On the other hand none occurred in fewer than 3.3% of cases. The most frequently reported categories were *emotional* (22.9%) and *aggressive* (17.5%). However, a greater total frequency (46.0%) was reported in categories of behaviour which were probably socially acceptable. 12.0% of such reactions were *non-active,* 9.5% *adult referent,* 11.6% *avoidance,* and 12.9% *positive.* Of the remaining categories 5.0% were *autonomous,* 5.1% *reflective,* and 3.3% *peer referent.* The findings appear to indicate that children's reactions to inconsiderate treatment are, in their own eyes, likely to be both varied and relatively moderate. Perhaps adults may have a view of children frequently reacting in somewhat uninhibitedly extrovert and offensive ways to provocation or ill treatment because such behaviour is easily noticed; by comparison more quiet or sensible reactions may tend to go unobserved (and perhaps unappreciated).

The frequency of categories of reaction to problem situations also showed variations from reactions to happy (and unhappy) situations. The most frequent reaction was *positive* (27.1%). However, children were just as likely to seek help as to rely on accepted norms for solving social moral difficulties. 15.6% of reactions were *peer referent,* and 12.0% *adult referent.* The relatively high frequency of peer referent reactions may perhaps be partially explained by the number of problem situations which occurred in a setting of informal play and hobbies (see Chapters 6 and 9). Reactions which in behavioural terms might have been socially unacceptable or unconstructive were relatively rare. 1·7% of reactions were *aggressive*, 6·1% showed *avoidance*, and 3·1% were *emotional.*

Overall, the pattern of children's reported reactions to happy, unhappy and problem situations must be fairly comforting to any who are pessimistic about the moral state of the nation's children. From the present study it appears that children see themselves, in the majority of types of situation considered, being prepared to act within a widely accepted social moral framework. Provided that adults are prepared to identify why children behave in particular ways, then there appears little reason for fearing that the moral behaviour of children should be eroded by lack of that caring understanding which necessarily must provide the foundation for satisfactory moral development of children.

If *others* in first reactions are considered (that is, others to whom children relate in their reactions) the following findings emerge. In reactions to happy situations (see Tables 24 & 26), *creatures* (10·2%), *objects* (21·2%) *and environment,* in total 38·7% were reported more than twice as frequently as the next *other* group, *parents* (17·3%). No other group (apart from *miscellaneous*, 15·7%) was reported more frequently than 10·2% (*children not close family members*). If all children are considered together, that is *siblings* and *children not close family members*, the frequency is 13·2%, still less than the frequency of the parental category and about a third of the frequency reported for the *creatures, objects, and environment* category. In fact, it appears that in reaction to happy situations children were over half as likely to react with non-human as with human *others* (38·7% as compared with 61·3%), and that they were much more likely to react with non-human *others* than with any indivi-

Table 22   Number of reactions to situations: happy, unhappy, problem situations

Number of reactions	Situations Happy	%	Unhappy	%	Problem	%
0 reactions	351	10·8	284	8·9	124	4·4
1 reaction only	1779	54·6	1441	45·4	1370	48·4
2 reactions	718	22·0	825	26·0	819	28·9
3 reactions	359	11·0	511	16·1	461	16·3
4 reactions	22	0·7	70	2·2	37	1·3
5 reactions	20	0·6	33	1·0	15	0·5
6 reactions	4	0·1	7	0·2	5	0·2
7 reactions	6	0·2	5	0·2	0	0·0
TOTALS	3259	100·0	3176	100·0	2831	100·0

Table 23   Frequency of categories of first reaction: happy, unhappy, problem situations

| Reaction | Situations | | | | | |
	Happy	%	Unhappy	%	Problem	%
Non-active	186	6·4	347	12·0	260	9·6
Adult referent	305	10·5	276	9·5	325	12·0
Peer referent	110	3·8	96	3·3	422	15·6
Aggressive	13	0·4	507	17·5	45	1·7
Avoidance	9	0·3	336	11·6	165	6·1
Positive	1628	56·0	374	12·9	733	27·1
Autonomous	251	8·6	145	5·0	250	9·2
Reflective	86	2·9	146	5·1	421	15·5
Emotional	319	11·0	663	22·9	83	3·1
TOTALS	2907	99·9	2890	99·8	2704	99·9

dual group of humans. It would seem reasonable to conclude that the natural (as opposed to the human environment) plays a significant part in the well-being of children in the 8—13 age range.

In reactions to unhappy situations (see Tables 24 & 28), the single most frequently reported group of *others* was *children not close family members* (21·2%). *Siblings* were reported by 13·1% of children, so altogether other children were reported by 34·3% of children, or in just over one third of all answers. *Creatures, objects and environment*, although not pre-eminent as in reactions to happy situations, were the second most frequently reported group (20·6%). *Parents* occurred in 15·0% of cases, and *adults not close family members* in 10·0%. Other groups did not occur more frequently than in 4·2% of answers (*relations*), except for *miscellaneous* (12·9%). It can be concluded from these findings that in reactions to inconsiderate treatment, the most significant role for children is played by other children, although other adults, and the natural environment remain significant.

In reactions to problem situations (see Tables 24 & 30), more than twice as many answers (39·3%) referred to *children not close family members* as to the next most frequently reported category, *creatures, objects and environment* (14·8%), (except *miscellaneous*, 15·0%). No other category occurred in more than 7·9% of cases (*parents*). Since *siblings* occurred with a frequency of 4·3%, other children were found in 43·6% of cases, or approaching half of all answers. The frequency with which other children were reported in reactions to problem situations is consistent with other findings in the present study which discovered in problem situations high frequencies of children as *others* in situations of *peer referent* reactions and *informal play and hobby* themes (see above, this chapter and Chapters 6, 9 & 10). Nevertheless, as in reactions to happy and unhappy situations, the non-human environment remained significant.

In conclusion, it is worth remarking that the non-human environment, in happy and problem situations, is relatively more frequently mentioned as *other* in reactions, than as *other* in situations; and in unhappy situations is as relatively frequently mentioned (see Tables 17 & 24). Thus, in happy situations *creatures, objects and environment* is the most frequently mentioned *other* category in reactions to situations, but the fifth most frequently mentioned *other* category in situations; mentioned in problem situations it is the third most frequently mentioned category in reactions, and the sixth in situations mentioned. In unhappy situations *creatures, objects and environment* is the second most frequently mentioned category both in situation, and in reaction. If *other* in situation is identified as the agent acting upon the child, and *other* in reaction as the *other* upon whom or which a child acts, then it can be seen that to children the non-human environment is more significant in circumstances in which the child is the agent than in circumstances in which the child is acted upon. But, even without making this distinction it seems clear that in a situational, interactional context, the child's world is not dominated entirely by the human environment.

Table 24   Other groups: in first reactions to happy, unhappy, problem situations

Other group	Situations Happy	%	Unhappy	%	Problem	%
Parents	504	17·3	433	15·0	213	7·9
Siblings	86	3·0	380	13·1	116	4·3
Relations	203	7·0	123	4·2	133	4·9
Adults not close family members	189	6·5	289	10·0	365	13·5
Children not close family members	298	10·2	614	21·2	1065	39·3
Supernatural, fictitious & well known figures	48	1·6	82	2·8	8	0·3
Creatures, objects & environment	1124	38·7	597	20·6	401	14·8
Miscellaneous	456	15·7	374	12·9	406	15·0
TOTALS	2908	100·0	2892	99·8	2707	100·0

15   Happy situations—reactions

In discussing the reactions of individual children to happy situations (and to unhappy and problem ones), a number of factors need to be considered. These are: first the category of reaction (aggressive, positive etc.); second the fact that a child might report more than one reaction to a situation (multiple reactions); and third, the category of *other* or *others* (if any) to whom a child related in his or her reaction or reactions. In order that these factors may each be appropriately analysed the following procedure has been adopted: initially answers are considered according to category of reaction (thus *aggressive* reactions are considered as a separate group, as are *positive* reactions, *adult referent* reactions etc.); next, multiple reactions and *others* are discussed within the context of each category of reaction.

As might have been expected, the great majority of reactions reported by children to happy situations were *positive,* while only a minimal number of children described *aggressive* or *avoidance* reactions. In considering the *positive,* and also the *autonomous* reactions, the general pattern comes more clearly into focus (which became apparent in analysing themes of happy situations), whereby children specified as happy those circumstances in which they were treated with consideration and were able to reciprocate such treatment. *Positive* reaction to considerate treatment by adults, particularly as exemplified in the giving of presents or treats could take the form of offering a gift in return. A 9+ London boy gave his mother a necklace.

The time when someone made me happy was when my mum bought a car, The car is a Ford anglia.
    What I did as a result I bought mum a necklace as a result.

Gratitude could also be shown by the performance of good deeds. A 12+ boy in his last year at middle school recalled an event far in the past.

What I am going to write happened about $8\frac{1}{2}$ years ago, It had been a big

151

surprise. It was coming up to my 4th birthday. and I was sitting down in the bedroom when in came dad wheeling a trycicle in, I had never been so over-joyed in my 4 years, after that I helped my mum and dad for at least 6 months.

Another child, a girl from a Newcastle middle school, likewise remembered a distant occasion.

Long Long agow when I was six I got A Set of Books I was very very happy the Book wher called hear we go and Janet and Jhon and the rubber ball and Dick the Bulldozer and the explosion so I went and done the Beds and then I dug the garden and I got fifty pence and I was very Happy.

A reaction which sometimes accompanied good deeds, and sometimes occurred on its own, was good behaviour. Children at times intentionally rewarded adults for their kindness by omitting to be a nuisance. A 10+ boy on holiday in Liverpool described such circumstances very explicitly.

At Easter we were on holiday and my grandad came to our place and said 'do John and paul want to come to the Liverpool musiam with me.' We said 'yes' and got dressed got some money and went. We got on the ferry at Birkenhead and went across the mersy. I usually mess about and moan but I did not this time.

Answers in which multiple reactions were reported, children both being good and performing good deeds, were given by a 10+ girl from London, and an 11+ boy from Dorset.

Table 25 Frequency of categories of reaction to happy situations

Reaction category	Reactions First	% of *	Second	% of **	Third	% of ‡
Non-active	186	6·4	81	7·2	37	9·0
Adult referent	305	10·4	88	7·8	28	6·8
Peer referent	110	3·8	43	3·8	9	2·2
Aggressive	13	0·4	3	0·3	1	0·2
Avoidance	9	0·3	7	0·6	0	0·0
Positive	1628	56·0	614	54·4	221	53·8
Autonomous	251	8·6	126	11·2	62	15·1
Reflective	86	2·9	64	5·7	18	4·4
Emotional	319	11·0	102	9·0	35	8·5
TOTALS	2907*	99·9	1128**	100·0	411‡	100·0

Somebody made me very happy when they took me to the Zoo Chessington
Zoo it was first time I had been to a Zoo and I was very excited. First of all
we saw the camels with the humps on their back some had one hump some had
two Then we saw the lion which looked very fierce and hungry. Close beside the
lion in another cage was a tiger with black and orange stripes. I was not all that
excited but still happy. Then we went to see the apes which was very funny.
My aunty kept making faces at them and all of a sudden the ape jumped up
and my aunty ran away. We all started to laugh. As a result I behaved my self
and often go and help my auntie at home who has a baby.

I was geting ready to go to out to play when mum siad we were going to the
pictures to see let live and die that made me feel happy and pleaced because
mum the day befor siad that I could not go. In return I washed the pots and
went on an errand and I was a good boy for the rest of the day.

Positive reactions could also consist of simply being polite, and saying
'thank you' (and possibly also of hugging and kissing, an *emotional* reaction).
A 9+ boy from Cardiff, in a multiple response reported that, as a reaction to
being given a go-kart he said 'thank you' (reaction 1) showed interest and care
for the present (reaction 2) and carried out a good deed (response 3).

Two years ago when Christmas was coming I always wanted a go-cart. When
Christmas came I had a go-cart, I was so pleased that I thanked my mother
and farther very much. The next day I went out on it. It whent very fast and
the brakes were good. Then I took it in and cleaned it.
Because I was so happy I washed the dishes.

A 10+ girl from a Chester middle school reported intense interest in a
present (reaction 1) and an *emotional* reaction (reaction 2).

I felt happy when my gran bought me a big doll and a pram. My doll had an
underskirt on, a dress a cardigan and some booties. The pram was brown it was
a big springy one. I have still got it now. My pram had a sheet, a blue and pink
silk eiderdown and a white silk coushon. The eiderdown has got a blue strip
of silk down the front with a bow at the bottom (The bow is blue). I looked
at the pram then ran and gave my gran a hug and a kiss.

There were times when children received presents with which they were
delighted, but for which they did not report saying 'thank you', or being
good, or performing good deeds; in such cases what they often did was simply
to show intense interest in the present. However, this was not necessarily a
result of selfishness, or lack of gratitude. Joy in the present could explicitly
be intended as a means of showing pleasure and thanks.

Table 26   Frequency of others in first reactions to happy situations

Other group	Other		No.	% of others
Parents	Mother		230	7·9
	Father		152	5·2
	Mother and father		118	4·1
	Parent		4	0·1
		TOTALS	**504**	**17·3**
Siblings	Sibling(s) same sex		61	2·1
	Sibling(s) other sex		23	0·8
	Siblings, both sexes		2	0·1
		TOTALS	**86**	**3·0**
Relations	Relation(s)		100	3·4
	Special close relation(s)		5	0·2
	Family group		98	3·4
		TOTALS	**203**	**7·0**
Adults not close family members	Teacher(s)		67	2·3
	Unknown, unspecified adult(s)		24	0·8
	Adult(s) in authority		65	2·2
	Adult(s), friend(s), neighbour(s)		33	1·1
		TOTALS	**189**	**6·5**
Children not close family members	Known child(ren) or cousin(s)		75	2·6
	Child friend(s)		211	7·3
	Unknown, unspecified child(ren)		12	0·4
		TOTALS	**298**	**10·2**
Supernatural, fictitious & well known figures	Fictitious figure		10	0·3
	Public figure		36	1·2
	Religious figure, God		2	0·1
	Spirits, ghosts		0	0·0
		TOTALS	**48**	**1·6**
Creatures, objects & environment	Object(s)		615	21·2
	Living creature(s)		298	10·2
	Something		2	0·1

	Environment		209	7·2
		TOTALS	**1124**	**38·7**
Miscellaneous	Somebody (s & pl)		26	0·9
	No-one, myself		325	11·2
	Activity group		105	3·6
		TOTALS	**456**	**15·7**
		OVERALL TOTALS	2908	100·0

An aspect of such reactions was that the *other* in the reaction was not the same *other* who had caused the happiness. Whereas, where a parent gave a child a present or a treat, and the child thanked, or gave a present in return or behaved him- or herself, it was the donor who directly benefited, and so was the significant *other* in the reaction, as well as the original significant *other*. Where a child showed involvement with a present, then the present was the significant *other* in the reaction, and not the donor.

These two points (that children might show intense interest in a present as a conscious way of showing gratitude, and that the *other* in reaction in such cases was not the donor but the present) are illustrated in the answer of a 10+ girl who was given a dog by her parents.

when it was my birthday I was very happy whe my mummy and daddy bought me a dog I shood how happy and please I was by feeding himing and playing when ever the dog felt like playing I called the dog lucky because the first week I had him and he ran out in front of the car but he was ok. and I was very pleased he was not hert so I watched him all the time.

Both the length of time over which children recalled the circumstances in which they enjoyed certain presents or outings, and the intensity with which they could write about them, indicated how significant such events could be in children's lives. Particularly the delight which children could reveal in the possession of and playing with toys and animals could lead to the formation of very real relationships. One 10+ girl wrote of her feelings for a kitten which had been given to her by her father.

There was a time when I was happy it was when my Farther came home with a kitten, it was black and white it was a lovely kitten it was my very own. I was aloud to take it to bed with me and it would play with me if I didn't have any one to play with me, and I could take it for a walk because it would never run away it would stay by my side, and it was very clean.

Although typically *others* in reactions were either the immediate cause of the happiness (a present) or the original cause of the happiness (a donor), this was not always necessarily so, particularly where the cause of pleasure was not a present or treat. For example, achievement could lead to satisfaction and a consequent *positive* reaction. In one instance a boy was pleased when he was picked for a team, and it won. His reaction was to perform good deeds for his mother, who did not appear to have been in any way involved in his triumph on the field of play.

I was happy when I was picted for the hockey it was the first time I had played for the school We were going to play Ferndown at Ferdown Steven Booth was our captain we scored two goals in the first half and we had to swap refs in the second half. We had a ref from Ferndown he did not play the same rules as our ref but we still hung on to our 2 nil lead until the end. I was pleased and helped my mum as much as I could that night.

Other *positive* reactions to achievement, or adult encouragement of a child, could be determination to continue or raise the level of achievement, and a desire to show gratitude to and please adults concerned usually by sustained effort in the activity with which the adults had helped or encouraged.

An 11+ girl showed her *positive* reaction to two adults who had encouraged her musical ambitions; the two adults were the *others* in the reaction.

When someone made me feel pleased and happy was when I new someone was interested about my futcher. Playing the guitar and folk singing. They took more interest in me than anyone elso had every befor. My first guitar lesson they had no hope for me because my hands were so small. But because they had pleased me. I stuck at it and the things they had showed me to do I did and did well that pleased them and I went on pleasing them and I still are they still please me. I not only got on well I won a gold meadle and two stifficats as well these people had pleased and made me happy their names are. Pete Franklin and Alan Right. I will all ways be happy to do any thing for them.

A 10+ boy indicated his determination to play football well as a result of a teacher putting his name in a school magazine. In this answer there was no *other* in reaction.

A time when somebody said something that made me pleased was when my teacher told me that my name was in a sports magazine my name had never been in any papper or magazin before so it gave me a great thrill. As a result I went on trying hard to play football well and now I have been in the same

magazine quite a lot of times, so I would like to keep it up. The teacher who
put it in made me pleased.

In general the *positive* reactions of children to each other were similar to
their *positive* reactions to adults. Children given presents or treats by friends
reciprocated in kind. A 9+ boy from a Chester middle school briefly indicated
his reaction to receiving a present from a friend. 'On Christmas my freind gave
me a present and I was pleased and I got him a present.' In greater detail a 9+
boy wrote about how he rewarded another boy for letting him have turns on
his bicycle.

The Boy named Jimmy let me have a go on his Bike. And I went Round The
Block, and as i was Riding I stoped to look at The shops as I went Past, and I
stoped at a Sports Shop And I saw This goalies cap for 56 Pence and I went in
and Bought it for Jimmy For letting me have sixteen goes on The Bike and
They had a macth and They won eight-Five. The end.

Sometimes more unusual events took place, but the reaction was similar.

One day I went to the swimming Pool and I lost a gold earing and a Girl found
it I was so happy. I had lost it when I was putting on my swimming cap. In
return I bught the girl an ice cream a the ice cream van.

On occasion an element occurred in children's relationships with each other
which was not present in their dealings with adults. The giving of presents
could involve a transactional aspect, whereby objects were exchanged, almost
ritualistically, to symbolize friendship.

my fred guve me some cars and i sad i will be your besd fred and I gave him
some vans and he sed i will be your besd fred and we went in my den and we
had s bred.

Autonomous reactions to happy situations included those where children
responded imaginatively, or with a degree of individuality which transcended
behaviour which might conventionally have been expected. One 10+ girl, on
hearing that she was to go riding regularly reacted both *positively,* by thanking
her mother (first reaction) and *autonomously,* by making and playing with a
pretend horse (second reaction). In the *autonomous* reaction the significant
other was an object, the play horse.

One thing that made me feel pleased and happy was when my mother said she
would book each week for me to go riding. I was very happy. and I helped my
mother with housework then I stuffed a sock marked eyes and imaged he was

a real horse I sat on the log in the garden, and fastend the sock onto a stick. I stuck the stick into the ground. and made strong reins and then had a good game. All that evening I was in a very good mood. I stayed in the garden for a very long time that evening playing with my horse.

Another girl, aged 12+, wrote about the circumstances in which she reacted to a girl, (in danger of going blind), who cheered her up when in hospital, by establishing a long lasting friendship. While her reaction was *positive,* in the sense that it was in accordance with what would have been socially approved, its achievement required a degree of personal choice, and commitment to that choice, which rendered it *autonomous.*

When I was five I had to go into hospital for an eye operation. While I was there a girl of about the same age as I was brought in. She had nearly lost her sight in one eye and was going to have an operation done on the other. It was all because of a firework she told me. I was'ent very happy in hospital as I had something against them. This girl told me a story about her brother who had lost his sight. I don't really know wether it was her friendship or her story but I felt happier.
    Her operation proved no good and she went blind. As a result I went to see her every week for two years and we still remain good friends.

Emotional reactions, such as hugging and kissing have already been mentioned, together with *positive* reactions, in multiple reactions to happy situations. Other *emotional* reactions included sheer physical exuberance resulting from a joy too powerful to be kept under control. An elder brother found himself the object of a friendly assault on one such occasion.

One day in October my friend, Robert Hyde, phoned me up to ask me if I wanted to go and see Bournemouth play Watford. I naturally accepted after asking my mum and dad. When they said yes I went baserk and ran round the lounge giving my elder brother a few friendly biffs in the chest. At about 2.00 in the afternoon I arrived at Roberts house with my bobble hat and scarf. We arrived at the ground and went through the turnstiles After showing two season tickets. Bournemouth won 1−0 and I thoroughly enjoyed myself.

A more muted type of *emotional* reaction was reported by a 10+ girl who, to her delight, won a swimming competition. She could not stop smiling. (She also, in a second reaction, told her mother when she got home, an *adult referent* reaction).

The day that made me feel pleased was when Miss Rigby told me that I was going to go through to the finals in the swimming gala that we had against different people from different schools. I couldn't believe it when I stood up after the race and saw that I had come first, I went into the changing rooms feeling all pleased about myself. I couldn't stop smiling every where I went I was smiling when I got home and told my mum where I had come she was pleased to.

Reflective reactions could be ones in which children first paused for thought, then decided how to react, and finally put their reaction into practice. *Reflective* reactions of this type always were reported as one of a multiple reaction. For example, an 11+ boy in his third year at a middle school described how he responded to the gift of a bicycle. First, he though (first reaction, *reflective*), then he kissed his mother (second reaction, *emotional*), then he gave her a present (third reaction, *positive*). In the *reflective* reaction there was no *other,* but in the *emotional* and *positive* reactions the *other* was his mother.

When my mum bort me a bicecul I wisht that she bort me a bicecul I sead that I was happy and I did not no wot to dow to show. I han grafull [am grateful] for when she gave me the bicell I thort and thort and then I kiss her and I whent to the sied bord and poled out a drowe and took some monney and gave it to her.

Another type of *reflective* reaction could be prompted by a more complex pattern of events. First, the child would perform a good deed; second, the beneficiary of the good deed, or a third party, would express gratitude or reward the child; third, the child would reflect how worthwhile it was to make others happy. Sometimes the child's reflection would be accompanied by the thought that being useful was preferable to being a nuisance. A 10+ girl from a London school was pleased at being able to help an elderly lady.

There was a time when somebody made me happy. It is when I was walking up the road, and I saw an old lady with a walking stick, she was trying to get a cardboard box out of her way. I said to her 'shall I take the box away for you she did not hear me I repeated it than she said 'Yes dear, please' so I did. It made me happy because I did a good deed, instead of being a nuisance to everybody.

Another girl, in her first year at a comprehensive, was rewarded by a shop-keeper for doing an errand for her mother. She reflected on the tangible and pecuniary benefits which could result from considerate behaviour: being good could pay!

There were three of us going to town we went into a shop and the shopkeeper told us we could have 20p worth of anything free as we were doing a good deed for our mothers. Which made me feel very pleased to know it was worth doing a good deed.

Other *reflective* reactions involved situations in which a child was made happy through anticipation of an event to come. The thoughts would concern the nature of that event. One boy for example was pleased because he and his mother were going on holiday together, without his father.

My Mum made me happy when she said we were gowing on holiday on our own.
This ment there wasent Dad to growl at you if you did somthig wrong.
When we got to Brighton we met a taxe which took us to a hatel.
The hotel over looked the sea-front and the pear.

From the observer's point of view it might be difficult to distinguish *reflective* reactions from *non-active* reactions. Such reactions to happy situations were ones in which, typically, children reported that they were pleased or happy, but did not express their feelings, either because they did not know how to, or because their emotion was so strong as to be, paradoxically, incapacitating. In a number of the *non-active* reactions it seems clear, from what the children wrote, that their feelings were in fact understood by observers. However the crucial point is that, from the child's point of view, the reaction was *non-active*. For example, a 10+ girl was given a rabbit. She wrote she and her brother (also given a rabbit) 'were so plesed we dident no wote to do.' But she also wrote that her parents 'was pleasd to see us both happy.' This was a case in which a child described her reaction as *non-active* although clearly others, noticed some reaction.

Whene I was young me and my brother dune some washing up and wiping up my sisster said thats anufe. thene she said come with me you two thers a surprise wating for you. So we went behind the conter and there in two boxes was two bybe white rabbits in theme it was one for my brother and there was one for me. we were so plesed we dident no wote to do. Our mum and dad was pleasd to see us both happy.

An 8+ girl however was apparently more genuinely *non-active*. Most atypically, she failed to describe the circumstances to which she was reacting. Probably they were too important and intimate for her to feel she could trust them to paper.

Well the people who made me feel happy at home was my mummy and daddy.
That day was one of my happest day in my life. I did not show it. It was all
inside me. All the joy and happy-ness was all a secret. It did show on my face a
bit. But not as much as it should of been. The impression on my face looked
like I was the most sadess girl in the world. But really I was the happist girl in
the world. The thing came right in a flash.

Reactions in which children referred directly to others (*peer* or *adult referent*
reactions), were infrequent in relation to other categories of response. In such
cases children might simply show gratitude for considerate treatment by love
and concern for the *other*; in these circumstances the *other* in reaction would
always be the same as the *other* who caused the happiness. A 9+ girl from a
Cardiff school, in a multiple response, wrote about her reactions to the kindness of another child. Two reactions were reported 'I've liked her more through
her kindness', and 'I am always doing my best to please her'; both reactions
were *peer referent.*

Julia she is the one who made me happy because to jion swimming club she
did so much and I've liked her more through her kindness.
She put my name down and encouraged me and told me not to give up hope.
I have always tried to be like that to her and I hope I have. Julia is younger
than me but she acts older so I am always doing my best to please her I think I
have sometime through out our friendship.

Another type of *peer* or *adult referent* reaction was that in which the child
turned to another for instrumental purposes, in order to enable a desired or
promised activity to take place. In a multiple reaction, a girl invited to join
another in riding lessons asked her mother for permission (*adult referent*),
ran up the stables (*positive*) and subsequently went riding (*positive*).

One day I arrived home from school with my friend, Lynn and she said to me
'Wait there a second, while I ask mum something. While Lynn was gone I put
my satchel down. I was thinking what Lynn would come out and say, 'It's not
her birthday party or anything, then Lynn came out, she said to me, 'I know
your a great lover for horses, so I wondered if you would come with me and
have horse lessons', at this moment I never knew weather it was a dream or not,
I rushed in and told mum. she said she would think about it, but I know she
would let me have lessons so Lynn And I rang up the ridding stables at Holt-
wood, and we booked in a lesson for for the weekend for an hour, for the
first time. When we got there the horses were ready I rode on chippy, Lynn
rode on Topper and Sue, the teacher told us what to do so we went out in the
field and we learnt how to handel the horse and to stear. When we finished we
booked again for next week for two and a half hours and we will learn how to

groom them and put the sadles and bridles on and clean the tack and know how to clean the stables out and to look after the horse. Now we have been a lot now and know how to trot and canter.

A number of both *adult* and *peer referent* reactions took place in situations in which children who had been made to feel happy or pleased, for whatever reason, reacted by going to somebody else, whether child or grown-up, to share and recount the situation. For such children happiness was an emotion to be shared, a reason for conviviality.

16   Unhappy situations—reactions

A frequently reported reaction to unhappy situations was *aggression; avoidance,* the alternative option in the 'flight or fight' choice, also appeared relatively frequently. *Avoidance,* as the term suggests, was a comparatively straight-forward and undifferentiated reaction, involving simply withdrawal from a situation, whether by walking away or running away, hiding, or refusing to look or to listen. The *other* in an *avoidance* reaction would be the *other* being avoided – usually, though not always, the *other* who caused the situation. Sometimes *avoidance* occurred in multiple reactions, and at times together with *aggressive* reactions. A 10+ girl described a time when her feelings were hurt, and she withdrew to be on her own for a day. The *other* in reaction was her aunt.

I remeber in the half term holiday. My sister and I made a paper mashey. When we had finished I put mine on the side to dry. The next day we painted them and let them dry. The next day we showed them to my mum who said they were very good. When my aunty came to our house we showed her them. She said that my sisters was very good but mine didn't have a lot of paint on. I was so unhappy I went up to my room and stayed in bed for a day.

Another child, a 9+ boy, was also upset by the behaviour of visitors. He tried two solutions to bring to an end the situation which was making him unhappy. His first reaction, though verging on the *aggressive,* was *positive.* His second was *avoidance;* he refused to listen. In both reactions the *others* were his father's friends.

One evening when I was at my dad's friend's house they started talking about ghosts, and my mum said that there used to be 2 ghosts at the bottom of my sisters bed. A little while after I said be quiet and put a cushion over my head so I couldn't hear. That is what I did as a result.

In *aggressive* reactions children deployed a wide variety of techniques, especially against adults. The distinction between the sophisticated methods used to deal with the grown-up world compared with the comparatively crude procedures adopted against peers is easily explained. Other children could be hit or shouted at; adults frequently (though not always) were either inaccessible or impervious to such modes of attack. Consequently, non-physical and more subtle techniques were often needed.

Children's *aggressive* reaction against adults varied from the impotent, through the irritating, to the effective. Children who were unhappy as a result of adult behaviour, but who felt it was outside their power to do anything effective to change circumstances might vent their aggression on some innocent person or object (a technique familiar in psychological jargon as displaced aggression). A 12+ middle school boy, furious with his father attacked a cushion with a knife (in this case the *other* in reaction was not the father but the object attacked).

The day I felt angry was when my dad would not let me make my airfix model because he was reading a book and he did not want me to disturb him.
So when he had gone out into the garden I got hold of a newspaper and I tore it to threads and I got a sharp knife and stabed the cushion and all the feathers came out and my mum smacked me and sent me to bed.

An example of a similar reaction, although not against familiar adults but against public figures, was given by a boy who watched an international foot-

Table 27   Frequency of categories of reaction to unhappy situations

Reaction category	Reactions First	% of *	Second	% of **	Third	% of ‡
Non-active	347	12·0	188	12·9	84	13·4
Adult referent	276	9·5	216	14·9	92	14·7
Peer referent	96	3·3	51	3·5	18	2·9
Aggressive	507	17·5	205	14·1	79	12·6
Avoidance	336	11·6	165	11·4	76	12·2
Positive	374	12·9	184	12·7	102	16·3
Autonomous	145	5·0	102	7·0	31	5·0
Reflective	146	5·1	105	7·2	56	9·0
Emotional	663	22·9	235	16·2	87	13·9
TOTALS	2892*	99·8	1451**	99·9	625‡	100·0

ball match. He wrote, from his own personal viewpoint, about the type of situation much discussed in the national press. His *aggressive* reaction (reaction 1) was followed in a multiple reaction by refusal to talk to anybody except his friend (*avoidance,* reaction 2). The *others* in the first reaction were objects, and in the second reaction the activity group, members of the coach party; in neither case was it the *others* who originally caused the trouble, the footballers. From the boy's angle it was a very frustrating situation, because he had no way of relating to the people who had caused him the anger and misery. Consequently he had no option but to displace his feelings onto the objects and people in his immediate surroundings.

We had gone to Wembley with the school, When poland scored I was so angry that I threw a can of drink down onto the spectators below when England scored I went a bit hazy for a few seconds and kept seeing Allan clarke score that goal when poland scored again I ripped up my programme and nearly broke the seat by jumping up and down on it. On the way back I didnt speak to anyone except my best friend, I was so upset.

More direct, but not much more effective techniques of expressing aggression against adults involved muttered expletives, and planned obstruction.

A 9+ boy from a Dorset middle school employed the first method against a teacher who had told him off.

In Fernch Mr . . . told me off i said I did not know And I fellt unhappy And then we went Back to PE I said pig under my breath.

A 10+ girl from West Bromwich used the second procedure against another teacher, albeit self-destructively since the irritation caused to the teacher by badly done work would undoubtedly be visited on the child. This answer in fact illustrates well by what a simple dynamic of interaction a vicious circle can be set up in the classroom, whereby teacher and pupil each behaves in such a way as to reinforce the other's expectation of unfair or undisciplined and inattentive behaviour.

The time that I felt when I felt unhappy was this afternoon when our teacher said we could not have P.E. again on a Tuesday. What I did was get all my sums (wrong) nor did I listen to what our broadcast said.

Children could also employ retaliatory procedures in the home. Those who had been denied what they wanted, particularly if they believed the prohibition to have been unnecessary or unfair, could embark on quite elaborate

Table 28   Frequency of others in first reactions to unhappy situations

Other group	Other		No.	% of others
Parents	Mother		225	7·8
	Father		150	5·2
	Mother and father		54	1·9
	Parent		4	0·1
		TOTALS	**433**	**15·0**
Siblings	Sibling(s) same sex		229	7·9
	Sibling(s) other sex		148	5·1
	Siblings, both sexes		3	0·1
		TOTALS	**380**	**13·1**
Relations	Relation(s)		93	3·2
	Special close relation(s)		5	0·2
	Family group		25	0·9
		TOTALS	**123**	**4·2**
Adults not close family members	Teacher(s)		67	2·3
	Unknown, unspecified adult(s)		102	3·5
	Adult(s) in authority		97	3·3
	Friend(s), neighbour(s)		23	0·8
		TOTALS	**289**	**10·0**
Children not close family members	Known child(ren) or cousin(s)		231	8·0
	Child friend(s)		255	8·8
	Unknown, unspecified child(ren)		128	4·4
		TOTALS	**614**	**21·2**
Supernatural, fictitious & well known figures	Fictitious figure		35	1·2
	Public figure		13	0·4
	Religious figure, God		0	0·0
	Spirits, ghosts		34	1·2
		TOTALS	**82**	**2·8**
Creatures, objects &	Object(s)		160	5·5
	Living creature(s)		216	7·5

environment	Something		79	2·7
	Environment		142	4·9
		TOTALS	**597**	**20·6**
Miscellaneous	Somebody (s & pl)		69	2·4
	No-one, myself		270	9·3
	Activity group		33	1·2
	Unclassified		2	0·1
		TOTALS	**374**	**12·9**
		OVERALL TOTALS	2892	99·8

Percentages have been rounded.

programmes of disruption. An example of such behaviour was given by an 8+ boy, whose daily television routine was interrupted by the Budget, an unwelcome intruder from the outside world. It is ironical to reflect that, in this case at least, the Chancellor's activities succeeded in bringing woe to children as well, doubtless, as to adults.

I was unhappy when my mum said that I and my sister could not go to our auntys house to wart B.B.C.2. because all childrens programes were on B.B.C.2. and the Buget was on B.B.C.1. And my aunty had B.B.C.2 on her T.V. And all that day I got in my mums way.

By no means all children were afraid or unable to face adults directly, and alter situations which were objectionable to them. Indeed a feature of a number of the answers was the confidence with which children confronted grown-ups, and the willingness grown-ups showed to modify their behaviour, if they felt the children's feelings were reasonable. No doubt the children's confidence and the grown-ups' readiness to treat them as people in their own right were connected.

Fathers of girls appeared prone both to cause trouble, and to be prepared to acknowledge themselves in the wrong with a good grace. A 10+ junior school girl found the combination of her father's assumption of a male dominant role, together with a provocative attitude, unacceptable. She struck back, argued (the father was the *other* in reaction), and won: he agreed to help with the washing up.

I was angry with my father because he had sent me to wipe the dishes, I went to wipe them and my father had a grin on his face, he got out his book and began to read. I grow angry with him and we had an argument. I won. In the end we both washed and wiped.

Another girl, age 9+, took more direct action when frightened by her father (again, the *other* in reaction was the father).

Yesterday I was in the hall it was very dark without the light on. and I was just going into a room when suddenly my daddy jumped up at me he made me very frightened, he made me so frightened that I chased him down the hall.

Where adults did accede to children's wishes their willingness to be reasonable might well be rewarded. One of the major sanctions enjoyed by children in dealing with the adult world was the threat of ill-discipline. Children might both use this to try and make adults change their ways, and lift the threat if adults complied. One 8+ girl, furious at her father's dilatoriness in carrying out a commission for her, issued a severe ultimatum: father duly came to heel. And he was rewarded, by obedience, for behaving himself.

One week ago I asked my Dad to bring me seven bangles to give to my friend. Every day when he came home I asked him were are my bangle he sad I left it at the shop. One day I was so angry that I said Dad if you do not bring those bangle I will not do a thing you say so the next day he bought them. So now I always do what he says.

Sons, in dealing with fathers, often employed physical rather than verbal *aggression*. An 11+ boy and his brother attacked their father (unsuccessfully) to punish him because he had switched over television channels unjustifiably.

One day a few week's ago Serch Control was just about to start on the telly but dad came in and turned it over to BBC2 and said that Agecutler was on so me and my brother got a little bit angry and when the program had finished I got mad because he wasn't on, so me and my brother had a little fight with dad and we lost.

Another boy, 9+ from Swindon, dealt by a multiple reaction with his father's attempt to frightem him. First he jumped on him (reaction 1, *aggressive*); next he frightened him (reaction 2, *aggressive*); finally he made his coffee with oxo (reaction 3, *autonomous*). It worked; father never frightened him again.

One night when there was an electric power cut about half past nine I blow the candle out ten minites later my dad came up quitely. (It was halowen.) The door opened it squeeked a little bit he was curverd in a white sheet I roled over and saw him out of the corer of my I when look round it was gon. When he come back I jumped on him. Later when they were going to bed when my dad was in bed I got a blanket and fritend him. I taler him in the morning I made him a cup of coffy with an oxo. But he never did it again.

A boy, aged 9+, did not apparently resort to physical violence, but he failed to make his father honour a promise.

One day my father said that by the end of the year I could have a ride in an aircraft. But by the end of the year I had not had not had that ride so I got very cross. But I still did not get that ride.

Children's *aggressive* reactions, particularly perhaps with their peers, were designed to achieve results. Sometimes a child would use verbal aggression alone, either because it was sufficient to do the job required or because he or she did not quite dare to reinforce it with physical aggression. One child, an 8+ boy from a Newcastle first school, was faced with the problem of an obstructive sister. In his first reaction he was *positive*; in his second he used verbal *aggression,* quite imaginatively.

One day I made a tent with ladders for a frame and covers and for a wall and you could sit one the top my sister always wanted to sit on the top I said you will have to give other people a turn. I said there are times when I would go to Manhatten go on top of the Empire state sky scraper and throw you off.

The intention of an *aggressive* reaction to other children could be to prevent bullying or intimidation, usually but not always in self-defence. One 9+ boy employed physical *aggression* in self-defence, with satisfactory results.

One day I was walking down my street and a boy started punching a calling me names I was geting angry and he he keeped calling names.
So I hit him a he fell and I kicked him, and he started to cry, About an hour later his mother was round my house. I felt frightened but it was ok. The boy never touched me again.

Another employed violence to ensure that a theft was not repeated.

There was one time when someone made me feel unhappy, and that was when someone pinched my gloves, so I chased him untill I got him, then I got my gloves back, and went back to my desk and put them in my desk, then I said, 'I am going to make sure he don't pinche them again'. So I had a fight with him and gave him a bleeding nose.

Another child, a 10+ boy, saw a boy being cruel to a dog. His first reaction, a *positive* one, was to tell the boy to desist. When this failed, he attacked him (reaction 2, *aggressive*), which presumably was effective.

One day a boy made me unhappy by throwing stones at a little dog so I went up to the boy and told him to stop it. But when I turned my back he started throwing the stones at the dog again so I bashed him up.

In some situations children could thus use aggression to achieve moral ends, such as support of the weak and defenceless. Children however also used aggression in a punitive, retaliatory or revengeful way. Girls seemed just as ready as boys to resort to violence. One 12+ girl used verbal and physical aggression on another girl who had stolen her boy friend.

Its about the boy I mentioned in Question 1. It was on a Saturday night I was supposed to meet him and go to the flicks but he did'nt come at least not with me. I saw him later with another girl this made me very angry. Because the girl was my mate.
As a result I waited until he had go home and I went up to the girl and told her what I thought of her and then I hit her.

Two girls playing rounders got into an altercation in which verbal aggression followed physical aggression.

One day I was playing rounders and I was talking to my friend about the other team was cheating because a girl pushed the ball out of the other girls hand. Then a girl from the other team came and push me so I pushed her back and we started to fight I hit her in her face and it went red and then she went away. After woulds I said that next time I would pull her hair out of her skull.

A 9+ girl from a Newcastle middle school described a very straightforward set to.

quite a long time ago my friend has thumped me and I thumped her Back she thumped me again and every time I thumped her She thumped me and I got very angry.

The role of 'friend' as it appeared in relation to *aggressive* reactions was of interest. On the one hand it seemed at times to be an almost formal designation, little related to any real underlying affection. One boy for example had a fight with a friend in which there was no evidence of any other than a casual play relationship between the children concerned.

an afternoon when we come out of school my freind came up and said do you want to play a game of foot ball, I said yes so we played. When we stoped he went home so when I went out of the gate he was going down the road. I went into the tuck shop when I got out of the tuck sope he out side he kiked me and ran of I chased him when caught him I beat him up. He went of crying so I went home.

On the other hand the most apparently ferocious encounters with a friend might be just another episode, if a somewhat rumbustious one, in a relationship of mutual esteem and affection. In fact the seriousness with which a child viewed a fight might well depend, not so much on the amount of blood spilt, as on the intentions and attitudes of those participating. A battle between two West Bromwich boys, worthy of a James Bond film, ended in amity.

This is the time that felt angry becuse my friend Andrew Hoult made me angry by making me trip over so I punchd him and we started to fight and he hit me right in the mouth so I punched him in the eye and we fighted and fighted he hit me in the belly I hit him on the nose he would get me on the grass and hit me but I hit him back allright do you now he fell over the stump that was in the ground and lafat and he said I hit you for that and hit me right in the eye and I sead take that and that but inthe end we made friends and walked down the street I had a black eye and he had a thik eare.

A 9+ girl, from London, also told of a fight which ended happily.

One day I went into my garden and one of my freinds came she said 'play to balls with we I said yes ok so we played to balls we were playing misses Brown I was on turnsy when she said I cheated but I did not so I gave her the ball and I said I was not playing and she started a fight with me she started to kick me I kicked her back and she started to cry she whent in to tell her mum her mum said it serves her right for starting it. When we were going to school I gave her some of me sweets.

However, a satisfactory ending to this episode was considerably assisted by the sensible behaviour of the mother involved. The attitudes and actions of adults could have considerable influence, for better or for worse, upon children's reactions. Understanding grown-ups could ensure that quarrels were defused and became minor episodes in childrens' lives; unsympathetic grownups could both create situations in which children got into trouble, and ensure that trouble, once started led to increased bitterness. One 12+ boy remembered a time when he was teased at school for having a short hair-cut, retaliated, and was reprimanded by a teacher. But the situation had effectively been created by a mother who had insisted on having his hair cut to her specifications.

It was a Tuesday afternoon when I arrived home from school when mum said

'Paul I've booked you up for a hair cut at 5.30 today.'

I was only young at the time and I hated having my hair cut. I said to mum 'I dont have to have it to short do I.' Mum said that I would have it as short as she would like it, Anyway when we got there mum said that she wanted it short at the front and back but not to short on the top. And that meant short.

When we came out of the shop I hardly had any hair on my head. When we got home dad was very pleased because he used to like short hair. My brother Jamie started to laugh at it so I wasnt very pleased. Next morning it was time to go to school. When I got there people started to make fun of me and call me names like baldy and skinhead, this got me very angry indeed so I hit one of the boys and he started to cry and went and told a teacher, and I got told off.

Many of the individual answers suggested that particular acts of aggression were specific to certain situations. Further evidence which suggested that some children reacted aggressively in given circumstances, rather than simply being aggressive children, came from comparing answers given by children to all three questions. A 10+ Swindon boy described a physically *aggressive* reaction to provocation in the unhappiness question.

Once andrew . . . made angry he cepet on telling the tecer lies aboat me and calling me names and I cept on geting tolled of so when the teacher went for her coffe I went over to andrew . . . and and hit him in the nose and when the teacer came back from the staf roon and I had to go to the head mitercis and I was toled of.

But the same boy, in the happiness question, recounted the pleasure he got from seeing an injured bird cared for.

there onece was a time when my cusin made me feel Happy. It was when me and him went for a ride and He fond a ingerd Bird and He pikt it up and look it to the neerest farm and the farmer said I will look after Him and we came Bac to him every Day to see How the Bird was geting on.

And in the problem question he recounted how he and a friend rescued another friend who had fallen in a lake.

I was winth my freind over the lake and one of my mates fell in the lake and I did not no wot to do soo me and my mate got in the lake and got this boy out and we took him home.

The only reaction reported more frequently than *aggressive* was *emotional.*

In a number of cases *emotional* reactions were accompanied by other reactions, such as *avoidance* or *aggressive.* Typically, the *emotional* reaction to unhappy situations was crying or loss of temper. Such reactions were often reported by girls. A wide variety of feelings, from fury to fright to grief could give rise to *emotional* reactions. A Swindon girl, in her first year at a comprehensive school, recalled a time when she returned home to find her younger brother savaging a beloved Teddy. In a multiple reaction her first response was *emotional*, her second *aggressive.*

I have still got a teddy from when I was one years old. When I was about six years old my mum had got my teddy from upstairs and gave it to my brother who was one, so he could play with it. My mum did'nt think I would mind because at that time I was at school. When I came home for lunch I saw a dreadful thing he was tearing and biting my teddy, I was crying and very unhappy. I was realy angry with my brother that I started to hit him, he started screaming and my mum came in and asked what the matter was. I showed her my teddy and she said that she would sew it and it would be alright. I have still got that teddy.

Crying, whether intentionally or otherwise, frequently resulted in adult intervention, to help or remonstrate depending on the circumstances. In such cases the *other* in reaction was usually different from the *other* who caused the situation. A 9+ boy from Cardiff told how he was frightened by a thunderstorm, and cried for his mother. In this case the *other* which caused the situation was the thunder (environment), while the *other* in reaction was the mother.

One night when I was in bed when I heard some thunder and it frightened me I was six at the time.
And I cried for my Mother. My Mother came up and said It only the fairys moving thier furniture and so I went to sleep.

A 9+ girl was frightened by her mother. Her reaction was to go to her bedroom (*avoidance*), and to cry (*emotional*). Later, although not as a direct reaction to the same situation, she refused to lay the table for her father.

won day my muther hit me I wos angry ye siad to me if I do it a gen I will get hit with the belt and I siad yes mumy and went up sters and sat dy my windo criin I went don and to woch tele my Father told me to lay the tadle I siad no my Dad hit my I went up stas I lad on my Bed.

A 10+ girl offended her mother, and attempted, in a sequence of reactions, to try to put matters right. First, she cried (*emotional*); next, she reasoned with her mother (*positive*); next, she cried (*emotional*); next she hugged her mother (*emotional*). Nothing, however, worked.

My brother is 15 and my mum has to fight him to do his homework, one day as I was eating some biscuits in the kitchen while my mum was peeling some spuds while she was doing so she was moaning about my brother not doing his homework, suddenly I said 'mum why do you always moan while I'm in the kitchen with you' and that was the worst thing I could have said. (for when-ever mum mum moans I always say the same thing) my mum went upstairs and started to cry and I followed her also crying I went up to stop my mum crying but it was no good. I went in my bedroom and cryed my eyes out and I kept saying 'why did I go and open my big mouth' later on I dryed my eye's and went out onto the landing where I saw my mum coming out of the bath-room I gave her a hug thinking that that would change things but my mum just said 'darling your going to have to learn not to keep telling me off every time I moan or say anything'
I was glad when that day was over.

Sadness and grief, for both humans and animals could cause intense emo-tional reactions. One girl, aged 10+, described her reaction to the illness of her grandmother.

A time when someone made me feel sad was when my mum told me that my nan had to go into hospital and when every time my mum and dad came back from visiting her they sometimes looked upset or worried. I senced something was wrong and sometimes I used to cry about it and even when I was having fun it didn't seem like fun anymore.

Another child, an 11+ boy, wrote of his feelings on the death of his grand-mother.

Someone made me unhappy when my nan died over 4 months ago. And I nearly tried to kill my self.

The death of animals could lead to mourning, and not only in children. An 11+ girl recounted how the death of her dachshund reduced not only herself, but her entire family to tears.

My dog brandy my me feel unhappy and angry he had been very ill my father spent a lot of money on him to pay the vet but that did't matter we all loved him from a puppy he was sausage dog or a dashound. it was on a saturday night

I fell asleep and was taken to bed the following morning I woke up and looked
for brandy and he wasn't there I went into my mothers bedroom and my sister
was there with my mother she told me that my dog had got up on his chair
and just died my father tried to wake him up but he would not my father
started crying so was my family. When she had finished I went to my room
bursting in tears it my me feel very unhappy.

Positive reactions to situations had in common a balanced and common-
sense response to distressing circumstances. A girl on holiday in Germany
helped her brother out of the swimming pool after he had cut his head
(reaction 1) — she also was crying (reaction 2, *emotional*) and later thought
about what had happened (reaction 3, *reflective*).

When we were on holiday in Germany we went to these swimming baths
which had a slide on which ended in quite shallow water. After I had a few
go's I got my brother to go down head first being eighteen at the time. But
when he came up he had gashed his head open. I got him out the pool because
his head was bleeding very badly and dad rushed him to hospital and while he
was there I was crying. It made me so sad to think that I had dared him to do
it and if it had not been for me he would'nt of have to stay two days in
hosiptal and then not aloud in the water. I then relised how much my brother
ment to me because I was so upset by what had happened.

An 8+ girl had to cope with the unsettling situation of her mother losing
her nerve on a ghost train. The child dealt sensibly with this role reversal, but
got little thanks for her actions.

One day we went to barry Island and I went on the goast train and my mother
was hanging on to me and i said dont be frightened mum it is only paintings.
and she said she knows oh i said im sorry. so after we got off and went on the
trampoline.

Another girl, faced with a father frighteningly playing the fool, kept her
head and instructed him to desist.

When somebody made me feel frightend it was when Daddy and Mummy and I
was walking down to our chicken farm in the night when daddy put the torch
on his face it made him look horibble I said turn it of.

Animals could be treated in much the same style as adults. An 8+ girl from
a Chester middle school wrote simply 'I was angry to the cat I am angry.'
Possibly the creatures concerned were duly grateful for not being chased or

hit, while benefiting from being told off.

Children might turn to others, not so much for help but rather as a means of sharing troubles. With adults such reactions might be, depending on the circumstances, *adult referent* or *positive*. Where this happened with toys or pets it was always, in the absence of an animal or object referent category, classified as *positive*. A 9+ girl, frightened in the dark, turned to her teddy bear for solace.

One day when it was halloween night and it was dark outside and I looked out the window and the moon was out and I went to bed lasht [last] and when I was in bed I was scard and so I went to get my bear and went back to sleep again and in the morning I told my mum all about it.

In a more complex situation an 11+ girl wrote about her reaction to her mother's preferential treatment of another girl. She explained matters to her cat, a sensible response in the circumstances. Later her mother exacerbated matters, and the girl's reactions became more drastic.

My mother has an anoying habit she invites my wroste enemy out with us to the beach, she ducked me under the water and I can't swim propally and put sand in my sandwitches, then my mother bought some sweets a huge box and offered her some, she did'nt just take one but 10 of the best, when mum and dad had taken a few the box came to me I took 3 and mum told me to give the rest to Suzanne this made me mad, I never gotanything off her so why should she get all these things, it would have been better if she was a friend, but she was'nt, when we arrived home she toddled off without even a thankyou, I'd had enough, I explained how I felt to my cat, that somehow calms me down, he's not like parents who but in all the time, being an only child I have no brothers to explean to nor sisters, so the cats the perfect victem, after my calming down my temper was roused again, by me hearing her say was'nt she a sweet little girl, as a resalt of this a went on a hunger strike, then I refused to sleep and got my clothes dressed and got out my bike and started peddaling round the block I came in exusted and was soon asleep, as a result of this I was very, very, tired in the morning.

More complex situations at times called for reactions which needed more than common sense and a conventional approach; a capacity to think for oneself was sometimes required. *Autonomous* reactions might need the intelligent practice of social skills. A 10+ boy from a Chester middle school reacted to trouble over the selection of a football team, (a matter in which he felt the captain had been unfair), by arguing, successfully, with the captain to change his mind.

I was angry when Peter left Gary and Graham out of our football team because he fell out with Graham and thought Gary was not good enough. So I convinced him to make friends with Graham and I convinced him that Gary was good enough and they both got back into our football team.

A 9+ girl, frightened by her cousins, reacted by thinking out and putting into practice an appropriate retaliation.

My cousins made me angry when I came out of the girls loos on the caravan site. They crept up on me and made me frightend and angry. It was a dark night and so I took their torch away and they had to find their own way back.

A 10+ boy was faced, in company with a friend, by the fear that a stranger was upstairs. (The boys were alone in the house.) In a multiple reaction he reassured his friend that nobody was there (reaction 1, *positive*); then he proved it to him by taking him to look up the stairs (reaction 2, *autonomous*); next, having heard something, he collected a weapon (reaction 3, *aggressive*).

Sometime last year I was all by myself apart from my next door neighbor Terry it was nine o'clock when my mother and father went out to a Dance. And they were not coming back intill about 1 o'clock. We sat down and started to watch the T.V. Then around about Ten o'clock a film started it was about a boy and a woman who had been murdered one night. Suddenly Terry turned and said did you here that, I said here what he said that noise comming from upstairs. I said there nobody up there. He said yes there is. I proved it to him by opening the door and looking up the stairs. Then I started to here something we went into the living room and shut the door then we both got something we could hurt the person with if he came in the room. But soon after we found out it was the boiler from upstairs.

Reactions in situations of deep emotion could also reveal an originality in children which transcended what might normally have been expected. A 9+ girl wrote about the time when her grandfather died. She told her grandmother how sorry she was (1st reaction, *positive*); and later she and her sister both gave their grandmother money which had been given to them, presumably to cheer them up (2nd reaction, *autonomous*).

The most unhappiest thing that any body had every said to me was when my grand-dad was dead. He died of 65 years of age in the hospital of a heart a tack. All my relations were at my nans house and I had to go to my Antie Jones house while my relation went to the hospital. That is the night when he died. When they had been to the hospital they all went to my nans house to keep her company. My dad came to collect me and I said good by to my cousins and I went to my nans. On the way home to my nans my dad told me that he was dead. When I got to my nans I went to my nan and said that I was sorry for her. When it was time to go home my relations all gave me and my sister some money and all the money we got we gave it to my nan. And that was the death of Mr Finch my mums dad.

Reflective reactions occurred as a rule either when an immediate reaction was not appropriate or not possible, but the child concerned decided that, when appropriate, he or she would react specifically; or when, after reflecting on a situation which had occurred, a child decided on a general rule to be followed if similar circumstances should arise again; alternatively, a child might reflect very quickly before taking action in circumstances which required an immediate response.

A 10+ girl recalled a time when, having got into trouble (unspecified), she thought about the situation, and decided that the best thing to do was apologize, which she duly did (second reaction, *positive*).

This is a short piece of writing of how I felt unhappy and frightened. Well one sunny day, I was only a little girl at the time, I got myself in serious trouble, everyone started picking on me, and I got all the blame.
As a result I got very depressed and went away, and thought of how miserable I looked. When I finished thinking of the great big trouble I caused. I went and apologised.

Children could react very angrily if they felt that generous behaviour by themselves to peers, which they considered should have been reciprocated, or which involved an actual promise of reciprocation, was not in fact reciprocated. A 10+ London girl was furious in such circumstances, and presumably intended – as a result of her reflections – to act hostilely to the girl whom she considered had swindled her.

It was a time when a girl made me feel angry because I made a skirt and it was to tight for me so she whated it so I gave it to her it costs $18\frac{1}{2}$p and I said she could have it for 4p so she gave me four pence. Then the other day she said she would bring me something. Then the next day she did not bring any thing. From then I think is a lier, cheat and a theive and she can pis off.

Principles to guide future action were deduced from various types of situation. A Swindon boy in his first year at comprehensive decided never to buy presents for anybody (his *reflective* reaction followed an *avoidance* reaction).

this year my brother was talking to my mum and I over herd them. my mum
had promist me a football I herd my mum say that I will not get a foot ball
for being nortey so I ran upstairs but I did not here what else she said after
that, and I said to my self I will never by a nover present for anybody.

Another child, who concluded a series of reactions by reflection was a girl
in severe trouble with her father, who slapped her for being naughty. She
screamed (*emotional*), she ran away (*avoidance*), and she decided she would
not misbehave again (*reflective*).

The person who made unhappy and sad was my father. The thing was when I
told of and was about to get slaped. I was very soory I did somthing wrong. It
was tierbile because I was afraid of geting slaped. When I did I screamed and
run in and out of rooms when I did this I also said please don't hit me. When
I had cooled down I said to my self, (but did not say it out loud) that did
teach me a lesson not to do wrong things like that again. After I begun to sob
and I nearly stared to cry again. but I did not.

A 10+ girl had her horse given away, against her wishes, by her mother.
She decided that she had felt so upset that she should never again commit
herself emotionally so deeply to an animal, and thus run the risk of being
similarly hurt.

The time when somebody made me feel very unhappy was when my mum sold
dusty. What was worse was that I had to lead him into the horse-box and he
reared and reared. Mum siad she sold him because I had grown out of him But
in a book it said that shetlands can tack a man his wife and there luggage 40
miles. that saturday coming he went to a carnival he had a boy dressed up as
an Indian on his back he won first prize. I will never for get him. The result
was I try not to like an animal to much if I know they mite have to go.

At times children reflected, either by working a reaction out for themselves
or by referring to rules, before reacting to a situation which required some sort
of immediate response. One West Bromwich boy was approached by a strange
man. Before deciding what to do he reflected upon how his mother had told
him to behave in such circumstances. Consequently (reaction 2, *positive*) he
politely refused the stranger's offer. This case illustrates clearly how useful
rules can be to children, and how sensibly they can apply them in difficult
situations.

this is a time when somewone made me frightend and angry. Becaus oneday I
was going a walk and a very strange man came to me he ask me if I wanted to

go in his car to go cadding for him on the golf coarse I thought back to wen my mother had told me never never go with a stranger even if he offers me enething. So I sed no thank you an went a walk and I will never never talk or go whith a stranger.

Of reactions in which others were directly referred to, reference to adults was considerably more common than reference to peers. This was because such references were usually made to obtain help and adults were, in general, seen as more likely to be effective in providing assistance than children.

Young children could go to considerable lengths to seek adult, and particularly parental assistance. An 8+ girl reported running home from school because she had no-one to play with.

I was unhappy because I had no friends and no people to play with and went it playtime I sat on a bench and I did it time and time agan and was so unhappy I run home from school at playtime and wood not like lot of school dinner because there was Jelly for pupping and people became my friends.

A 9+ girl recalled running home because of the unpleasant behaviour of her teacher.

I was in the last year in the infants and ther was a hordel ticher [horrible teacher] her name was Miss . . . I ran out of the school to my Mum she sent me Back Miss . . . did not like me a all she pall the boy ers [pulled the boys' ears] put sellertap over ower mouth and put us in the bin.

A 10+ girl from a Chester middle school wrote about her reactions when she found the boy next door assaulting her beloved teddy bear. She wanted to hit him (*aggressive*); she cried (*emotional*); she ran indoors and told her mother (*adult referent*), who sorted things out. In each reaction the *other* was different – in the first the boy, in the second nobody, in the third the mother.

I was unhappy once when Steven . . . (next door) had a big cane and he poked Ian (My teddy Bear) with it and he split down the middle I got Ian out of the pram and I saw he was split I started crying and I ran in and told my mum she said she would sew him. I felt angry and felt like bitting him because he is the oldest thing I've got (He is 9 years old this Christmas) I had him when I was one and now I am 10, He as only got one small hole behind his ear (He is white). I love him as much as my mum. (He sleeps with me at night).

Although adults were often referred to for help, they did not always provide it. A 10+ boy was not believed by his father, when he told him of his brother's breaking his loudspeaker. The boy was angry that the support he expected was not forthcoming.

I was angry when I came home from shopping one day and Keith my brother had put his hand through my loud speaker cone that runs of my radio and broke it. I did not find out untill a day after when I told dad he din not believe me and said that I must of done it. That made me made.

A girl, who went to her mother when her sister had an accident was blamed for what had happened, and became very upset.

On Friday my sister had red spots on her face. and she looked ugly and it frightened me becaus I though she was nerel dad, and my mum called the Docker. and he said it is not measles. and I wos very glad. and when the Docker want she had mor spots on her face and I came mor frightened then I was befor. and then she went into the Kickin and the budud [cupboard] wor open. and she bumtuer her head. and she want white as a Goster and I wors very very frightened and I want up stare and my sister folad me and she nele fall down the stare and band her had and I want and told my mum and she wos very angry and I want up stay and I fall on the bed and I started to cry.

When necessary, many children were quite prepared to go to the relevant authorities for help. A 9+ boy, approached by a man, refused (*positive*) and told the park keeper (*adult referent*).

On day I was over the park when a man started to follow me. And asked me if I wanted a rid in his car. But I said no and warked off and told the parky. And he found the police. And the policmen came but when they got to the bench he was not there. So the policeman said go home and tell your mother and father. So I told my mum and Dad. And they said if you see him again tell me and we will go to the police. so I said yes I will.
    And the next day I seen him so I told my mum and she called the police. And they cot him and as a result I had to go to court but on the way to the bus stop we mist the bus so we walked there.

A girl, chased with her friends by a man, ran away (*avoidance, other*: the stranger), and told the police (*adult referent, other*: adult in authority).

One days I was walking down the road when I met a girl who I knew she said to me there is a man with a stick who has been running after us for no reason. I had some friends with me we all felt frightened because we saw the man coming down the road with the stick in his hand we all heard him say hay you lot. Then we began to run very very fast down the road till we reached home he wasn't there any more now. As a result I told the police.

Non-active reactions shared the common characteristic that children appeared to take no action in response to a situation. However, such non-action could result from a variety of motives. It could, for example, be the outcome simply of passivity. An 11+ girl, who knew her knitting pattern had been taken by another girl, said nothing about it — even when blamed by her teacher. The teacher in this case put to right any trouble she might have caused by apologizing to her for having wrongly blamed her. Such readiness by teachers not to stand on their dignity occurred quite frequently, and usually succeeded in improving the classroom atmosphere.

In school I was knitting a bunny so was Mandy my arch enemy. I was beating her and mine was'nt too bad but hers UGG. She knew this and was jealous and she was more popular than me so she turned everyone against me then she stole my knitting pattern. That was IT. My friend Kay told me about it. My needlework teacher went mad with me she thought I had lost it in the end Mandy turned up with it by mistake. Then the needlework teacher told Mandy off for stealing and apoligized to me, And settled the matter by getting another pattern and then we were friends for once although it made me very cross.

Non-activity might be a result of intentional restraint, the outcome of a desire not to exacerbate a difficult situation. A boy in his first year at a Nottingham comprehensive wrote about how he avoided reacting to provocation and becoming involved in a fight.

I was playing foot ball when one of my frends tript me up and kiket me this made me angrey. But as a result I left it at that and did not carry on becaus things would only get worse.

Another boy, 8+ from a Newcastle first school was provoked by his sister. He contemplated aggression (*reflective* reaction, *other*: sister), but decided to restrain himself (*non-active* reaction, *other*: sister). His reasons for non-activity were not given, but were possibly fear of consequent trouble, or a dislike of fights and tears.

Along time ago I was makeing my jigsaw, when my sister got a piece of my jigsaw and she snaped it and I was very very angry and I had a good mind to hit her on the arm but I did no do it.

Non-activity might be a reaction to being involved in an accident (frequently accompanied by an *emotional* reaction). In such circumstances children might be non-active either because they were physically incapable of taking action, or because they did not know what to do. As a rule other children or adults, familiar or unfamiliar, would come to their aid. An 8+ girl cracked her head open, while playing, and a stranger, 'a black man' came to her aid.

Once I was walking along the wall on my way to the park all alone a brick wall it was and some people walked past me and some more children were walking along the wall but they had there mother with them and they went away now and I sudenley sliped and split my head alittle and a black man saw me and he phone the ploice ambelance then he picked me up and put me on to the benck until they came and they took me to hospital and aksed me my phone number just be for I fanted and they rung my mother up when she didnt go to work and she came to see me.

Non-activity included not only situations in which outside circumstances accidentally made it difficult for children to offer active reactions, but also situations in which children themselves intentionally arranged circumstances so that they became non-active. Some of such reactions could well be cate-gorized as psychosomatic. A 10+ girl from a Hertfordshire middle school was very upset when her friends said that her party was horrible (due to her younger brother's misbehaviour). She became ill, making the causal connection between her brother's naughtiness and her suffering explicit.

One day I was very happy and I was playing with my friends. In the after noon they came to my party when I was 5 years old I had 6 of my friends come. But my brothers were really horrible when we were playing games they always spoilt it. When all my friends home I cryed. my said to me your brothers are younger than you and they can't help it. But the next day wen I went to school my friends were saying how horrible the party was so when lunch come I went home and I really become ill mum put me to bed and phoned the doctor up and when he come up he said I was ill because I be very sad and children had be shouting at me and that I was going a bit death and I had trouble with my ears. So I had to go into hospital and it was really horrible of my brothers and I was very unhappy. but after I came out every body was kind to me after all that time.

More briefly, a 12+ boy from a Cambridge comprehensive school explained that, as a result of not getting his way in a football game, he was injured.

When I am forst into somfink when I wanted to go in gole but they would not let me. So I got ingerd in a fue minits.

17 Problem situations—reactions

In a number of answers concerning problems children described the situation, and then immediately defined their reaction without explicitly stating the problem. However, since the answers were given in response to a question which required description of a time when children were not sure what to do, it is assumed in such cases that the problem was how to react to the situation described.

Avoidance reactions were more frequently reported than *aggressive* reactions. An 8+ girl described a situation in which her friends were cruel, and she ran away: (this was an instance in which her problem was not explicitly defined, although obviously it was what to do when her friends were unpleasant). The girl also cried (second reaction *emotional*), and, as happened to other children, her crying was interpreted as an appeal for help. A friendly stranger (*other* in reaction) helped to cheer her up.

One day I went out with six of my frendes and ther names Carol Debbe and so on we went to the prak and carol and Debbie war croll so I ran a uwa a I was friunt and I was criing but they was a lady with a blak dres on a red hair and she seid wot is ur nemes and I said Debbie she said Bebbie is a prity name so I seid wot is your name she seid carol. and I said that is a prety name to.

Avoidance could be the only sensible reaction. A self-possessed 10+ girl found herself and a friend confronted by some decidedly unfriendly horses.

One day last year My friend and I went for a walk to the woods, We decided to go to the place where horses were when we got there the horses were in the open bit of land my friend had her dog with her, When we got there the horses started to come over to us her dog was very frightened when the horses came they started to get very nasty so we ran but I told her not to cause the horses were chasing us so we stopped but the horses were bucking And I didn't no what to do In the end we ran up a hill and hid in a big bush until the horses went away When they did we went home.

An 11+ boy found himself, like many another before him, caught red-handed stealing apples. He could have tried to explain or apologize, but discretion proved the better part of moral valour.

Table 29   Frequency of categories of reaction to problem situations

Reaction category	Reactions First	% of *	Second	% of **	Third	% of ‡
Non-active	260	9·6	133	10·0	45	8·7
Adult referent	325	12·0	193	14·4	64	12·3
Peer referent	422	15·6	117	8·8	29	5·6
Aggressive	45	1·7	21	1·6	10	1·9
Avoidance	165	6·1	83	6·2	49	9·5
Positive	733	27·1	503	37·7	218	42·1
Autonomous	250	9·2	140	10·5	57	11·0
Reflective	421	15·5	101	7·6	31	6·0
Emotional	83	3·1	44	3·3	15	2·9
TOTALS	2704*	99·9	1335**	100·1	518‡	100·0

One day I was with David . . . and John . . .. David . . . did'nt have a bike so I gave him a lift on mine. We went to a place where there had been some lovely apples the year before. We climbed on the fence we saw the owners of the house were out. We also saw that all the apples had gone. Then this man who was whizzing along the road suddenly he stopped and started to reverse. He was looking at us, so we presumed he was the owner of the house. We scarped! We went down this gravel lane. David . . . jumped off John . . .'s bike. Dave and me thought the man had given up, but he came through the other entrance. We cycled up to a big estate and got on the pavement. The man chased us half way through the estate, then he lost us. When we knew he had given up the first thing we said was, phew!

Unpopular or difficult school work could cause problems. An 8+ Swindon girl was set to do 'six a day' (presumably sums) but did not want to. She avoided it, first by doing something else, and secondly by messing about.

about a muth a go in school my teacher told me to do 6 a day and I did not wont to do it so when my teacher whent for her cofey I stoped working and I looked at my reading book and when my teacher came back it was Pe time and when we came back I hat to do 6 a day and I mut a rond [mucked around] I I hat to stay in when we had play.

Table 30 Frequency of others in first reactions to problem situations

Other group	Other		No.	% of others
Parents	Mother		131	4·8
	Father		54	2·0
	Mother and father		27	1·0
	Parent		1	0·04
		TOTALS	**213**	**7·9**
Siblings	Sibling(s) same sex		72	2·7
	Sibling(s) other sex		43	1·6
	Siblings, both sexes		1	0·04
		TOTALS	**116**	**4·3**
Relations	Relation(s)		81	3·0
	Special close relation(s)		4	0·1
	Family group		48	1·8
		TOTALS	**133**	**4·9**
Adults not close family members	Teacher(s)		92	3·4
	Unknown, unspecified adult(s)		127	4·7
	Adult(s) in authority		91	3·4
	Friend(s), neighbour(s)		55	2·0
		TOTALS	**365**	**13·5**
Children not close family members	Known child(ren) or cousin(s)		173	6·4
	Child friend(s)		814	30·1
	Unknown, unspecified child(ren)		78	2·9
		TOTALS	**1065**	**39·3**
Supernatural, fictitious & well known figures	Fictitious figure		1	0·04
	Public figure		6	0·2
	Religious figure, God		1	0·04
	Spirits, ghosts		0	0·0
		TOTALS	**8**	**0·3**
Creatures, objects &	Object(s)		213	7·9
	Living creature(s)		68	2·5

environment	Something		5	0·2
	Environment		115	4·2
		TOTALS	**401**	**14·8**
Miscellaneous	Somebody (s & pl)		60	2·2
	No-one, myself		264	9·7
	Activity group		82	3·0
		TOTALS	**406**	**15·0**
		OVERALL TOTALS	2707	100·0

Percentages have been rounded.

Aggressive reactions were the least frequently reported of all categories of response to problems. On occasion children, failing to get their way or being angry for other reasons, were faced with a problem of how to express their feelings. A 10+ boy remembered a time when he decided to vent his anger on a wash bowl, (*other* — object).

one day last year some time I was in a mood with my brother becuse he was sposed to have his wash frist, so this is how it happend my mum brout some hot water up in a bowal and I was so in a bad mood I got the bowal a hit it a gante the door and made a big crack it is still there new.

A girl was reduced to impotent beating of a bed in which she found an unsatisfactory solution, but the best she could manage.

It was when I was so angry I didn't know what to do I was thumping the bed like anything I just didn't know what to do I did it my hardest but I didn't do it hard enough I was so angry.

The most frequent category of reaction was *positive*. Positive reactions included those in which children made explicit references to known moral and social norms, usually of the adult world; but occasionally, in the case of older children, of the world of their peers. A 10+ girl refused to assist in attacking another girl because she felt that her membership of the Guide movement militated against such behaviour.

When we (me and my freind) were going for a walk and this girl asked me to help beat up someone else because she had broken freinds at school. I said no because Im a guide.

Another 8+ girl found herself in a quandary because her parents were not available to offer advice. She found herself doubtful whether to behave as her friends expected her to, or as she thought her parents would expect her to. Finally she reacted by reference to her parents, although trying to hide the fact from her friends.

When I was with my friends they asked me to go swimming with them only for half an hour I could not swim and I did not know what to do because my parents were out so I did not know wheather I should go or not go. I had the key round my neck at the end I said to my friends shall I go but I never.

In some instances children reacted to problems in accordance with adult norms, and by seeking adult support for their actions. Two 9+ girls, in a multiple reaction to two other girls fighting at school first watched (*non-active*), second went away (*avoidance*), third returned and stopped the fight (*positive*) and last took the offenders to their teacher (*adult referent*).

one day at school Sally and Sonia had a fight me and my friend was watching it. I did not no what to do so I watched. then I we a way with my friend. then I came back and I stop the fight I told Sonia to mrs zoher and Maxine told Sally to mrs zoher.

Positive reactions to etiquette problems typically involved attempting to act in conformity with the expectations of the person or group in whose company children found themselves. A 9+ boy, staying with his grandmother, found himself having to deal with visitors. First he offered them a cup of tea (first *positive* reaction), then — this having been rejected — he settled down to occupy himself quietly (second *positive* reaction).

One day when I was down my Nanas I didnt have anything to do because she had visotors and I had to stay in the same room and talk then I thought that they would like a cup of tea but they didnt then I saw a pen knife and I decided to make a calender so I cut the front and made one.

A 9+ boy did not know what to do at a party, because he knew no-one there except one friend. So he tried to look and act in the same way as all the other children.

The last time I was with someone was when I went to my friends party. The only person I knew was my I friend first me and my friend had some thing to eat and then some other people came I did not know what to do because

their was know one else but me and my friend. We did not know what to do so
we just joined in the games and looked happy. Then we played postmans
knock then I had to go out of the room and my friend started to laugh because
he had not been out yet. Then we started to join in with the fun after that we
play squeek piggy squeek and I was third one out. Then we played spin the
plate and I was one of the last to get out.
Then I joined in the fun and was happy.

Problems of how to occupy oneself could be exacerbated by the arrival of
visitors. One child, a 9+ girl, tried a sequence of reactions in such a situation.
She looked for something to read (*positive*); she tried sitting with the visitors
(*positive*); she tried talking to her mother (*positive*); she tried asking her
mother what to do (*adult referent*).

One day my mum had some visitors and I didnt know what to do. So I went
into my bedroom to see if I could read or something but I had red all my books
and I did'nt feel like doing any thing I tryed to sit quitly in lounge while they
talk but that was boring so I started talking to mum but when I had finished
talking about somthing then I said to my mum what can I do and she said go
and play with your toys but I said back to her I dont want to so she said go
and play with your friend so I went to my friend and I knocked but she was'nt
in I told mum and she said just go and find something to do so I went into the
garage and I found a box and I made it into a slide for my dolls.

Children were occasionally faced with very unusual social situations. To
these they might react partly instinctively, partly in accordance with social
norms. A 12+ girl was staying away from home, when news of a death in the
family arrived. Her first reaction, to comfort, was *positive*; her second, to
withdraw (*avoidance*), was perhaps the best thing to do in the circumstances.

A time I have not been sure what to do was when I was at my cousins and the
word came that their grandfather (opposite side of the family) died. I honestly
did not know what to do, it was very difficult. First I tried to comfort them
then went downstairs to wait until they had calmed down.

At times children found themselves in circumstances where, instead of
themselves needing help from adults, the positions were reversed. An 8+ girl
on an outing found that her teacher had forgotten her sandwiches. The child
reacted positively.

One day when I came home from school I was so excited. Why? Because I was
going to Crystal Palace and whats more the coucil was paying for me and some

other children as well. So my mummy said when are you going tomrowo. Well said my mummy you'd better go and buy some bread and some ham and some sweets that you are aloud to bring on the jouney. Soon I came back and I had brought some ham, bread, Crisps and some drinks (in plastic bottles). Not long from then my daddy came home and I shouted dad—dad I am going to Crystal Palace tommrow and the cousils is paying for me and some other children as well.

Soon tommrow came and the coach came to the school. But when we got there are teacher had forgotten her sand whiches so I gave her some of mine. And I hope you people can arange for class 6 in Saulsbury school to go some were nice.

Problems in informal play situations frequently resolved themselves into questions of how children should occupy themselves and typically were resolved positively by finding some pastime acceptable to both adult and child norms. However, other sorts of problem, requiring a different style of reaction some-times occurred when children were at play. In particular, other, unknown, children might get into difficulties and need help. A 9+ boy from a Nottingham Junior School encountered a child with a broken toy. He did his best to put matters right.

When I was playing with my freinds and a boy came along he was runing in his heand he had a toy and as he past me I axadentley knokt him and He dropt His Toy The Toy Bkock and the Boy started crying I didunt now wot to do I picked the toy up for Him and I promist Him I wood mend it for Him. so He gave me the Toy I I walked away not nowing wot to do when I got home I asked my Dad if He wood mend it.

A positive, helpful reaction was also the response of a girl 12+ who noticed that some people near her were in difficulties over harnessing a horse.

I was on a holiday in Wales in a romany caravan. I had been once before and the horse that we had had that time we had asked for again. I had just fetched her in from the field and I was just about to harness her up when I realised that I was being watched. The people who had left the base nearly the same time as my family did not know how to put their horses harness on. They were trying to copy me but they were getting in an awful mess because my horse was wearing my grandfathers carthorse harness which was very different from their harness. I thought I should go and help them so I did. I could not get their harness out of the tangle though so I called my grandfather over to do it.

Sometimes the nature of circumstances made it difficult, or virtually impossible, to apply ready made rules or norms to the solving of problems;

in such cases children could show a capacity to work out solutions independently for themselves. Such *autonomous* reactions at times revealed considerable resourcefulness and ingenuity.

The fact that autonomous behaviour is not necessarily in accordance with prevailing social morality was illustrated by a number of answers. One 9+ boy, for example, had to solve the problem of how to retrieve a lost ball; his solution was effective, but did not show respect for property.

When I was down my nans I was playing with my freind Gerald I was playing hide and seek then we started to play football then the ball went over a very big hedge then Gerald said will I go over there to get it but I was not sure how to get it then I went in the house and got my sheaths nife then I stood on a thin brans and cut my way through the hedge then I went into the garden but first I could not find it but then I saw it then I picked it up and went back through the hole in the hege.

Another 9+ year old, provoked by insensitive relations, exacted revenge as if he had never encountered the New Testament morality; 'a tooth for a tooth' appeared to be his philosophy.

A time in my life when I felt I was a fool was when fell flat on my face in front of some realitvas they all burst out lauing I did not no what to say in the end I went out the room subbely I had an ibie [idea] I put a bit of wood by the door then I ran in the room and my unkcle ran after me I jumped ofer the wood but my unkcle never and he fell over it I burst out lauing.

A 10+ boy recalled a party where insufficient occupation was provided. The problem of what to do was solved by those present with a plan which occupied them all, showed a masterly appreciation of tactics and strategy, and no doubt caused discomfort to the person who was to blame in the first place for failing to provide something to do. However, it cannot be claimed that the children's solution would have been acceptable to the prevailing morality.

Last year I went to somebodys party after a couple of games we didnt no what to do so we all went in a corner and we made a plan of the house so we could spy on Johns Mother then John showed us all the hideing places and gave us a water piston So when his mother was looking for us she would go in the rooms and we could get out of are hideing places and skwert water at her.

On the other hand a number of children exercised their judgement in order to help others. A 12+ girl recalled an incident many years in the past.

When I was 4 my brother broke his leg. The day he came back from hospital I was in bed with a fever. Mum had to go next door for something and she said she woulden't be long. Trev thats my brother thought he'd be clever and go downstairs. On the way down he fell and I could hear his cries of agony. I just could'ent think what to do. I tried calling for help but that did'ent work. So I pulled myself up to the window it was already open. I droped the nearest thing to me out of the window. It broke on the pavement below. Mum looked round and came in. Trev had to go back to hospital.

Sometimes children had to work a difficulty out for themselves, because their problem arose from breaking adult rules (advertently or not), and they were afraid to go for help. In some cases children rose to the challenge, and all worked out for the best — the children possibly having benefited from having to think for themselves. But there was always the possibility that they could not cope, and might get into serious difficulties. A 9+ girl found herself, through being careless in her father's garage, in a position where her friend was in a predicament, and she dared not go to her father. Fortunately, things turned out all right, but there might have been an unpleasant accident as a result of *autonomous* rescue work.

One day I went out with a friend of mine and we went in to my dads garage and I forgot to tell my friend about a hole in the floor and befor I could tell her she fell down It I did not no how to get her out I could not ask my dad because he would be very cross. Then I found a rope and I lowerd the rope down my friend caugh hold of it and I pulled her up.

Adult policy, preoccupation, lack of awareness or overwork could lead to children being left to help themselves when they might have preferred to be assisted. A 12+ middle school boy explained how at times he had to try and find his own solutions in class work.

When I am in class sometimes I don't understand how to do things so I try to work it out if I couldn't I ask the teacher, and sometimes teachers don't explain work enough.

A number of children were faced with problems which primarily concerned their own safety. One 9+ boy lost himself at a fair.

One time I was alone except for lots of people all around me when I was lost at a fair and i did not know what to do. So I thought and I thought until I came up with an idea I asked a person who was saying over a migaphone roll up roll up come and see the strongest man on earth. So I asked him to broadcast over a megaphone lost boy his name his Simon . . . will his parents please come and collect him from the strongest man on earth show. I waited there and waited and waited until they came. Finally they came and told me where have you been and I said Ive only been looking round the fair ground. They said I should not have wondered off.

Another boy, aged 12+ in his last year at a middle school, found himself in danger of losing his way on a scouting exercise.

Our Scout group had been to Europe camping but some of us younger ones were not allowed to go, so we went camping near Salisbury.
One of the tests we had to pass was make a 6 mile hike with a friend of your own age. I picked a sensible boy who was a year younger than myself. We set of with a map and compass and followed the footpaths till we came to a road. We crossed the road and walked on down the footpath until Ashley and I came to the top of a hill, here the footpath petered out. We wondered what to do, we looked at the map and we were certain we were in the right place, after a discussion I said lets use the compass. So we set the compass and following the bearing to the right place, about 3 miles away. We discovered we were the only pair to use the correct route.

Social problems could confront children with dilemmas which ranged from the relatively trivial to the very serious. Peers who made conflicting or unwelcome demands were one source of difficulty. A 12+ boy had to reconcile the requirements of two of his friends who were mutually antagonistic.

I was with a friend when another freind came they both did not like each other. And I liked them both they said they whould leave if I did not go with them I did not disapiont any off them I made them make friends.

A less moral solution to a problem posed by an unfortunately timed and unwelcome invitation from another girl was found by an 11+ girl in her first year at a comprehensive.

Our Gang have one member which I just can't get along with I was walking along the university wood when she came up to me and started talking. She is one of the most unusual people I've ever met she talks about some silly things and asked me whether I would go to disco with her as it was I had all ready been asked out to the flics with Gareth Nigel and Louise but I did'nt want her to know. I was'nt at all sure what to do so I ended up lying which I did'nt like at all I said I was going to wash my hair.

Children could become involved in the conflicts of adults. A 10+ girl discovered that her divorced father did not intend to return her and her sister, after a holiday, to their mother. The girl's solution to this problem, (since she wanted to return to her mother) was resourceful, and it worked.

When I was on holiday with my real dad, we enjoyed our sels until he told us he was not going to take us home. My sister and I did not know what to do. The next day I had thought of what to do. Lynne was to phone grandma up and ask grandma to tell mummy or Colin my step father to come and fetch us. While my sister was in the phone box I looked out for daddy or any other of his family. When we had phoned we went back in doors, and acted if nothing had happend. After tea I got ready to go to bingo with daddy and Margret. When I was ready mummy and Colin appeared on the door step to take us home. Mummy had left my other sisters and brother at home.

If children considered themselves to be in the right, they were quite capable of explaining the reason for their actions. An 11+ boy stood his ground when approached by an irate workman.

One day when I was sheltering in a not yet built house, when the rian was pouring down we saw a workman come running in all my friends ran but I stayed because I new we haden't don any thing wrong so he grabed hold of me and asked me what I was doing I told him and he siad I could go.

Children also might decide to justify behaviour which had irritated adults, or others, rather than simply taking flight or fetching someone else to help. An 8+ boy told an unknown man how it had come about that he and his friends had broken the man's window.

One day I was with 5 boys. We were walking home and one of them throw a stone at me I duck and the stone hit a window I man came out. The 4 boys run I was not sure wether to run to to say how did it.
I did make up my mind I stayed a told the man the story I he let me go I did not go home that way again nor go home with the 4 boys.

The exercise of independent judgement by children took place, at times, in strange circumstances. One 8+ boy in London was playing with friends on a railway line. He decided that to jump on the rails immediately after a train passed would be dangerous, since the lines would be hot; he did not jump. A friend who did tripped over and hit his head. Of course the boy was wrong both about why it was dangerous to jump on lines, and about the inferred reason for his friend's mishap. But he had, in his own convoluted and mistaken fashion, been exercising his own judgement and acting accordingly.

One day I was playing foot ball. and we got bored. So my friends said why dont we play on the rails. So I did. and a train come we jump of the rails. and then my frends said do it again. I thought that the rails could be hot becouse a train went by but my friends said they would I thought and said it would be dangerous and I said no and they went on the rails and one fell a bashed he head on the rails and we help him up and I said it was his fort and he said he would never go on the rails again.

When children *reflected* on their problems they might do so on their own, or in discussion with others. An 11+ boy ran away from home, and then considered his predicament.

ones I ofend tried to run away frome home becouse of geting told of ones I ran out of the house and ran down the canel I felt mad and angree but I wasen't quite sure what to do. I said to my self I must go back and a pologenisd so I did.

A 10+ boy, with a friend, saw smoke coming from a building: the problem was, was there a fire? The two reflected on the matter, and eventually decided there was. Their next reaction (*positive*) was to go to the police (*other* adult in authority). Having reached the police station, they hesitated because of un-familiarity with such places. This suggests that children's willingness to help when there is trouble could be inhibited through lack of contact with authorities who have to deal with emergencies such as fire and accident.

As we pass the tolots [toilets] there was all smok come in out of the Lades so we stead there thinking if it could be a fire at last we made up our mind and went as fast as we could to the police Staiton round the coner. Both of us had not been in the police station before so we stop out side and thort of a few seconds and a other boy on bike came up and went in font and tooked the police and there phone for the engine. So we wash [watched] the fire be put out.

A 9+ girl, together with a number of friends discussed how money which they had saved should be spent. The *reflective* discussion offers an example of how children amongst themselves could practice techniques of democratic decision taking. (Having reached a decision to follow the suggestion of one of the girls, it was duly put into practice. Consequently, for the child writing the answer the second reaction was *positive,* acting according to norms agreed by the group.)

One day my friend Jeani called for me we went to call on 'Jane, Amanda, Lucy, Ann and Anthea.' This was our Gang. We went to our usual 'Gang hut'

and had a 'meeting'. We all put 10p into the tin we kept. 'Now' said Anthea
we shall see how much we have got we have been saving for Ages. Crums
£5.99½ said Lucy what shall we do with it all. I know lets go to Barry said
Jeani. No I said we shoudent well we cant, you know what our parents woud
say. I know what theyd do muttered Ann. Cissys Cissys said Jeani bet your
scarrd enyway I'm going. It our money as much as yours said Amanda. I know
what we'll do said Ann listen we whot [want] a proper gang hut all we have
now is blankets hung up by sticks lets get a small toy wendy house we could
have that with money left over right. We got it and it was much better than
Barry.

Non-active reactions were explained by a variety of motives. Prudence, for
example, could lead children to hold their peace. A 10+ boy on an outing
with his aunt and uncle decided to stay silent for fear of making a *faux pas.*

not long ago my uncle and anty took me out for a ride up the forest of dean
and you now how it feels your not sure what to do you might do something
rong or you might say something rong. So I cept quite.

Children could become confused by being offered too great a range of
choices and end up by deciding to do nothing as happened to one 9+ girl.

On a day I think it was a Thursday I was not sure what to do becuse my
techer said do enything and I had to much to finish so I did nuthing intill my
teacher told us what to do.

Inevitably, too, children might find themselves rendered inarticulate and
inactive through shyness — like a 9+ boy from a Chester middle school.

I was with my friend in his house and his mum said to me what do you want
for your tea and I was nervous to say and when I was going to get my coat I
was nervous.

Failure to resolve a problem, such as the perennial difficulty of finding
something to do, could likewise result in inactivity. However, bored children
sometimes attracted benevolent attention, and at times from unexpected
quarters. The girl friend of an elder brother saved a 10+ boy and his friend
from a tedious afternoon.

Last summer when Nigel Harris my friend came up to play he had had his
dinner (when)•before he came up but we hadn't so he watched the horse
racing. When I had finished I went in the living room to watch telly with him
after about an hour my brothers girl friend came up and Nigel and I didn't

know what to do we were just board then Adrians girls friend came out and
had a game of football with us she went in goal and Nigel and I tried to get
the ball in with the calfs we were playing for about half an hour and then Nigel
past the ball to me and I kicked it over into the calfs and we didn't go in
because the calfs would kick. When dad feed them he threw it out.

Reference to adults was not uncommon, especially for help in overcoming
difficulties. Younger children could go to considerable lengths in refusing to
find the answer to a problem without adults, and particularly parental support.
One girl, aged just 8, would not go on a short expedition with a friend without
her own mother's specific permission.

When I went to the park with my friend and my mother my friend said I want
to go the pond down the lane my mother said she was going home when she
cross the road I was not sure to go I said no and comeing a cross the road was
her mother she said to her mother can I go to the pond down the lane her
mother said yes I was not sure because my mother did not no my friend
mother. I said no my friend said why I said because my mother do not no your
mother she went to the park and I went home.

Other young children referred to adults because it seemed the most sensible
way to get out of an unpleasant situation. An 8+ girl found herself surrounded
by older, hostile children. In a multiple reaction she first called for her friend
(*peer referent*), to no avail. She then appealed to a passing stranger (*adult
referent*), but he ignored her. In the end, the girl was rescued by her sister. It
is evident from this answer, as it was from some others, that the parable of The
Good Samaritan could have particular relevance for children. However it is
perhaps unusual for teacher and parents to interpret the parable in terms of
children as victims, robbers, and Samaritans, and of adults as those who pass
by on the other side.

I was once in the midle of five or six children who were much much older than
me they mad a big cicle round me and I didn't know what to do I tried to call
my freind but she was rite up at the end of the road and non of my faimly
came out and I did not know what to do about it and I wounded what to d a
man came past he took no notice and I went to speak to him but he went strait
past but in the end my little sister came out of the house and saw the boys and
wounded what they were doing and she looked inside the cicle and ran in and
told my dad and he came out and they all dicerpired because they saw him and
they all ran away.

Reference to adults for help could however have much happier results, as a
9+ London boy discovered.

> one day I went up to the park to play football and when I got up there I went
> onto the football pitch and then a gang of people came towards me and said
> that they wanted my ball I said no then they said if I did not they would beat
> me up I did not know what to do I ran down to the park keeper, I told him
> about them and he sent them out of the park.

In situations where rules or procedures had not been made clear, children
might refer to the best known and most reliable authority figure available. A
10+ girl, not sure whom she ought to accompany on a school outing, did not
even ask the teacher in charge; she simply joined the teacher's group.

> The time somebody was with me and I was not sure what to do was when I
> was at the juinior school. We where on a outing and I was puzeld I did not
> know if I was meant to go with the stewdent or not. I went with my teacher
> and not the stewdent and every thing was all right. We went in a museum.

Children could refer to adults where they knew they had broken rules, or
became involved in circumstances which might annoy adults, but usually only
when either adults were likely to find out the misdemeanour any way, or
adult help was seriously needed. Usually adults referred to in such circumstances responded in a balanced and sensible way. Very possibly children only
referred to those adults who, in their experience, would be unlikely to be
particularly hostile. A 9+ girl, in a common enough type of domestic incident,
broke some crockery.

> About a month ago I was in the kitchen when suddenly I coughed and I
> droped the plate that I was holding and I did not know what to do. But then
> I thought that I should go and tell mum so I did and she told me to sweep it
> up.

Peer referent reactions included both those in which children referred to
their peers for assistance and those in which, perhaps against their better
judgement, they followed the example of other children.

An 8+ child from a Newcastle first school had a social etiquette problem.
She simply copied her cousin (or friend).

> When I was not shur wat to do was when I was with my auntie put for tea
> at here house.
> And then I just done wot cristepher did.

A 10+ boy from West Bromwich found himself, with friends, arguing about
the correct route on a walk. The boy's first reaction was *positive* — to point

out the correct route, which he knew. But his second reaction was *peer referent,* because he followed the advice of another boy; they got lost.

Once I was going a walk whith my friends to barr bicon and one of my friends said that it was one way but I had been here befor and I knew the right way but he would not listen so I whent whith him and we got lost I said to him I told you the right way befor but you would not listen so you have to get us lost after all I did not know what to do but after we whent to a house and the lady at the house phoned the police and the police took us home I will never go of again.

Part VI
In conclusion: questions arising

18 Interrelationships of variables

Method and presentation

Descriptive research does not readily lend itself to a concise summary of
findings. In the present study, as in most such investigations, more questions
were generated than answered. However, pertinent hypotheses were systema-
tically identified and proposed prior to analysis of data (see Appendix D).
Children's answers provided information for happy, unhappy and problem
situations concerning context of situation (place, time and involvement),
themes of situations, others in situations, reactions, and others in reactions (see
Chapters 5, 6, 10 and 14). All of these factors were examined in relation to
obtained personal and social details of the children in the sample (see Chapter
3, p. 20).

The findings described below cannot claim to be more than indicative of
the relationships between the variables, and it was not possible — given the
necessarily limited nature of the time and other resources available — to consider replicative studies. In order to test the many hypotheses the data have
been analysed by non-parametric statistical techniques using parts of the SPSS
computer package (see Appendix C, p. 231). The main findings to be described
are those deriving from a statistical significance of 5% or less. Findings are
presented in the same sequence as was employed for consideration of descriptive data (e.g. *Context, Themes, Others,* etc.), and under appropriate detailed
headings so as to enable particular areas and cross references to be identified
as required. A general discussion of findings is offered in the concluding
section of the chapter. Elsewhere interpretation is offered only where meaning
may require clarification or where conclusions may be of particular interest.
It is hoped by this procedure both to make findings available in a readily
comprehensible, if compact, format and to identify the major issues arising.

Context — place

In this section the associations are investigated between place (the environment in which children reported situations occurring) and other major variables (see Appendix D). The categories of place employed in the study (see Chapter 5, p. 36) are school, neighbourhood, abroad, seaside, medical environment, multiple (any combination of the preceding places) and elsewhere (places not included in the previous classes).

Region   Answers of children in the South East gave a high frequency of school environment both for unhappy and problem situations. Answers of children in the North West gave a very high frequency of seaside environment for happy situations, and answers of children in the North West and Wales gave a high frequency of seaside environment in problem situations.

Sex   In happy situations there was no major difference between the replies of boys and girls. However, in both unhappy and problem situations girls gave home as the environment more frequently than boys, while boys gave neighbourhood as the environment more frequently than girls. In problem situations girls gave school environment more frequently than boys.

Age   For happy, unhappy and problem situations school was reported more frequently by older children, whereas home was mentioned more frequently by younger children. The neighbourhood was reported less frequently for happy situations by older children. The seaside was reported with decreasing frequency as age increased.

Reading quotient   The very low ability children (RQ 60–69) mentioned both school and home less frequently than other children, and neighbourhood very much more frequently. Very high ability children (RQ over 140) reported multiple environments more often than other children.

Paternal occupation   No significant associations were discovered in either happy or unhappy situations. For problem situations children of fathers from social class 1 mentioned home as the focus of situations more frequently than other children, while children of fathers from social class 5 reported home less frequently than other children.

School size and type   For happy, unhappy and problem situations, the larger the school the more frequently it was mentioned. Similarly, in school type, comprehensives 11–16 and 11–18 (which tended to be larger than other schools) were mentioned for happy, unhappy and problem situations more frequently than other types of school. Since older children also reported school for all types of situation more frequently than younger children, there appear to be strong reasons for concluding that as children grew older school played an increasingly significant role in their lives.

Context — time

In this section the associations are investigated between time (time when children reported situations occurring) and other major variables (see Appendix D). The categories of time employed in this study (see Chapter 5, p. 37) are very recent (within the last month), fairly recent (within the last year), distant (over a year), and early childhood (six years old or younger).

Region   For happy, unhappy and problem situations children in the North East tended to write about situations which had not occurred recently; while, on contrary, children in the North West tended to write about situations which had occurred recently.

Sex   For no type of situation were any significant differences discovered between the replies of boys and girls.

Age   For all types of situation, the older the children, the more likely they were to report events which had not occurred recently.

Reading quotient   Children with RQ below 80 were more likely than other children not to record when events occurred; this was true for happy, unhappy and problem situations.

Paternal occupation   No significant associations were discovered in any type of situation between social class of children's fathers and time when reported events took place.

School size and type   For happy, unhappy and problem situations, pupils in larger schools and pupils in schools for the older age range were more likely to report events which had not occurred recently. This coincides with the similar finding, in relation to age, that the younger the child was the more likely he or she was to write about recent happenings.

Context — involvement

In this section the associations are investigated between involvement (the estimated degree of emotional involvement in a situation revealed by children's answers) and other major variables (see Appendix D). The categories of involvement employed in this study (see Chapter 5, p. 38) are mild, medium and intense.

Region   For happy and unhappy situations, children in the North West were more likely to give answers with an intense degree of involvement than children elsewhere. For problem situations, children in Wales and the South

West were more likely to give answers with a mild degree of involvement than children elsewhere.

Sex   For happy, unhappy and problem situations, girls very much more frequently than boys gave answers showing an intense degree of involvement.

Age   There was a tendency, in all types of situation, for the degree of involvement shown to become more intense as children grew older.

Reading quotient   For happy, unhappy and problem situations, the degree of involvement tended to become more intense as RQ became higher. It is worth emphasizing that this finding relates to children's ability to express intensity of involvement through writing or drawing, not necessarily to the real degree of intensity felt in the actual circumstances by children.

Paternal occupation   No significant associations were discovered in any type of situation between social class of children's father and degree of involvement revealed in children's answers.

School size and type   For happy, unhappy and problem situations, larger schools and schools for the older age range were associated with a tendency for answers to show a more intense degree of involvement. This is consistent with findings related to age.

Themes

In this section the associations are investigated between themes (the main subjects of children's answers) and other major variables (see Appendix D). Such associations are considered in relation to groups of themes which are categorized in this study (see Chapter 6) as *personal and home life, other children, activities and pastimes, special occasions and occurrences, behaviour difficulties, critical situations, problems* and *expectations.*

Region   For happy, unhappy and problem situations *activities and pastimes* were reported less frequently in the North East than elsewhere. For problem situations the themes in the *critical situations* group were lowest in the North West.

Sex   For all three types of situation themes concerning *personal and home life* were higher for girls, while themes concerning *activities and pastimes* were higher for boys. In happy and problem situations there was no significant difference between boys and girls for themes of *behaviour difficulties,* although in unhappy situations boys reported *behaviour difficulties* with greater frequency than girls. For all types of situation girls' answers revealed a higher frequency of themes of *expectation* than boys'. Since *expectations* were essentially concerned with issues of social moral awareness (e.g. concern for others, striving, taking responsibility) it can be argued that girls were more sensitive in this area than boys.

Age   For unhappy situations no significant relationships with age were discovered. For happy and problem situations themes concerned with *behaviour difficulties* and with *expectations* were reported with increasing frequency as the children grew older.

Reading quotient and paternal occupation   No significant relationships with reading quotient or paternal occupation were discovered.

School size and type   For unhappy and problem situations *behaviour difficulties* were reported more frequently in 11–16 comprehensives, and less frequently in 5–11 primary schools. This tends to confirm the age-related findings that *behaviour difficulties* increase as children grow older.

Time   For happy and unhappy situations both *behaviour difficulties* and *activities and pastimes* tended to be reported as having occurred recently or very recently. For problem situations critical situations were more frequently reported as having occurred at least a year ago. Specific problem themes (e.g. What do I do? What do I choose? etc.) were frequently associated with early childhood.

Place   For all types of situation, as would be expected, *personal and home life* themes were most frequently associated with home; *other children* themes were most frequently associated with school and neighbourhood. For all types of situation unexpected happenings (an individual theme category) showed a high association with medical environment. For happy and unhappy situations school was frequently associated with *activities and pastimes* (for problem situations, however, school was not reported significantly frequently). *Special occasions,* for happy situations, were frequently associated with home, abroad and elsewhere; for unhappy situations *special occasions* were associated with sea and abroad; for problem situations *special occasions* were associated with sea and elsewhere. For unhappy situations *behaviour difficulties* were found with equal frequency associated with school, home and neighbourhood. Thus there appears to be little support for arguing that the incidence of children's behaviour difficulties varies significantly according to environment.

Involvement   For happy situations no significant associations were discovered. For unhappy and problem situations intense degrees of involvement were found associated with *personal and home life* themes more frequently than medium degrees, and medium more frequently than mild; on the other hand mild degrees were found associated with *behaviour difficulties* more frequently than medium, and medium more frequently than intense. *Critical situations* tended to show higher degrees of involvement, as did *expectations*. For problem situations only, themes concerning older children were associated with degrees of involvement which increased in frequency as they became more intense.

Others

In this section the associations are investigated between *others* (those reported as initiating interaction with children) and other major variables (see Appendix D). Such associations are considered in relation to groups of *others* which are categorized in this study (see Chapter 10) as *self, activity groups, family, children not close family members, adults not close family members, creatures, objects and environment* and *supernatural, fictitious and well known figures*.

Region   For happy, unhappy and problem situations no significant association of region with *family* was discovered. Other regional differences were either small or contradictory.

Sex   No major differences in reaction were discovered between boys and girls. Girls showed a slight tendency in unhappy or problem situations to report *family* more frequently than boys; while boys in the same types of situation showed a slight tendency to report *children not close family members* more frequently than girls.

Age   In happy and unhappy situations there was a tendency for *activity groups* to be mentioned with increasing frequency as children grew older. For all types of situation *family* was mentioned with decreasing frequency as children grew older. Within the family group there were interesting variations. In happy situations parents were mentioned more frequently by younger children, while in unhappy situations they were mentioned more frequently by older children; siblings on the other hand were mentioned less frequently in unhappy situations by older children, while in happy situations they were mentioned more frequently by older children. *Children who were not close family members* were mentioned in unhappy situations with greater frequency as age increased. For happy, unhappy (with the exception of 12 and 13 year olds) and problem situations, mention of *adults not close family members* increased with the age of the respondent. If frequency of the use of the categories of children and *adults not close family members* are pooled, than a pattern of increasing contact outside the family as children grow older is suggested. In unhappy situations reports of *super-natural, fictitious and well known figures* decreased with age.

Reading quotient   No significant associations were found between reading quotient and *others* in unhappy and problem situations. In happy situations children below RQ 80 were more likely to mention *children who were not close family members. Adults who were not close family members* were mentioned with greater frequency as children's RQ increased. If individual groups of adults are considered, it is found that teachers were mentioned more often than other adults in relation to increasing RQ. This would seem to suggest that, the higher a pupil's reading ability, the more likely it was that considerate treatment by teachers would be mentioned. In other words, in children's perception, the brighter (in reading ability) the child, the more likely he or she was to be looked upon favourably by the teacher.

Paternal occupation   No significant associations were found, for any type of situation, between social class and *others* mentioned by children.

School size and type   For happy, unhappy and problem situations children in larger schools, and in schools for older children showed a tendency to mention *creatures, objects and environment* less often than children in other schools. This seems to indicate that children in these environments perceived a more person-centred world, although the findings relating to *others* in association with age did not indicate an association specifically between age and mention of *creatures, objects and environment.* .

Time   For all types of situation children mentioned themselves as the *other* (see Chapter 10, p. 112) in the situation with high frequency either in relation to situations from early childhood or non-recent events. In contrast, for all types of situation, *children who were not close family members* were recalled relatively infrequently in association with early childhood.

Place   For all types of situation, *activity groups* were reported with high frequency in association with school and abroad. As might be expected *family* was often reported associated with home and seldom in association with school. *Children who were not close family members* were frequently reported in a context of school and neighbourhood. *Adults who were not close family members* were very frequently mentioned in association with school. This is probably due to the frequency with which teachers in school were mentioned in relation to other adults who were not close family members. For happy and unhappy situations, *creatures, objects and en-vironments* were infrequently mentioned at school; for happy situations they were frequently mentioned at home.

Involvement   No major associations were observed for happy, unhappy or problem situations between *others* mentioned by children and degrees of involvement.

Reactions

In this section the associations are investigated between reactions (the way in which children reacted to others' treatment of them) and other major variables (see Appendix D). The categories of reaction employed in this study are (see Chapter 14) *non-active, adult referent, peer referent, aggressive, avoidance, positive, autonomous, reflective, emotional.* Analysis of findings is concerned primarily with first reactions; but, where categories of reaction are markedly and interestingly different in second or subsequent reactions (an infrequent occurrence), these are also discussed.

Region   For happy, unhappy and problem situations answers from children in the North East showed a rather high frequency of *adult* and *peer referent reactions. Positive* reactions were reported with high frequency for unhappy and problem situations in the South West.

Sex   For happy situations girls reported *emotional, positive, autonomous, reflective, adult referent* and *non-active* reactions more often than boys; boys on the other hand showed *aggressive, peer referent* and *avoidance* reactions more often than girls. For unhappy and problem situations boys likewise more frequently showed *aggressive* and *avoidance* reactions than girls. For unhappy situations, as for happy, girls were more likely than boys to show *emotional* reactions. Although boys were more likely than girls to show *aggressive* reactions to all types of situation the level of statistical significance was fairly low. In general, the reported reactions tend to confirm conventional views of behavioural differences between the sexes. However while boys, – if only marginally – were more liable to 'fight', it is interesting that they were likewise more liable to 'flight'.

Age   For all types of situation *adult referent* behaviour decreased with age, while *aggressive* behaviour, *avoidance* and (perhaps paradoxically) *reflective* behaviour increased with age. *Peer referent* behaviour was only marginally associated with age in happy and problem situations, while for unhappy situations no firm trend was established, such behaviour being associated with the 10+ and 12+ age groups. Neither *positive* nor *autonomous* behaviour were age related. As far as autonomy is concerned, this perhaps tends to suggest – in support of Williams (1970) – that the concept of autonomy as a stage of development following necessarily preceding stages (Kay, 1968; Kohlberg, 1969) needs to be re-examined.

Reading quotient   For all types of situation, in the first response there was no significant association between reading quotient and behavioural reaction. None of the first three reactions showed any association for unhappy situations. Only second reactions for happy situations and third reactions for problem situations showed any associations. In happy situations (second reactions) *autonomy* tended to increase with RQ, while in problem situations (third reactions) *autonomous* and *positive* reactions were associated with higher RQ. Nevertheless, the present study gives little support to any suggestion that children's behavioural reactions to treatment can be related to their ability to perform well or badly at reading.

Paternal occupation   With reactions to unhappy situations there was, except in second reactions, no significant association with paternal occupation. With reactions to happy situations there were no significant associations for second reactions, and in problem situations there were no significant associations with second and third reactions. Such evidence of association as did exist tended to be contradictory. However, social class 5 was significantly more frequently associated with *positive* reactions in problem and happy situations and with *aggression* in unhappy situations. In happy situations *autonomous* reactions tended to be associated with social classes 1 and 2.

School size and type   For happy, unhappy and problem situations *positive* reactions tended to be associated with smaller schools, while *emotional* reactions were associated with larger schools. (*Positive* reactions were not, as discussed, age related). *Emotional* reactions likewise tended to be reported in association with schools for older children. *Non-active* reactions occurred relatively infrequently in children attending schools for younger pupils. *Aggressive* reactions were not found associated with any type of school, and only minimal and inconsistent associations were discovered with school size.

Place   For all types of situation *non-active* reactions were frequently reported in medical settings. For unhappy and problem situations *avoidance* was often associated with neighbourhood; *aggression* showed no striking association with any particular environment.

Involvement   For all types of situation the degree of reported involvement in *adult referent* and *positive* reactions was low. *Autonomous* reactions however, while showing low involvement in happy situations, revealed high

involvement in problem situations. *Aggressive* reactions showed low involvement in unhappy situations, but high involvement in problem situations.
Emotional reactions showed an increasingly intense pattern of involvement
in all types of situation.

Others in reactions

In this section the associations are investigated between *others* in reactions
(those whom children involved in their reactions) and other major variables
(see Appendix D). Such associations are considered in relations to groups of
others as described in the section on **Others**, above. First reactions are
discussed unless otherwise stated.

Region   For all types of situation children in the North East recorded
relations very frequently.

Sex   Only marginal differences between the replies of boys and girls were
observed.

Age   For problem and unhappy situations mention of *parents* decreased with
increasing age. For all types of situation frequency of mention of *siblings*
increased with age.

Reading quotient   No associations were obtained for unhappy situations and
few and inconsistent associations for problem situations. For happy situations children of very low reading quotient (60–69) mentioned *parents*
infrequently, while children of very high reading quotient (140–149)
mentioned *parents* frequently.

Parental occupation   No significant association between parental occupation
and *others* in reaction was discovered for any first or second reactions.

School size and type   No consistent patterns of association were obtained.

Time   No consistent patterns of association were obtained.

Place   As might be expected, for all types of situation *parents* were frequently
mentioned at home, and infrequently at school.

Involvement   Reactions in which *siblings* were the *others* showed a significantly low degree of involvement for all types of situation.

Children's ability to report reactions

In this section the associations are investigated between children's ability to report reactions and other major variables (see Appendix D). In so far as a sequence of reactions may be indicative of experimental behaviour (see Chapter 14, p. 145) the investigation of these associations can indicate whether such behaviour is found in relation to any particular factors.

Region   No consistent patterns of association were discovered.

Sex   For all types of situation — happy, unhappy and problem — girls reported a greater number of reactions than boys.

Age   For all types of situation there was a tendency for older children to report a higher number of reactions (These findings may be compared with those of McPhail et al (1972) who reported a significant and similar increase in experimental behaviour in boys and girls from 12 to 15).

Reading quotient   For all types of situation the number of reactions reported increased with higher RQ's.

Paternal occupation   For happy situations, but not for unhappy or problem situations, there was a tendency for the number of reported reactions to increase in relation to higher social class.

School size and type   For happy, unhappy and problem situations higher numbers of reactions occurred more often in larger schools, and schools for older children.

The evidence from the study of numbers of reported reactions shows some consistency. It suggests that experimental behaviour is associated with girls, with older children, and with children of higher reading ability. Such children may find it easier to cope with the behavioural requirements implicit in moral interpersonal situations: or alternatively, they may simply be more aware of those implicit requirements.

Discussion

The analysis of variables identified in relation to the moral situation of children offers an interpretation of the personal and social moral context within which may be located the varying individual experiences discussed earlier in the present study. In general, the findings do not contradict either the conclusions of other research, or indeed the suggestions of common sense. They do, however, in certain areas indicate a development of previous work, or isolate new points of interest.

Situations reported by children tend to support a traditional view of sex roles and behaviour. It does not look as if women's liberation had any marked effect on the boys and girls in this sample. Girls were more home and family oriented than boys, while boys were more neighbourhood inclined. Boys in general were more combative, while girls showed a greater tendency towards experimental behaviour. As far as feelings were concerned, in every type of situation girls were more likely than boys to report strong emotion.

The findings suggest that, as children grew older, their moral education in school might have become both more difficult for teachers and more crucial for themselves. Older boys and girls were more likely to be aggressive, to become involved in problem situations, to respond with strong feeling to others' behaviour, to be concerned with relationships in school and with teachers, and to practise experimental behaviour. Some encouragement for the moral educator was offered by the evidence that, as children's age increased, so did their ability to think about moral interpersonal situations.

The findings concerned with reading quotients need to be treated with reserve, both because measured ability refers only to a limited specific capacity, and because a variety of different tests were employed (see Chapter 3, p. 21). However, in so far as these tests do offer a measure of ability in a field which is both educationally and socially very important, the findings may well have some significance. Children with a very low reading quotient were more likely than others to be concerned with the immediate present, to be active in the neighbourhood, and to record a mild degree of emotional involvement. On the other hand, boys and girls with low reading quotients were only marginally differentiated from other children by the way they reacted to considerate, inconsiderate or problem posing treatment. Children with high reading quotients were more likely to receive favourable treatment from teachers and to show experimental behaviour.

Social class by paternal occupation was a factor of negligible significance. For example, children's behavioural reactions were hardly affected by class, nor was their tendency to show experimental behaviour, nor were the others with whom they interacted, nor was the nature of the situations in which they became involved. Furthermore, children of different class backgrounds revealed no tendency to feel more or less strongly, nor to be more or less prone to live in the present. The only clear and consistent finding was that children of higher social class were more likely to meet social moral problems at home, while those of lower social class were more likely to meet them in the neighbourhood.

To finish on a practical and educational note — while the conclusion to be drawn from the analysis of children's individual answers was that each moral situation should be viewed without preconception and in the context of all relevant circumstances, the evidence of the statistical analysis suggests that almost regardless of social background, moral education in school becomes more difficult yet more necessary as children grow older. Further, differences exist between boys and girls which teachers, and indeed parents, would be foolish to ignore!

Appendices

Appendix A
Participant schools

PRE-PILOT SCHOOLS (242 pupils)

Overmead County Primary, Oxford
John Fisher RC Primary School, Oxford

PILOT SCHOOLS (487 pupils)

Bishop Kirk Junior School, Oxford
Blackbird Leys Junior School, Oxford
Greenmere Junior School, Didcot
North Hinksey CE Junior School, Oxford
Preswood Junior School, Great Missenden
St. Mary and St. John Junior School, Oxford
Wolvercote Primary School, Oxford
Carterton Comprehensive School, Oxon.
Headington County Secondary School, Oxford
Milham Ford Secondary School, Oxford
One educationally subnormal unit (school wished to remain anonymous)

POST-PILOT SCHOOLS

Westleyn Middle School, Bury St. Edmunds
Caldecote Junior School, Abingdon
Blackbird Leys Junior School, Oxford
Alec Hunter Comprehensive School, Braintree, Essex

NATIONAL SURVEY SCHOOLS (3475 pupils)

North East

Newcastle-on-Tyne
Centre leader: J. W. Brimer, Religious education adviser, county of
   Northumberland

Newbiggin Hall Cheviot County First School (Mrs. A. Chayton, headteacher)
Throckley Vallum County First School (Miss B. E. Severs, headteacher)
West Denton County First School (Miss M. Tate, headteacher)
Newbiggin Hall Cheviot County Middle School (N. McGuinness, headteacher)
Throckley County Middle School (W. Anderson, headteacher)
West Denton County Middle School (W. Brown, headteacher)

East Riding of Yorkshire
Centre leaders: S. Londesborough, General education adviser, East Riding of
   Yorkshire
                     C. Wigglesworth, Headteacher, Grove Street School

Langton School (Mrs. M. Wellard, headteacher)
Settrington School (E. Windle, headteacher)
Westow School (J. Bateman, headteacher)

North West

Workington
Centre leader: P. Gartside, Teacher Centre Warden, Workington

Northside Junior School (Miss I. M. Harnan, headteacher)
Victoria Junior School (W. Kerr, headteacher)
Moorclose Boys' Secondary School (C. Wright, headteacher)
Newlands Girls' School (Mrs. J. E. Bottomley, headteacher)

Cheshire
Centre leader: K. Williams, Senior organizer for religious education, Cheshire

Bishops Middle School (G. G. Phillips, headteacher)
Cherry Grove Middle School (G. W. Platt, headteacher)
Newton Middle School (D. H. M. Roberts, headteacher)
St. Thomas of Canterbury Middle School (W. I. Holyoak, headteacher)

Midlands

Lichfield
Centre leader: G. Hughes, County adviser, Stafford

Charnwood Junior School (F. W. Wall, headteacher)
Chase Terrace Junior School (H. T. Earlham, headteacher)
Chase Terrace Comprehensive School (G. V. Pinnell, headteacher)

Nottingham
Centre leader: D. E. Bennett, General educational adviser, Nottingham

Carlton Gedling Stanhope Junior School (D. W. Wing, headteacher)
Kimberley Comprehensive School (F. Collier, headteacher)
West Bridgeford Comprehensive School (B. A. Marden, headteacher)

West Bromwich
Centre leader: R. Leach, Remedial and advisory teacher, Child Psychology
Service, West Bromwich

Yew Tree Junior School (Mrs. M. B. Jukes, headteacher)

South East

Cambridgeshire
Centre organized by project
Sawston Village College (G. Elsbury, headteacher)

Hertfordshire
Centre leader: Miss P. Firkins, Religious education adviser, Hertfordshire

Barkway School (Miss I. Catley, headteacher)
Icknield Walk Junior School (Miss C. Bull, headteacher)
Bridgewater School (H. Bellchambers, headteacher)
The Greeneway Middle School (K. G. Charles, headteacher)
The Thomas Bourne Middle School (M. Irwin, headteacher)

ILEA

Centre leader: J. Kettle, Adviser for compensatory education, London Borough
of Brent.

Furness Junior School (D. McIntosh, headteacher)
Salisbury Junior School (J. Harris, headteacher)

Wales

Cardiff
Centre leader: Dr. T. Jones, General educational adviser, City of Cardiff

Llanedeyrn Primary School (E. Powell, headteacher)
Marlborough Junior School (Mrs. K. Jones, headteacher)
Roath Park Junior School (H. Harris, headteacher)
Llanedeyrn High School (G. Jones, headteacher)

South West

Dorset
Centre leaders: R. Cocks, Religious education adviser, Dorset
             B. Oastler, Warden, Wimborne Teachers Centre

Cranborne County Middle School (P. Prosser, headteacher)
Ferndown County Middle School (J. Last, headteacher)
St. Michael's CE School (M. Neave, headteacher)

Devon
Centre leaders: P. King, Religious education adviser, Devon
             J. Dumpleton, Warden, Crediton and Tiverton Teachers' Centres

Bow Primary School (F. W. Coombs, headteacher)
The Queen Elizabeth's Comprehensive School (J. H. Brown, headteacher)

Swindon
Centre leaders: A. Greenwood, organizer Gorse Hill Teachers' Centre
             T. Phillips, organizer curriculum study and development centre

Eldene Junior School (P. C. Jinks, headteacher)
Walcot Junior High School (A. D. Bott, headteacher)

Appendix B
Questions to pupils

PRE-PILOT SURVEY

1   Tell me of a time when somebody frightened you, or made you angry.
    What did you do?

2   Tell me of a time when somebody made you happy.
    What did you do?

3   Tell me of a time when you were with somebody else (or other people)
    and you weren't sure what to do.
    What did you do?

PILOT SURVEY

1   Write or draw about a time when you were unhappy
    — What did you do?

2   Write or draw about a time when you were happy
    — What did you do?

3   Write or draw about a time when you needed to choose what to do
    — What did you do?

If you draw, write on your drawing what it is about.

NATIONAL SURVEY – QUESTIONS, INSTRUCTIONS, GUIDELINES
Questions to pupils

1   Write and draw about a time when somebody made you feel pleased or
    happy.

    DESCRIBE WHAT YOU DID AS A RESULT.

2   Write and draw about a time when somebody made you feel frightened, angry or unhappy.
DESCRIBE WHAT YOU DID AS A RESULT.

3   Write and draw about a time when you were with somebody else (or other people) and you were not sure what to do.
WHAT DID YOU DO?

For 11+ and 12+ pupils drawing is optional. Accordingly, questions start 'Write, and draw if you wish to, about a time . . .'.

Instructions to pupils

Teachers are asked to read out the following instructions to their classes. After this reading, teachers may, if necessary, use their own words to explain instructions.

How to answer the questions
a   You will be asked to answer three questions.

b   What you write and draw will be completely private. No-one will know it is you. Your name will not be on the sheets. Write and draw what you want to. Nobody from this school will look at it.

c   Only write and draw about things which are real, which have actually happened to you.

d   You can write and draw about things which have happened in school, or at home, or anywhere else.

e   It does not matter when the things you write and draw about happened; it might have been quite a long time ago or not at all long ago.

f   When you have finished, all your envelopes will be put in one large envelope and posted to Cambridge. Other schools all over the country will be doing the same as you and their answers will be sent to Cambridge as well. The answers will help people know what kinds of things matter to children. When all the answers have been looked at, games or books will be made about the things which matter to you, to help you in school.

g   Do not talk about what you are going to write and draw with other children.

h   Here is/are the question(s). (The teacher will read out the question or questions to be answered during the period, and write it, or them, on the board).

i   Try to answer each/the question.

j   Before you start each answer, write the question number on the answer sheet. Make sure that any drawing sheets are also numbered.

k   Start each answer on a new sheet.

l   When you have finished each question, put your answer in your envelope. When all the answers are finished, stick it down.

Guidelines for teachers

1   Sufficient time should be allowed for pupils to answer questions adequately. (More than one period may well be necessary, particularly for younger pupils).

2   Pupils should be given lined sheets for writing and blank sheets for drawing. Writing and drawing will be done on separate sheets.

3   All teachers involved in any one particular school should arrange to give the questions simultaneously. If teachers fail to do this, children may talk among themselves, and those who have answered the questions may suggest ideas to those who have not.

4   Questions should be given to complete classes in normal classroom conditions. (e.g. if children usually sit in groups, they will sit in groups to answer their questions.)

5   Children are likely to raise points about the questions. These should be answered by the teacher but without giving any examples and without allowing any discussion amongst the children. All points should be made direct to the teacher.

6   In general the time preceding the answering of the questions by the children should establish an atmosphere in which the children:

   (a) feel that they are doing something rather different, special, worthwhile.
   (b) feel secure and able to express themselves freely.
   (c) are prepared to think about answering the questions without having entered into any detailed discussion.

   In particular it may be necessary, especially with the younger children, to spend a few minutes ensuring that pupils are ready to think about the questions. During this time, it is essential both that teachers do not suggest any specific incidents to children (e.g. as 'examples') and that the children themselves do not voice specific incidents. Further, the time must not be long enough for any group leader, or leaders, to suggest particular ideas or attitudes. With younger children, one method which could be used is to suggest that they think of particular incidents and use facial mime to express their feelings.

7   There will be some children who are unable or unwilling to answer one or more of the questions. These children should not be encouraged or persuaded by the teacher to respond. Non-response is as significant as response. Children who do not answer any of the questions should put into their envelopes one blank sheet. (This does not apply to children who do not respond through absence.)

8   Teachers will need to have an alternative occupation ready both for children who do not answer and for those who finish answers early. Such occupation should not be so popular as to make children neglect or rush their answers.

9   (a) Children may want help with spelling and other minor details during answering of the questions. This help should be given without other children overhearing. (A key word or phrase such as 'Dad's car' might, if overheard, suggest ideas to other children).

(b) Some children may want help in putting down in writing what they want to express. If absolutely necessary, teachers can write what children require on the answer sheets, and initial what they have written. Envelopes of children so helped should be marked by the teacher with an 'H'.

(c) Children should not be told that they can discuss with the teacher what they have done. However, if they ask of their own initiative to do so, time for this purpose should be provided at the end of the period, when the questions have been completed.

10   (a) When the last question has been completed, children's sealed envelopes will be put into the master envelope; this in turn will be sealed immediately and posted, if possible by a child.

(b) Teachers must put their own name and the names of their school and class on the outside of the master envelope. If this is not done, it may not be possible for the Project to identify where the responses come from.

(c) All pupils' envelopes, before they are first given out to the children, will be given a code number. Teachers will code envelopes themselves; the first name on the register will receive '1', the second '2' and so on. Code numbers should be put in a convenient place on the envelope. (But not on or under the flap!)

(d) Before sealing children's envelopes into the master envelope, it would be a great help to the Project if they could be put into numerical order.

Appendix C
Methods of analysis

CLASSIFICATION PROCEDURES

Two related but separate approaches to classification were employed. The first approach, a convergent one, required the development of a systematic classification of data obtained. The second approach, a divergent one, required the classification of individual answers which either illustrated particularly vividly and aptly, or suggested further consideration of issues raised within the context of the general classification.

In the convergent approach, the major categories of data were predicated by the way in which the questions asked were formulated. These categories were the theme of each situation, the *other* in the situation, the type of reaction in each situation and the place where each situation occurred. In addition, as a result of analysis of pre-pilot and pilot surveys certain other categories were found to be necessary: *other* in reaction, number of reactions, degree of involvement and time when situation took place.

Within the major categories, the individual classes were differentiated and developed inductively. The classification was developed through the use of pupil data cards which, as they were revised, specified in increasing detail the differentiated categories. Initially, prior to analysis of the pre-pilot survey answers, a simple 'pupil data card' was designed; this was revised as a result of use. During analysis of pilot and National Survey random sample a further five revisions took place before a final 'National Survey coding card' proved satisfactory. Each pupil's answers were coded on separate cards; the cards were designed so that the coded data could be punched onto computer cards for computer analysis. The classes discovered, within their categories, are tabulated in the appropriate chapters (Part II Chapter 1, Part III Chapter 1, Part IV Chapter 1, Part V Chapter 1).

In the divergent approach to classification a 'National Survey topic' card was designed. This provided for a brief description of the context of a specific answer, a comment on the specific answer, and a brief tabulation of any general issues raised by the answer (of the full sample, excluding the control group 1260 answers (36·2%) were topic carded).

The intention of the procedures of classification followed was to enable the project to offer an overall interpretation of data obtained, together with reference to individual points of view as revealed in specific answers.

NATIONAL SURVEY RANDOM SAMPLE

A random sample of the answers in the National Survey was obtained (for the national survey sample, see Chapter 3, p. 18) primarily so that the development of the classification could be completed and classification procedures coordinated but also to provide a cross check ensuring that procedures for giving questions to pupils had been correctly carried out by teachers. (In fact, all sets of answers from schools were also briefly checked on arrival at the project.)

In order to obtain an approximate 10% sample a table was provided showing the number of children in each age group, school by school, who had answered the questions. Each set of answers was then numbered from 1 to 3755 by entering the accumulative total in the appropriate cells of the table. A set of 400 random numbers between 1 and 3755 was obtained by using an existing subroutine (IRNUNI) in the Cambridge computer library. This resulted in 385 distinct integers (sampling with replacement) each of which represented a particular script within the appropriate cell of the table. The random sample of size 385 is 10·2% of the total number of all participants (i.e. pupils given questions both by teachers in the full sample, and by project members in the control group).

COORDINATION PROCEDURES FOR CLASSIFICATION

In order to achieve consistency between the four project members responsible for classification of data the following procedures were adopted. From the random sample, first three groups of children's answers were selected so as to provide a variety of responses: secondly, at a team meeting the first group of answers was classified by discussion, until a concensus was achieved: thirdly, following this meeting the second group of answers was classified individually by each team member, without consultation: fourthly, at a second group meeting the results of the four separate classifications of the same group of ten answers were compared and discussed: fifthly, the same procedure was followed with the third group of children's answers. From a comparison of classifications made of the third group of children's answers by individual team members it was concluded that the required degree of consistency had been achieved. Subsequent to coordination procedures the full random sample was classified. During the classification of the random sample regular team meetings were held to ensure that consistency in classification procedures was being maintained.

ANALYSIS OF ERRORS IN PUNCHING AND CODING

Subsequent to coding and punching onto computer cards of the complete sample an analysis of errors was made. A random sample of 421 answers was obtained (11·2% of the complete sample) by the same methods as were employed for obtaining the initial random sample. The answers were recoded, and the results compared with the original coding and punching. 73 punch errors were discovered (0·17 errors per card). This was well within the conventionally accepted range of error. 157 coder errors were discovered (0·37 errors per card). This also was well within the conventionally accepted range of error. The two error categories together give an average rate of one error per 160 items of information. A further analysis was carried out of consistent errors. It was discovered that 12 consistent errors had been made; consistent errors were removed by editing the full set of data cards.

COMPUTER PROGRAMS

The computer analysis of the data

All the computer programs were run under the auspices of the University of Cambridge Computing Service on their IBM 370/165 installation.

Those parts of the pupils' responses which were amenable to numerical coding were punched onto cards, one card per pupil. Each card consisted of fifty-three variables, thirteen of these being personal data or details associated with the school attended; the rest of the card was taken up with coded response data.

This coding onto prepared coding sheets was undertaken by team members prior to punching and verification of the cards.

The computer programs

The first program was specially written in order to produce a rearrangement and a listing of the data. At the same time the program checked for some possible errors in coding and, in the later version, incorporated an option which tabulated the data in relation to each of the major variables. A copy of this program is given below. The program is written in Fortran IV and was run using the Watfiv 1 compiler. (University of Waterloo.)

Once the coded data had been listed then a sequence of error checks became possible. Two sources of error are those made by the coders firstly in coding the raw data and secondly in entering the code on the coding sheet. Errors in punching had already been corrected by the card verification process.

In order to detect types of errors made by the coders a 10% sample of the data cards was randomly selected using the Fortran routine IRNUNI from the Cambridge Subroutine Library. This prints out an integer random number drawn from a uniform distribution whose end-points have been determined.

Some consistent errors between coders was revealed as were errors in the coding of school size and some themes. Because the data were stored on disc by this stage, very quick global corrections of the entire data bank were possible, using on-line facilities. Those errors which were specific to the sample enabled an estimate to be made of the proportion of errors in the unsampled data.

Concern for a high level of accuracy of the coded data following the checking of the sample led to the evolution of a comprehensive error-checking Fortran program.

The final stage of the analysis involved the teasing out of associations between the variables. The majority of this work was done using the Statistical Package for the Social Sciences (SPSS) package produced by the University of Chicago (Version 1.4).

Both the specially written tabulation and checking programs, and the SPSS 'Fastabs' sub-program were used on four subsets of the total set of pupils: the 7+ sample, the control group, the random sample and the total less the controls and less the 7+ group.

Appendix D
Proposed hypotheses

Prior to the analysis of data eight sets of hypotheses were proposed (The investigation of these hypotheses is undertaken in Part VI, Chapter 18). Each group was related to the main aims of the study. The proposed sets were as follows:

SET 1

The place (environment) in which children reported situations involving considerate treatment by others/inconsiderate treatment by others/social moral problems initiated by others will be associated with region/sex/age/ reading quotient/paternal occupation/school size and type.

SET 2

Time when situations reported by children occurred, involving considerate treatment by others/inconsiderate treatment by others/social moral problems initiated by others, will be associated with region/sex/age/reading quotient/ paternal occupation/school size and type.

SET 3

The degrees of involvement reported by children in situations involving considerate treatment by others/inconsiderate treatment by others/social moral problems initiated by others will be associated with region/sex/age/reading quotient/paternal occupation/school size and type.

SET 4

Themes of situations reported by children involving considerate treatment by others/inconsiderate treatment by others/social moral problems initiated by others will be associated with region/sex/age/reading quotient/paternal occupation/school size and type/context (place, time, involvement).

SET 5

Those whom children report as treating them considerately/inconsiderately/causing them social moral problems will be associated with region/sex/age/reading quotient/paternal occupation/school size and type/context (place, time, involvement).

SET 6

Reactions reported by children to considerate treatment by others/inconsiderate treatment by others/social moral problems initiated by others will be associated with region/sex/age/reading quotient/paternal occupation/school size and type/context (place, involvement).

SET 7

Others with whom children related in reported reactions to considerate treatment by others/inconsiderate treatment by others/social moral problems initiated by others will be associated with region/sex/age/reading quotient/paternal occupation/school size and type/context (place, time, involvement).

SET 8

The ability of children to report reactions to situations involving considerate treatment by others/inconsiderate treatment by others/social moral problems initiated by others will be associated with region/sex/age/reading quotient/paternal occupation/school size and type.

Appendix E
Control group

Control groups were established in order to compare the effect, in three particular areas, of the giving of questions by teachers with the giving of questions by members of the project team (see Chapter 3, p. 9). Control groups consisted of classes from the following schools and year groups, matched for age, sex and ability: Icknield Walk First School (8+), Charnwood J.S. (8+), Eldene J.S. (9+), Bishops M.S. (9+), Llanedeyrn P.S. (10+), Ferndown M.S. (10+), Kimberley Comp (11+), Moorclose Boys School (12+), Sawston Village College (12+).
The following hypotheses were tested:

1   Answers to questions given by pupils' teachers will reveal a higher frequency of school placed situations than answers to questions given by persons from outside the school and unknown to pupils.
2   Answers to questions given by pupils' teachers will more frequently mention teacher as others in situation than answers to questions given by persons from outside the school and unknown to pupils.
3   Answers to questions given by pupils' teachers will more frequently reveal an intense degree of involvement than answers to questions given by persons from outside the school and previously unknown to pupils.

From the data obtained the findings were as follows:

1   The first hypothesis was supported: school was mentioned slightly more frequently by the teacher administered group than by the project administered group. For every 100 occasions when place was mentioned, the place was a school 10·7 times in the teacher administered group compared with 9·7 times in the project administered group.
2   The second hypothesis was supported: teachers were mentioned rather more frequently as others in the situation by the teacher administered group than by the project administered group. For every 100 others 12·4

were teachers in the teacher administered group, and 8·9 in the project
administered group.

3   The third hypothesis was supported: the intense category of involvement
was found to be more dominant in the teacher administered group than in
the project administered group.

In general, the differences observed were small. Nevertheless they indicate
the presence of an influencing factor which should be taken into account when
interpreting children's answers.

Appendix F
Moral Education 8–13 Project:
Teaching materials

Moral Education in the Middle Years – a teachers' guide

Photoplay 1 – photoposters, plus short teachers' notes including stories

Photoplay 2 – photocards, work cards, labels and teachers' notes.
   (*Photoplay* is a sensitivity approach, stressing non-verbal communication.)

Choosing – six 24-page books which describe a variety of situations and suggest
   follow-up work

Growing – resource material in three parts related to *Photoplay 1, Photoplay 2
   and Choosing:*

   (a) *How it Happens* – 54 situation cards
   (b) *Making it Happen* – 62 activity cards
   (c) *Setting the Scene* – cut-out figures and objects to stimulate simula-
        tion and drama

(*Growing* can be used alone or together with *Photoplay* and *Choosing.*)

Published for the Schools Council as *Startline* by Longman, 1978

Bibliography

Buber, M. (1958). *I and Thou*. Edinburgh: T. & T. Clarke (2nd Ed.).

Central Statistical Office (1974). *Social trends*. HMSO.

Crawford, D. G. and Signori, E. I. (1961). 'An application of the critical incident technique to university teaching', *Canadian Psychologist*, **3**, 4.

Department of Education and Science (1973). *Schools* (*Statistics of Education*, vol. 1). HMSO.

Hirst, P. (1974). *Moral Education in a Secular Society*. University of London Press.

Kant, I. (1948). 'Groundwork of the metaphysic of morals' (tr. Paton, H. J.), in *The Moral Law*. Hutchinson, 1966.

Kay, W. (1968). *Moral Development*. Allen & Unwin.

Kay, W. (1975). *Moral Education*. Allen & Unwin.

King, R. (1973). *School Organisation and Pupil Involvement*. Routledge.

Kohlberg, L. (1969). 'State and sequence: the cognitive-developmental approach to socialization' in *Handbook of socialization: theory and research*, ed. Goslin, D. A. Chicago: Rand McNally.

MacIntyre, A. (1967). *A short history of ethics*. Routledge.

McPhail, P. (1967). 'Adolescence: the age of social experiment.' Unpublished paper delivered to the British Psychological Society.

McPhail, P., Ungoed-Thomas, J. R. and Chapman, H. (1972). *Moral Education in the Secondary School*. Longman.

Mead, M. (1952). *Sex and Temperament in Three Primitive Societies*. Routledge.

Moore, G. E. (1903). *Principia Ethica*. Cambridge University Press.

Opie, I. & P. (1959). *The Lore and Language of Schoolchildren*. Oxford University Press.

Opie, I. & P. (1969). *Children's Games in Street and Playground*. Oxford University Press.

Peters, R. S. (1966). *Ethics and Education*. Allen & Unwin.

Piaget, J. (1929). *The Child's Conception of the World*. Routledge (also Paladin, 1973).

Sugarman, B. (1973). *The School and Moral Development.* Croom Helm.

Tillich, P. (1964). *Morality and Beyond.* Routledge (also Fontana, 1969).

Ungoed-Thomas, J. R. (1972). 'Patterns of adolescent behaviour and relationships in Northern Ireland', *Journal of Moral Education, 2,* 1.

Ungoed-Thomas, J. R. (1973). 'Educational research and curriculum development', *Journal of Moral Education, 2,* 2.

Ungoed-Thomas, J. R. (1974). 'Dissemination, process and training', *Cambridge Journal of Education, 4,* 2.

Williams, N. & S. (1970). *The Moral Development of Children.* Macmillan.

Wilson, T., Williams, N. and Sugarman, B. (1967). *Introduction to Moral Education.* Penguin.

Wright, D. (1971). *The Psychology of Moral Behaviour.* Penguin.

Members of the project consultative committee

Chairman   Professor P. H. Hirst, Department of Education, University of Cambridge.

T. I. Ambrose, HMI, Department of Education and Science.

Miss P. M. Bell, Deputy Head, St. Anthony's C of E Primary School, Newcastle-upon-Tyne.

G. W. Cooksey, Director, Stantonbury Campus, Milton Keynes.

C. R. Jacobs, Headmaster, Shepherd's Hill Middle School, Oxford.

Sir Desmond Lee, President, Hughes Hall, Cambridge.

K. McWilliams, Senior Organizer for Religious Education, Cheshire County Council Education Department.

J. Malone, Director, Schools Project in Community Relations, The Queen's University of Belfast.

A. I. L. Morgan, Newport High School, Monmouthshire.

A. Razzell, Headmaster, Ravenscote County Middle School, Frimley, Surrey.

D. Reid, Deputy Director, Education & Training Division, The Health Education Council.

Miss. A. Richards, Research Officer, Needs for Slow Learning Children Schools Council Project (until 1975); Remedial Teacher, Wolverhampton.

G. W. Scotney, Headmaster, West Lodge Junior School, Pinner, Middlesex.

T. Scrivener, Head of Centre, Elmbank Teachers' Centre, Coventry.

Mrs. N. Spinks, Birchwood Middle School, Lincoln.

I. Sutherland, Director, Education & Training Division, The Health Education Council.

J. R. G. Tomlinson, Director of Education, Cheshire County Council Education Department.

C. Wigglesworth, Headmaster, Norton County Primary School, Yorkshire.

Miss M. Wileman, previous President, Hughes Hall, Cambridge.

The project team

Peter McPhail (Director, 1972–1976): has worked in secondary modern and grammar schools and teacher education; was Director of the Schools Council Moral Education Project 13–16+ at the University of Oxford (1967–1972); MacKenzie lecturer on moral education in New Zealand (1974) and Institute for the Development of Educational Advancement lecturer in education in the United States (1975); worked on research into the social psychology of adolescence at Oxford University (1964–1969); has an Oxford M.A. in Modern Greats, specialising in philosophy, and a Diploma in Psychology.

Jasper Ungoed-Thomas (Deputy Director, 1972–1975): has taught in special and secondary modern schools; was a research officer in the Schools Council Moral Education Project 13–16+ at the University of Oxford (1969–1972). He has a doctorate in education from Oxford University.

David Ingram (Research Officer, 1973–1975; Deputy Director, 1975–1976): has taught in grammar schools and has an M.A. in education from London University. He is responsible for the dissemination of the project's work until August, 1978.

David Middleton (Research Officer, 1973–1976); has taught in primary and comprehensive schools, and is currently an SSRC research fellow at Cambridge University. He has a Diploma in Visual Arts and an M.A. in education from London University.

Caroline Rennie (Research Officer, 1973–1975): has taught in primary schools and at Shiraz University, Iran. She is Froebel trained and has a B.Sc. in social anthropology from the London School of Economics.

Charlotte Bird (Information Officer and Research Assistant, 1973–1976): has a background in office management and an M.A. from the University of Edinburgh.

240

John Sutcliffe (Statistical adviser, 1973–1976): has taught in grammar schools, was formerly BP research fellow at the Department of Education, Cambridge University, where he is currently a lecturer in mathematics. He has an M.Sc. in mathematical psychology, and is working on a doctoral thesis on 'Teacher decision-making in the classroom'.

Sarah Williams (Secretary, 1974–1976): has taught English as a foreign language and been an editor. She has a B.A. from Wheaton College, Massachusetts.

Peter Hudson (Visiting scholar, 1975–1976): Principal, Silver Birches Senior School, North Bay, Ontario, Canada. He has a B.A. from McMaster University, Hamilton, Ontario.